PREPARING CHARITY ACC

Second Edition

PREPARING CHARITY ACCOUNTS

Second Edition

Adrian Randall
Anthony Epton
Fiona Young

abg
professional
information

40 Bernard Street
London
WC1N 1LD
Tel: 020 7920 8991
Fax: 020 7920 8992
Website: www.abgweb.com

ISBN 1 84140 156 0

British Library Cataloguing-in-Publication Data
A catalogue record for this book is available from the British Library.

Typeset by Type Study, Scarborough, N. Yorkshire
Printed in Great Britain by Bell & Bain, Glasgow

Preface

In 1999 we wrote the first edition of *Preparing Charity Accounts* to provide assistance, advice and information for all those involved in preparing charity accounts, whether as an accountant, auditor or treasurer. It was based on our experience of advising charities on how to comply with the Charities Statement of Recommended Practice (SORP) – *Accounting by Charities*, published in October 1995. It was, we hoped, intensely practical with numerous examples drawn from the published accounts of charities and checklists, which we used in our work as auditors.

Since 1999 there have been quite a few changes in the charity accounting world, particularly following the publication in October 2000 of the revised Charities SORP – *Accounting and Reporting by Charities*, and the subsequently updated Regulations. The second edition seeks to look in some detail at the changes that have occurred.

There have not been any accounts produced at the time of writing this edition that comply with SORP 2000, and therefore we have reproduced in Part IV all the examples published by the Charity Commission as CC66 SORP 2000 – *Example Reports and Accounts.* Throughout the text extracts from these accounts have been used to illustrate significant points and the checklists have been revised to take account of the changes in the legislation.

We have been able to draw upon a unique mix of experience in this field. Adrian Randall has worked as the Finance Director of a major charity (Cancer Research Campaign), as a Charity Audit Partner (with Moores Rowland, subsequently BDO Stoy Hayward) and as a member of the Committee that produced the 1995 Charities SORP. Fiona Young, currently Charity Unit Audit Manager at BDO Stoy Hayward, has worked with a number of both national and local charities. She has conducted special assignments for charity clients including internal control reviews and designing and implementing budgeting and financial reporting structures. Anthony Epton is a partner at Goldwins and has specialised in charity accounting for several years.

We believe that *Preparing Charity Accounts* is an essential reference work for anyone responsible for producing or monitoring the accounts of charity. As a one-stop guide it provides clear, relevant commentary and guidance and, like its predecessor, is full of practical worked examples.

Adrian Randall
Anthony Epton
Fiona Young

June 2001

Contents

Abbreviations

APB	Auditing Practices Board
ASC	Accounting Standards Committee
CFDG	Charity Finance Directors' Group
DTI	Department of Trade & Industry
ED	exposure draft
FRS	Financial Reporting Standard
FRSSE	Financial Reporting Standard for Smaller Entities
s	section
SAS	Statement of Auditing Standards
Sch	Schedule
SOFA	Statement of Financial Activities
SORP	Statement of Recommended Practice
SSAP	Statement of Standard Accounting Practice
UITF	Urgent Issues Task Force

Table of statutes

All references are to chapter and paragraph number, e.g., 9.1.2 refers to Chapter 9, section 1.2. Statutes are listed in chronological order.

Table of statutory instruments

All references are to chapter and paragraph number, e.g., 8.1 refers to Chapter 8, section 1. Instruments are listed in chronological order.

Part I
Scene setting and background to the industry

Chapter 1 Introduction

Not all voluntary or non-profit making organisations are charities. Tax legislation defines a charity as 'any body of persons or trust established for charitable purposes only', but does not define 'charitable purposes'. To find out what are considered 'charitable purposes' we need to go back to an Act of 1601 and a line of court decisions that have further developed and extended the definition.

The *Pemsel* case decision in 1891 sets out four general headings for charitable purposes, which are still accepted today. These are:

1. the relief of poverty;
2. the advancement of education;
3. the advancement of religion;
4. other purposes of a charitable nature beneficial to the community not falling under any of the other headings.

Where a charity's purposes are within one of the first three headings, they are assumed to be charitable and for the benefit of the community, unless it is shown otherwise, but in the fourth category, a purpose must be shown to benefit the community in a way the law regards as charitable. A purpose contrary to public policy cannot be for the benefit of the community; not only will it not be charitable, but it will be void. Charitable status will not be accorded if the purposes:

- contain an over element of self help; or
- are not exclusively charitable; or
- are substantially political; or
- involve profit distribution.

A wide range of purposes have been accepted in the past as charitable, which means that similar purposes of new organisations will also be accepted as charitable. These include for example:

- the relief of sick, mentally or physically handicapped, disabled or old people, the rehabilitation of offenders or drug abusers and similar purposes;
- the provision of land and buildings for public use, such as recreation grounds and community halls;
- the conservation of the national heritage;
- the care of animals needing protection;
- the provision of sports facilities open to the public;
- the provision of recreation facilities, so long as they are in the interests of social welfare and aim to improve the conditions of life for the people for whom the facilities are intended.

All these purposes are limited and defined by decisions of the courts. The Charity Commissioners for England and Wales (Charity Commission) will give a preliminary ruling on whether proposed purposes are charitable before an organisation is actually formed and a formal application for charitable status is made. However, it is worth noting at this stage that the Charity Commissioners have no jurisdiction in Scotland or Northern Ireland. The legislation in Scotland relevant to charities is the Law Reform (Miscellaneous Provisions) (Scotland) Act 1990, whilst in Northern Ireland charities are governed by the Charities Act (Northern Ireland) 1964 and the Charities (Northern Ireland) Order 1987. There is no Charity Commission for either

Scotland or Northern Ireland and the charity authority in the former is the Inland Revenue whilst in the latter it is the Department for Social Development.

A charity receives its status by virtue of its objectives and not its legal form. Therefore a charity can be set up for example as a trust, an unincorporated association, a limited company, a friendly society, a housing association, or by an Act of Parliament. A trust is normally used where one or more individuals want to settle property that will be used permanently for charitable purposes. This property is effectively what is known as 'permanent endowment'. In simple terms, an unincorporated association is a club whose members aim to achieve a common charitable purpose. In most cases a limited company will be incorporated as a company limited by guarantee without share capital.

A charity must have a governing document and the nature of this depends on the legal form of the charity. People who wish to form a charity are advised to engage a solicitor to prepare the governing document, although some model governing documents exist (examples are obtainable from the Charity Commission/Charity Law Association).

The individuals in charge of running a charity are called trustees in the legislation governing charities, although they may go under other names in the charity's governing document. For example, a charity that is established as a company limited by guarantee has directors who are therefore the trustees.

Trustees of a charity have the duty to ensure that the charity's income is used only for the charitable purposes of the charity and that the charity complies with all the legal requirements imposed on charities. The Charities Acts 1992 and 1993 made many changes to the law relating to charities, which came into effect in several stages. Their provisions cover charity accounts, charity documents, annual returns to the Charity Commissioners, public collections, the sale of land owned by charities and many other areas. Charity trustees and administrators are recommended to read The Charity Commission's guide to the law, *A Guide to the Charities Acts 1992 & 1993,* which is very clearly written.

Most charities' accounts are reasonably well kept and need no major improvements. However, some charities do not keep adequate records. Is it important for them to do so? Professional and financial management is essential in the operation of any successful business whether or not the ultimate goal is to make a profit. This is even truer for charities.

In spite of all the changes in accounting regulations and recommended practices, too many charities are still not keeping proper records. Whilst successful commercial businesses will inevitably have good professional and financial management, many in the charity world continue to ignore this. It is of course true that a good set of accounts will not in itself lead to an efficiently run organisation, but it most certainly helps. The principal aim of the first edition of this book, *Preparing Charity Accounts*, was to provide a useful tool to managers of charities and those advising them to enable them to operate efficiently and effectively. This second edition, following the further revision to the regulations and the Statement of Recommended Practice, aims to continue that principal aim.

1.1 Developments leading to the Charities Acts 1992 and 1993

- In 1984 the Accounting Standards Committee (ASC) issued a discussion paper on charity accounting.
- In 1985 the ASC issued an exposure draft (ED 38) of a statement intended to provide some uniformity in charity accounts.
- In 1987 the Woodfield Report 'Efficient Scrutiny of the Supervision of Charities', commissioned by the Government, highlighted a number of deficiencies regarding the monitoring and control of charities by the Charity Commission.

- In February 1988 the Committee of Public Accounts issued a report 'Monitoring and Control of Charities in England and Wales', which was highly critical of the way in which charities were monitored and of charity financial management generally.
- In May 1988 the ASC issued Statement of Recommended Practice No. 2 *Accounting by Charities* (SORP 2). It is interesting to note that SORP 2 went beyond the requirements of the Charities Acts of 1960 and 1985, a development that was welcomed by both Woodfield and the PAC.
- In the summer of 1988 the Charity Commission published *Charity Accounts – Consultation Paper*, seeking views of the sector at large. In September 1988 the Home Office issued a consultation paper, *The Regulation of Charitable Appeals in England and Wales.*
- On 16 May 1989 the Government presented its white paper *Charities: A Framework for the Future,* which included many of the recommendations made by Sir Philip Woodfield in his report.
- There then followed a considerable period of Government inactivity after this flow of public documents. However, those in the charity world, particularly the Charity Finance Directors' Group (CFDG), continued to try and improve charity financial management.
- At the beginning of May 1990 CFDG launched a campaign with the slogan 'Charities Act 199?' in an attempt to raise the issue with those MPs known to have associations with charities to try and get the Government to act. However, this did not amount to anything, as *The Times* (July 1990) reported:
  'Two Bills put forward by Government departments are thought to have been rejected for next year's programme, they include a Home Office Bill to reform the law covering charities . . .'.
- Towards the end of July 1990, the parliamentary members of the All Party Charities Panel put down an Early Day Motion in an attempt to get the Government to bring forward legislation on charities as soon as possible. Like previous attempts this met with no success.
- However, on 5 November 1991 the much sought after Charities Bill was finally published. In welcoming the Bill, the Charity Finance Directors' Group (CFDG) expressed sorrow that, after 30 years since the last attempt to seriously legislate for charities, discussion on this Bill was to be somewhat curtailed. (By this stage CFDG's campaign had been running for over 18 months and, putting that into context, the fact that the second reading in the House of Lords of the Bill was to be on 19 November and the debate was to be completed by 30 November was, to say the least, somewhat rushed.)
- Strangely, all the discussion on the Bill took place in a committee of the House of Lords and it eventually went to the House of Commons in the final days just before the 1992 Election. In fact, no discussion took place in the lower house and it was effectively rushed through in well under three minutes on 16 March 1992.

The Charities Act 1992 was effectively a combination of several years work and was subsequently consolidated into the Charities Act 1993.

1.2 Charities Acts 1992 and 1993

As a result of these acts there was little immediate change in the way in which charity accounts were prepared and presented. However, since 1993 there have been considerable challenges for charity financial management in these areas. Why?

To ascertain this, we must consider a few specific aspects. Section 45 of the 1993 Act requires that every registered charity, over a certain size, should submit to the Charity Commission within 10 months of the end of its financial year a full set of accounts professionally audited or independently examined, as laid down under s43.

Accounting records, sufficient to show and explain the transactions so as to disclose with reasonable accuracy the financial position, have to be kept. These records must show details of receipts and payments and of assets and liabilities, and they have to be kept for a period of at least six years after the end of the relevant financial year. However, if the charity ceases to exist it can, with the approval of the Charity Commission, dispose of those accounting records.

Some charities have had to face, for the first time, having their accounts audited, as s43 states:

> 'By a person who:
>
> (a) is in accordance with Section 25 of the Companies Act 1989 (Eligibility for Appointment) eligible for appointment as a company auditor; or
> (b) is a member of a body for the time being specified in regulations under Section 44 below and is under the rules of that body eligible for appointment as auditor of a charity.'

The practical effect is that the friendly bank manager of the charity, or whoever had looked at its accounts and 'audited' them in the past, may no longer have been eligible. If the charity's gross income or total expenditure exceeded £250,000 for the relevant year or either of the two previous years, then of course it was no longer good enough, unless of course the individual happened to be qualified as outlined above.

However, where the charity's gross income or total expenditure is less than £250,000 but more than £10,000 then it can choose to have the accounts independently examined. This is of course provided that its governing document does not call for audit, in which case it would still have to have its accounts audited. Section 43(3) of the Charities Act defines an independent examiner as 'an independent person who is reasonably believed by the trustees to have the requisite ability and practical experience to carry out a competent examination of the accounts'.

Some charities will have also found for the first time that they had to produce an annual report. This again must be prepared and then submitted to the Charity Commission within 10 months of the end of the financial year. This probably meant not much change for efficient, well-run charities, but for many thousands of others it created problems. Effectively, for most charities the report and the accounts would be produced as one document.

Section 42 of the 1993 Act dealing with the Annual Statement of Accounts lays down that a charity's accounts must comply 'with such requirements as to its form and contents as may be prescribed by regulations made by the Secretary of State'.

Section 47 states quite clearly that the public are given the right to request a copy of the charity's most recent report and accounts. Although the charity may charge a reasonable fee for this, it must supply this information within two months of receiving the request.

We have already touched on some of the requirements in s42, which also states that where the gross income of the charity does not exceed £100,000 in any year, then that charity need only prepare a receipts and payments account and a statement of assets and liabilities. This of course for the purist accountant is probably an anomaly – how can you have an asset/liabilities statement if you do not do accruals and only produce a receipts and payments account? This figure of £100,000 can be amended at any time by the order of the Secretary of State and where the figure is exceeded then full accrual style accounts will have to be produced.

1.3 Statement of Recommended Practice (SORP) 1995 – *Accounting by Charities*

Following much consultation, SORP 1995 was issued in October 1995 just before the regulations. Although the charities SORP had no recommended start date, it was suggested by the Charity Commission that charities should adopt it as soon as possible. Accounting practice is such that to present a true and fair view, all standards, SORPs etc. should be followed from the first accounting period following their production. This effectively meant immediate adoption. This section looks briefly at some of the significant changes from the original 1988 SORP 2.

1.3.1 SORP aim

The Charity Commission's prime aim and objective in publishing the SORP as set out in the document was:

> 'To help improve the quality of financial reporting by charities and to assist those who are responsible for the preparation of the charity's annual report and accounts. The intention is that these recommendations will reduce the current diversity in accounting practice and presentation' (para 12).

1.3.2 Prescriptive approach

There was considerable debate about this particular approach but it was felt to be the best way to proceed in order to provide simplicity and ensure consistency. One of the principal aims of accounting by charities must be to improve accountability and make comparisons by members of the general public easier. It should also be borne in mind that the regulations, which are in themselves prescriptive, made much of the SORP mandatory.

1.3.3 Words

The formal narrative statement was expanded considerably, which meant that the trustees' report must include information about the charity's objects, activities and achievements as well as a commentary on the financial position of the charity. This reinforced the importance of the annual accounts and reports by strengthening the existing recommendation in SORP 2 (paras 26–28).

1.3.4 Numbers

Perhaps the most radical change was the introduction of a 'statement of financial activities' (SOFA). This essentially amalgamated the old income and expenditure account with the reconciliation and analysis of the movement of funds. The main purpose of the SOFA is to bring together all transactions in a single statement in order to present a complete picture that will give a true and fair view of the charity's affairs.

The assessment of the financial position of a charity is quite different to that of a business venture where profit is the main motive. A business raises capital which it uses to generate profits, which it either then distributes to those who contributed the capital, or retains in order to expand its profit-making capacity. On the other hand a charity administers funds received for the purpose of its charitable objectives. Historically accounting by charities has been based on a commercial type profit and loss presentation where a surplus or a deficit on the income and expenditure account did not necessarily reflect the actual position of the charity.

This proposal therefore attempts to give the reader an understanding of how the incoming resources have been applied and is a step in the right direction, because it illustrates more clearly the way in which charities operate (paras 22 and 69–165).

1.3.5 Investments

Under SORP 2, investments held for long term purposes could be shown on the balance sheet at either cost or market value, whilst SORP 1995 recommended that they be shown at market value under the general heading 'fixed assets' as a separate category. It was felt that market value best represents a true and fair view of the value of these assets to the charity, given the duty of the trustees to administer the portfolio of investment assets so as to obtain the best investment performance without undue risk.

It went on to recommend that if investments were held as current assets, e.g. where they were to be sold without reinvestment, then they should be valued at the lower of cost or net realisable value in the same way as other current assets (paras 174–182 and 192–198).

As far as the treatment of gains and losses is concerned, SORP 1995 recommended a separate section, after the 'income and expenditure' section, setting out in full detail both the realised and unrealised gains and losses (para 132).

1.3.6 Overhead costs

The definitions of fundraising and administration costs were amended and improved. It is curious that in SORP 2, although there were several references to publicity costs, these were not defined anywhere. The opportunity was taken to do so by combining them with fundraising (App 1.10 and 1.16).

A new category was introduced so that much of what was reported under the heading of administration would, where appropriate, effectively be described as 'support costs', which are those costs incurred in respect of supporting direct charitable activities (paras 150–153 and App 1.22).

1.3.7 Summarised accounts

Where produced, these have to be approved formally by the trustees and accompanied by a statement from the auditors that they are consistent and accurate by reference to the full detailed accounts. Many charities issue publicity material, containing accounts information, which is often highly abbreviated and partly in graphical or other pictorial form. All such information now has to follow the rules laid out in SORP 1995 (paras 213–222).

1.3.8 Trading activities

The trading results of a charity's subsidiary/ies have to be shown in the main on the face of the SOFA, under the separate heading 'trading activities'. Where only the net income/expenditure is shown then there has to be a full disclosure in the notes showing the profit and loss account for each trading activity. This is an attempt to provide a systematic approach to dealing with trading activities, particularly where this is done through a subsidiary company (paras 121–127).

Although this relates to the SOFA there has to be a full consolidation of assets and liabilities on the charity's balance sheet (para 66).

1.3.9 Branches

This change is one that had a considerable effect on the way in which a number of charities produced their accounts. Accounting for branches was tightened and all branch transactions must now be reflected in the charity's own accounts, whether or not the funds were received by the parent charity by the year end. Similarly all assets and liabilities of the branch should also be incorporated into the charity's own balance sheet.

Many charities did not include all their branches' transactions in their accounts in detail and often the money that the branch remitted to the charity was included net of costs and shown under donations. SORP 1995 effectively recommended a change to this way of operation which led to an increase in the accounting effort required both by the volunteers at branch level and at the head office of the charity (paras 45–49 and App 1.1).

1.3.10 Accounting concepts

In 1988 SORP 2 made little reference to fundamental accounting concepts. The 1995 version makes explicit reference to them and, with the notable exception of smaller charities whose gross income is less than £100,000, all charities now have to prepare their accounts in accordance with the accounting concepts of an accrual basis, consistency, going concern and prudence. In the case of those smaller charities which are permitted by law to produce receipts and payments accounts, only the concept of consistency applied (paras 32–33).

1.3.11 'Light touch' approach

The effective removal from the SORP regime of the majority of charities occurred with the cut-off for the preparation of full accrual accounts being set at £100,000 gross income per year. Furthermore, those charities with an annual income of less than £10,000, i.e. those eligible for the 'light touch' regime, need not have their accounts reviewed (by independent examination/audit), nor submit them to the Charity Commission unless they are specifically asked for them.

To allay the fears of many in the charity world, two separate guides to the SORP for these smaller charities were published in 1995 by the Charity Commission. These charities only need to refer to paras 13–21 of the SORP. The standard format of accounts, shown as an appendix, complied with the recommended practice for receipts and payments accounts.

1.3.12 Glossary

SORP 1995 included a very comprehensive glossary of definitions which was provided to enable readers not familiar with certain accounting terms to follow the document more easily (App 1).

1.3.13 Conclusion

The prescriptive approach taken in SORP 1995 undoubtedly changed the way in which many charities managed their finances and led to many more disclosures in the published accounts.

1.4 Review of SORP 1995 leading to SORP 2000

As promised three years earlier, the Charity Commission launched, in September 1998, a review of the SORP to which charities and those interested had until 7 December 1998 to submit their comments and views. The major points on which the Charity Commission requested opinions were:

- **Editorial**. Parts of the SORP need to be rewritten to remove potential ambiguities. There is also scope to improve the layout and the example accounts and to provide some commentary on how the SORP relates to individual accounting standards.
- A number of aspects of **consolidation, branches and combined charities** need to be rethought.
- **Trading**. Apart from consolidation issues when trading subsidiaries are involved, there are more general questions on how to categorise income and expenditure from some types of trading.
- **Accruals accounting for incoming resources**. There is a need for greater detail on how to account for certain categories of incoming resources, particularly legacies.
- **Expenditure classifications**. Further thinking is needed about the nature of administration and support costs and the disclosure requirements for allocated and apportioned expenditure.
- **Measurement and valuation principles**, in particular how these apply to fixed assets (including investments), investment gains and losses and the recognition of liabilities and grants payable within the accounts.

- **Summary income and expenditure account and summary accounts**. The question of when and why these are needed should be clarified.
- **Fund accounting**. Additional guidance is felt to be required in a number of areas relating to the use of restricted and designated funds.
- **Reserves**. Guidance on the disclosure of reserves should be expanded in line with the Commission's leaflet.

The Charity Commission produced a short report in the spring of 1999 drawing together all the comments that they had received. A committee was appointed with the task of reviewing the operation of SORP 1995 in light of the comments received.

1.4.1 Charity commission SORP consultation

Generally it was recognised that SORP 1995 had largely met its aims by both improving the quality of financial reporting by charities and reducing the diversity in charity accounting and presentation. Out of a total of 234 respondents, 104 expressed opinions on the general view of SORP 1995, of which 77 were supportive, 15 limited in that support, and only 12 did not approve.

Whilst it was agreed that fundamental changes were not required, there was a view expressed that certain areas of SORP 1995 needed clarification, and that ambiguities which existed should be removed, but that the SORP should not be amended to the detriment of the majority just to please a small minority.

1.5 SORP 2000 – *Accounting and Reporting by Charities*

1.5.1 The changes

This SORP has been completely rewritten, although there are no major changes to the structure of the accounts, nor are there any requirements that should be regarded as difficult. However, as a result, those preparing and reviewing charity accounts will need to look at all the paragraphs that apply to the charity for whom they are preparing or reviewing accounts. The Charity Commission make the point that, whilst the document is regarded as recommended best practice, charities are at liberty to provide additional information in order to give the reader an enlarged view of the activities and achievements of the charity concerned.

Unfortunately, because of the diversity of the sector in terms of size, structure and activity, SORP 2000 has increased in length. In addition, certain sections have been included at the specific request of charities to deal with special situations, although there are few, if any charities, to which all parts of SORP 2000 will apply. Charities should therefore ignore those sections that do not apply to them. Disclosure requirements have been separately identified throughout the SORP with those that are applicable to all charities, marked as AA, which should be included in the accounts or the annual report as required. As it is not possible or indeed desirable to be prescriptive on every issue, those who prepare and review charity accounts will, as ever, have to exercise their judgement in certain areas.

SORP 2000 is principally a guide for those who prepare or audit or examine charity accounts. It has been written in accounting language and as a result may not be easily understood by those who have little or no knowledge of accounting principles and standards. However, trustees are of course ultimately responsible for the resources and finances of their charity as they are reflected in the accounts. Therefore those trustees who have little or no knowledge of accounting matters will need to seek reassurance themselves on these matters from colleagues, staff or professional advisors who do have the necessary financial and accounting background.

All the anomalies in SORP 1995 have been removed, for example those relating to consolidation requirements, the need for a separate income and expenditure account and the definition of trading activities. As long ago as September 1997 former Charity Commissioner John Bonds was on record as agreeing, in respect of accounting for investment gains and losses, that:

> 'If in such a case a charity decides to disclose total investment gains/losses (both realised and unrealised) under one heading "net investment gains/losses" on the Statement of Financial Activities, the Charity Commission will not raise any objections nor will it use its power to return accounts for rectification and resubmission provided that this departure from the SORP is adequately disclosed and justified.'

Therefore this change has been made in SORP 2000. All issues on which the Charity Commission specifically made it clear that they intended to change or improve have been amended.

Probably the most significant change is in the name of the document. In both the 1988 and 1995 versions it was *Accounting by Charities*, which has now become in the 2000 version *Accounting and Reporting by Charities*. This was a deliberate attempt by the Charity Commission to ensure that more emphasis is placed by charities on the Trustees' Report, which the Commission felt was not being given the effort it required.

One issue that many would like to have seen resolved is that of the inherent inconsistencies between the accounting treatment required by a charitable company and that of an unincorporated charity. These in particular relate to the conflicts between the Companies Act 1985 and the Charities Act 1993. There are also inconsistencies between the reporting thresholds and the need for audit. There are further inconsistencies in areas such as the auditors' duty of whistle blowing (which under the 1993 Charities Act only affects unincorporated charities). Although some of the points under this particular issue went beyond the strict parameters of the review, many of these fundamental issues have been addressed.

1.5.2 What is new

A very detailed and self-explanatory section specifically dealing with charitable companies should resolve all the anomalies and problems flowing from SORP 1995 (see Chapter 10). Subsections dealing with transactions with trustees (including their expenses) and connected persons certainly answer all the queries received in response to the Charity Commission request of September 1997 (see Chapter 14).

In the trustees' annual report, trustees are asked to comment on their reserves (the policy, the level and the justification), their investment and grant making policies and their internal controls (see Chapter 2). Very detailed cross-referencing to Statements of Standard Accounting Practice (SSAPs) and Financial Reporting Standards (FRSs) has been added, as has an appendix which is a summary of all existing accounting standards, showing their application to charities (see Chapter 6).

For smaller charities it is proposed that the threshold for reporting resources expended as set out in SORP 2000 should be increased from £100,000 to £250,000 per year (see Chapter 7).

1.5.3 Revised/extended

The detailed requirements for narrative information (as distinct from legal and administrative information) in the trustees' annual report have been reduced in order to encourage charities to expand on their activities rather than answer a series of questions (see Chapter 2).

In the Statement of Financial Activities (SOFA), the presentation of incoming resources and resources expended has been altered to provide a more logical layout to fit in with the way in which charities handle their transactions and prepare their accounts. Incoming resources and resources expended of a similar nature will be grouped together and will be consolidated where there are subsidiary undertakings (instead of summarising the results of non-charitable trading activities of subsidiary undertakings on a one line basis). This will make the accounts more transparent (see Chapter 3).

The rules for recognising incoming resources have been restated with the emphasis now placed on three factors: entitlement, certainty and measurement. The information on accounting for legacies has been extended from one paragraph to six paragraphs, which deal more clearly with the thorny issue of what to disclose, when to disclose and the accrual situation. The guidance in relation to dealing with intangible income and donations in kind, e.g. donated facilities, beneficial loan arrangements, donated services or services from volunteers, have been clarified. They now need only be recorded where another party is bearing the financial cost of those resources as supplied and the benefit is quantifiable and measurable (see Chapter 3).

The section on trading has been completely revised and brought up to date, and trading is now more accurately defined as 'operating activities' using accounting rather than taxation rules. All income from non-charitable trading is combined under one heading (see Chapter 3).

The requirements for disclosing grants are set out more extensively with the emphasis on providing the analysis and explanation necessary to understand how the grants made by a charity relate to its objects. Disclosure is required when grants total £250,000 in the year or at least 5 per cent of total resources expended (see Chapter 16).

The definition of fundraising costs has been improved and replaced by the more correct terminology of 'cost of generating funds'. Fundraising costs became an area open to considerable misinterpretation in the four years of accounts that have so far been produced under SORP 1995. Investment management fees should now be included under 'costs of generating funds' provided that they are disclosed separately in the notes to the accounts. This disclosure requirement also applies to all material items of cost included under this heading (see Chapter 3). Accounting for separate funds has been further explained (see Chapter 11).

The balance sheet section is one area where radical changes have taken place. However, these changes are only radical in the sense that there is a considerable extension from what currently appears in SORP 1995. The changes take account of FRSs 11, 12 and 15, which deal respectively with 'Impairment of Fixed Assets and Goodwill', 'Provisions, Contingent Liabilities and Contingent Assets' and 'Tangible Fixed Assets'. These three FRSs have all been issued since SORP 1995, which was updated to take account of them, particularly in relation to inalienable and historic fixed assets, liability accounting and the revaluation of fixed assets (see Chapter 4).

The section on the Cash flow Statement has been amended and updated to take account of FRS 1, which was revised in 1996 after the publication of SORP 1995 (see Chapter 5). The section on smaller charities has been extended and a greater emphasis placed on accounting aspects (see Chapters 7 and 8). The consolidation of subsidiary undertakings section has also been expanded to overcome the problems previously faced (see Chapter 15).

1.5.4 Charity Commission aim

All charity trustees have a duty to keep proper accounting records for their charity that set out and explain all the charity's transactions. SORP 2000 effectively provides guidance on how this should be undertaken annually in relation to the resources entrusted to the charity and its activities. SORP 2000 applies to all charities regardless of their size, constitution or complexity except in those cases where a more specialised SORP applies, e.g. that for registered social landlords. Therefore the Charity Commission expects charities to comply fully with this or any other applicable SORP, and where they do not then the charities' accounts should identify this and provide a full explanation. Where the Charity Commission feel that the explanation is unsatisfactory or no explanation is given then the matter may be raised with the charity concerned and, in exceptional circumstances, the Charity Commission may institute an enquiry.

Quite clearly the Charity Commission's objective in publishing these recommendations is to improve the quality of financial reporting by charities and to assist those who are responsible for the preparation of the charity's annual report and accounts. The intention is that these recommendations will reduce the diversity in accounting practice and presentation. In all but exceptional circumstances, charities preparing accrual accounts should follow SORP 2000 in order for their accounts to give a true and fair view. However the impact of SORP 2000 will be different depending upon the size and complexity of a charity's operation. To help smaller charities in particular the Charity Commission produces a range of simplified guidance booklets.

1.5.5 General principles

Accounts intending a true and fair view must be prepared on the going concern assumption and the accruals concept, and they must provide information that is relevant, reliable, comparable and understandable. Where charities can choose to prepare receipts and payments accounts, then the information must be comparable through the application of consistent policies. In meeting the obligation to prepare accounts that show a true and fair view, consideration has to be given to the standards laid down in Statements of Standard Accounting Practice (SSAPs), Financial Reporting Standards (FRSs) and Urgent Issues Task Force Abstracts (UITFs) issued or adopted by the Accounting Standards Board which are relevant to the charity's circumstances and accounts. SORP 2000 provides guidance and interpretation of the most suitable application of accounting standards for charities, *but* it is supplementary to those standards and does not repeat all of their requirements.

The main purpose of the accounts is to give an overall view of the total incoming resources during the year and how they have been spent in the balance sheet to show the overall financial position at the year end. There are additional requirements for charities that have to account for more than one fund under their control. The accounts should provide a summary of the main funds, differentiating in particular between the unrestricted income funds, restricted funds and endowment funds. The columnar format of SOFA is designed to achieve this. Charities need to account for the proper administration of the individual funds in accordance with their respective terms of trust, and accounting records must be kept in such a way that will adequately separate transactions between different funds. Some charities may hold one or more restricted funds, some of which may be permanent or expendable endowment funds. Depending on the materiality of each, the notes to the accounts should group the restricted funds under one or more headings (see Chapter 11).

1.5.6 Timing and publications

The Charity Commission committee to review the SORP completed its work in June 2000 and clearance from the Accounting Standards Board was obtained in July 2000. SORP 2000 was published on 16 October 2000 and became effective for accounting periods beginning on or after 1 January 2001. However, early adoption was encouraged by the Charity Commission.

Charity Accounts 2001 *The Framework* (CC61), aimed specifically at non-accountants, Charities SORP 2000 *What has changed* (CC62), SORP 2000 *Example Reports and Accounts* (CC66) and other publications which have been revised following SORP 2000, are available on the Charity Commission's website (www.charity-commission.gov.uk) or by telephoning the publications order line on 01823 234427.

1.6 Regulatory framework

The accounting rules flowing from Part VI of the Charities Act, the Charities (Accounts and Reports) Regulations 1995 (SI 1995/2724), were published by the Home Office in October 1995 and a revised version was published in October 2000. Significant points of interest arising from the regulations that are not covered by SORP 2000 (except in so far as the regulations refer to it) include the following.

Table 1.1

The limits for unincorporated registered charities are:

Annual gross income	***Type of accounts***	***Type of review***
Below £10,000	Receipts and payments	None
Above £10,000 but below £100,000	Receipts and payments	Independent examination
Above £100,000 but below £250,000	Accruals	Independent examination
Above £250,000	Accruals	Audit

In addition charities with an annual income of less than £1,000 which do not have a permanent endowment need not register with the Charity Commission. All registered charities with annual income in excess of £10,000 have to submit a copy of their accounts to the Charity Commission. Charities whose annual income is less than £10,000, i.e. the 'light touch' regime, need not submit a copy of their accounts to the Charity Commission unless they are specifically asked for them.

However, all registered charities have to submit an annual return to the Commission. For the smaller charity this is a fairly simple document merely to keep the record straight. Any charity can of course choose to impose upon itself more rigorous rules than Table 1.1 sets out, e.g. a charity with an income of less than £250,000 can, if it wants, elect to have its accounts audited rather than independently examined (see Chapter 9).

Independent examination is a less onerous form of scrutiny than audit, both in the terms of the depth of work that is to be carried out and the qualification necessary to undertake such work. The examiner is not required to form an opinion as to whether the accounts show a true and fair view but reports instead, based on the examination carried out, whether specific matters have come to his or her attention.

However, in order to comply with their own constitution/ trust deed, many charities still require audit whatever their size. This is a problem that the trustees will/should have to resolve if they want to make use of the independent examination procedures.

Changes in company law as regards audit and audit exemption have left some charities with a problem. As shown in Table 1.1 the threshold for audit at £250,000 is the same whether the charity is incorporated or unincorporated. However, below that figure there could be a problem. Charities who have an income in the range £10,000 to £90,000 will, if they are unincorporated, require an independent examination, but if they are companies they will require no verification by an auditor or preparer of audit exemption reports.

Table 1.2 sets out the situation with the inconsistent problem area clearly highlighted. This matter still needs to be resolved and discussions continue between the Charity Commission and the Department of Trade & Industry. The situation could have deteriorated following the proposal from the Department of Trade & Industry in early 1997 to abolish the 'accountant's report' for businesses with turnover between £90,000 and £350,000 (the threshold for audit for non-charitable companies). As reported in *Accountancy Age* on 30 January 1997, this would have created a larger loophole for unscrupulous individuals to carry out fraud under the cover of charitable companies.

Table 1.2

Annual income	***Unincorporated charity***		***Incorporated charity***	
	Audit	*Independent examination*	*Audit*	*Audit exemption report*
Less than £10,000	No	No	No	No
More than £10,000 to £90,000	No	**Yes**	No	**No**
More than £90,000 to £250,000	No	Yes	No	Yes
More than £250,000	Yes	No	Yes	No

Fortunately, the DTI listened to the Charity Commission and to the charity sector generally and agreed not only to exempt charities from this new ruling but also to look at ways of reviewing the existing anomaly. As the official report said:

> 'The current arrangements will be retained for those charities which have chosen to incorporate, pending an *early consultation* on options for harmonisation of the financial reporting requirements under charities legislation on the one hand and companies legislation on the other.'

The italics are added as the report was issued early in 1997. One would have hoped that as a result of SORP 2000 and the regulations this problem would finally be resolved. All charitable companies will of course have to produce their accounts on the accruals basis and comply with company law regulations (see Chapter 10).

In following SORP 2000 the regulations on annual reports section is probably somewhat over detailed although it is perhaps better to be this way than leave things out. However, the reports of a charity whose gross income does not exceed £100,000 may be a brief summary of the main activities and achievements of the charity during the year in relation to its objects and not the fuller version previously recommended. Any remuneration paid to trustees or persons connected with the charity must be shown in the notes to the accounts (Part IV para 1(c)) and like SORP 2000 there is a requirement to show the number of employees within set salary bands of £10,000 from a base of £50,000 upwards.

Some of the recommended changes in SORP 2000 required changes to the Regulations and therefore the Home Office issued for discussion Draft Regulations on Charity Accounts and Reports on 22 February 2000. Comments on these Draft Regulations had to be submitted by 30 April 2000 to the Charity Commission. The consultation document was very technical but in summary it covered:

- whether to raise the annual income threshold for simpler arrangements for preparing annual reports and accounts from £100,000 to £250,000;
- how best to cover Governance arrangements and investment and reserves policies and practices in the annual report, at least for larger charities;
- how to make the detailed analysis in the accounts of incoming resources less prescriptive;
- how to revise the expenditure analysis to bring it in line with the Exposure Draft of the SORP;
- how to cover historic or inalienable assets, for reflecting in a recent accounting standard and the Exposure Draft of the SORP;
- how to revise the rules on related party transactions in the light of a recent accounting standard and the Exposure Draft of the SORP;
- how to make various other minor and technical changes to maintain consistency with the Exposure Draft of the SORP;

- whether to make a minor amendment on the rules on accounts scrutiny to allow the Charity Commission to give a dispensation at an earlier stage;
- where exactly to draw the boundary of the special accounting regime for Common Deposit Funds and non-pooling scheme Common Investment Funds;
- how to carry out technical updating of the rules for registered social landlords and certain designated education institutions, including making explicit that the accounts for these bodies must give a true and fair view; and
- whether provision needs to be made for any additional classes of charity to be allowed to treat accounts prepared under some other statutory accounting regime as also being their accounts for the purposes of the charity accounting regime; and whether that treatment should be conditional on the alternative accounts giving a true and fair view.

The Charities (Accounts and Reports) Regulations 2000 were laid before Parliament on the 25 October 2000 as Statutory Instrument 2000 Number 2868. The Regulations came into force on 15 November 2000 for statements of accounts prepared by the charity trustees of a charity in respect of the financial year that began on or after 1 January 2001. Where the trustees wished earlier adoption it was undertaken. In fact early adoption was obligatory if the trustees had not either approved the accounts of the charity or authorised the signature of the annual report for accounts ended before that date by 15 November 2000. The Regulations follow very closely the Statement of Recommended Practice and in particular have dealt with all the issues raised above.

A copy of the 2000 Regulations (SI 2000/2868) is available from HMSO or can be downloaded from their website at www.hmso.gov.uk.

Part II
Commentary and guidance on elements of the financial statements

Chapter 2 Trustees' annual report

SORP 2000 takes a similar view to the 1995 SORP in relation to the principles required in the trustees' annual report. However, there is a distinct decrease in the amount of detail required for narrative information. Trustees are encouraged to make the annual report both concise and comprehensive in its contents. A reduction in the prescriptive requirements within the report should enable trustees to focus more firmly on the charity's activities and achievements rather than merely complete a routine questionnaire or checklist. The need for qualitative non-financial information is reinforced within SORP 2000. Although in general the amount of narrative information that is required to be included in the trustees' annual report has been reduced, there are additional areas of disclosure for reserves policy and risk appraisal.

Section 45 of the 1993 Charities Act states that 'charity trustees should prepare in respect of each financial year of the charity an annual report containing:

(a) such a report by the trustees on the activities of the charity during that year; and
(b) such other information relating to the charity or its trustees or officers as may be prescribed by Regulations made by the Secretary of State.'

The Charities (Accounts and Report) Regulations 2000 (SI 2000/2868) contain the framework for disclosure requirements within the trustees' annual report. More detailed guidance to these Regulations is contained in SORP 2000.

Paragraphs 3 to 5 of SORP 2000 outline the purpose of the charity's annual report and accounts which is to discharge the trustees' duty of public accountability and stewardship. SORP 2000 outlines the basic recommended best practice for trustees to follow when preparing the annual report and accounts. Trustees are nevertheless encouraged to provide any further information to give their various stakeholders a deeper insight into the charity's activities and achievements in the year.

Paragraph 4 requires the reports and accounts to 'provide timely and regular information.' The purpose of this is to enable the 'reader to understand the charity's objectives, structure, activities and achievements.' This in turn will allow the reader 'to gain a full and proper appreciation of the charity's financial transactions during the year and of the position of its funds at the end of the year.' This paragraph lays down the philosophy and framework under which trustees should embark upon preparing the report and accounts.

The Regulations make a distinction between charities whose annual income is below £250,000 and those that exceed £250,000 in a year. There are additional requirements for those charities whose income exceeds £250,000 in a year as can be seen by the checklist at the end of this chapter.

2.1 Duty to prepare annual report and accounts

All of the charity's trustees are jointly responsible for the preparation of the annual report and accounts (para 26). The report should state the charity's aims and how it has attempted to achieve these aims. The report is a separate legal document but is usually presented with the main accounts. Trustees should confirm within the report and accounts that they have complied with current statutory requirements, the governing document of the charity and the

SORP 2000 (para 27). Both the annual report and accounts should be approved by the trustee body and the date of approval should be stated (para 28). Any dissenting trustees who cannot resolve their differences with fellow trustees or the auditors have an option to go the Charity Commission and state their concerns (para 28).

2.2 Legal and administrative information

These are very similar requirements to the 1995 SORP. Information that should be included in the trustees' annual report is as follows:

- Name of the charity;
- Nature of the governing document and how the charity is constituted, charity registration number and company registration number, if applicable;
- Names of all the charity's trustees on the date the report was approved or at least 50 trustees where there are more than 50 trustees. Name of any other persons who served as trustees in the year, together with their method of appointment. The name of the person or body entitled to appoint trustees should be stated;
- Address of the principal office of the charity;
- Names and addresses of relevant organisations or persons e.g. bankers, solicitors and auditors;
- Any specific restrictions imposed by the governing document; and
- Any specific investment powers.

2.3 Narrative information

The trustees' annual report should be sufficient to explain what the charity is trying to do and how it is achieving this. It should tell the story of the charity for the financial year in question. The report should show the extent to which the objectives have been achieved and explain clearly the charity's plans for the future. In addition, the report should be able to explain how the numerical part of the accounts interact with the organisational structure and activities of the charity. It is therefore sensible that detailed written information should match the Income and Expenditure headings in the main accounts. Paragraph 31 requires the narrative information to include:

(a) Explanation of the charity's objects which may include its mission statement. This is the reason the entity has been granted charitable status and the trustees' annual report should focus on how the charity has endeavoured to meet its objectives.
(b) The organisational structure should be detailed, together with a description of the decision making process within the charity.
(c) To the extent the charity has relationships with other related parties and organisations to help it achieve its charitable goals, a statement should be made in the trustees' annual report to reflect this. This requirement will effect many charities as it is quite common for charities to enter into partnerships with other charities or funders to maximise all available resources.
(d) A review of the activities of the charity to include:
    - significant changes;
    - developments and achievements in the year;
    - subsequent events affecting the activities since the year end; and
    - plans for the future.

This section of the report can include the contribution of volunteers and the extent to which fundraising activities have been successful in enabling the charity to fulfil its charitable objectives. Again, this can easily be cross referenced to the SOFA.

(e) The trustees' annual report should include the principal policies of the charity such as:
  (i) **Reserves Policy** – which should state the level of reserves held and should justify and explain why this level is necessary for the charity. This requirement follows the Charity Commission's publication of CC19 *Reserves' Policy* and should also include how the charity is going to maintain these reserves and the processes it adopts for monitoring and reviewing its reserve levels. This will be part of a planning process in which the charity will need to project future income and expenditure. To achieve this, it will need to analyse its future needs, opportunities, contingencies/risks (see (g)) and assess the likelihood of the above arising with related consequences.
  (ii) **Investment Policy** – which reflects the charity's investment needs and risks. It should show to what extent the trustees have put in place a policy that suits the charity's objectives and financial situation. The policy should be stated within the light of the Trustee Act 2000 which widens trustees' investment powers. The Act came into effect on 1 February 2001.
  (iii) **Grant Making Policy** – where relevant this should show how the charity's grant making is in line with its charitable objectives. It should also show how the application and monitoring process works.

(f) If certain funds are in deficit, the trustees' annual report should explain why this is the case and what action is going to be taken to rectify this matter. A restricted fund may be in deficit where project expenditure has been made in anticipation of future incoming funds. Whilst this situation is justifiable, should unrestricted funds or total funds be in deficit, then a more detailed explanation and analysis would be required.

(g) Quite significantly, a new measure has been added to the requirements within the trustees' annual report. This is a statement by the trustees confirming that major risks to which the charity is exposed to, have been considered and reviewed by the trustees. The risk management that is required should include not just financial risks but also strategic, operational, environmental and regulatory ones. Trustees may consider using risk maps or risk modelling to enable them to identify these risks. The level and significance of the charity's exposure to these risks needs to be outlined, together with any systems that the trustees have put in place to reduce these risks to the charity.

This requirement within SORP 2000 is a watered down version of the original requirement outlined in the draft SORP. It is based on the commercial sector requirement originally outlined in the Turnbull Report which requires officers of a legal entity to consider the wider legal and commercial context in which the entity operates. Included in this statement is the requirement to provide details on corporate governance and disclosures on internal financial controls within the charity. The statement should comment on the level and suitability of the internal financial controls within the charity and mention any formal management processes the charity has adopted to monitor risk and this should also be recorded at trustees' meetings.

The additional risk analysis required by SORP 2000 is a natural progression from the principles laid down by the Charity Commission in their booklet CC3 *Responsibilities of Charity Trustees*. This states that trustees should act reasonably and prudently when dealing with charity matters. The risk analysis approach should focus the trustees' attention to sensitive areas and this may enable them to be in a more informed position to perform their duties more efficiently.

2.4 Funds held as custodian trustee on behalf of others

Where a charity or its trustees acts as a custodian and holds property on behalf of another charity, the trustees' annual report should (para 32):

(a) provide a description of the assets held;
(b) state the objects of the charity whose assets they hold and how these meet the charity's own objectives; and
(c) provide details of safe custody and segregation of custodian assets held within the charity.

2.5 Responsibilities of trustees

The Auditing Practices Board (APB) Practice Note 11 (October 1996 – currently being revised) adopts SAS 600 *Auditors' Reports on Financial Statements* to include trustees' responsibilities as follows:

> 'Charity law requires the trustees to prepare accounts that give a true and fair view of the state of affairs of the charity and of its income and expenditure for the financial year. In doing so, the trustees are required to:
>
> - select suitable accounting policies and apply them consistently;
> - make judgements and estimates that are reasonable and prudent;
> - prepare the accounts on a going concern basis unless it is inappropriate to presume that the charity will continue in operation.
>
> The trustees are responsible for maintaining proper accounting records which disclose with reasonable accuracy at any time the financial position of the charity and to enable them to ensure that the accounts comply with the Charities Act 1993 (Companies Act 1985 for charitable companies). They are also responsible for safeguarding the assets of the charity and hence for taking reasonable steps for the prevention and detection of fraud and other irregularities.'

If this statement is not included directly in the auditors' report, it should be included within the trustees' annual report.

Table 2.1 Charity accounts compliance checklist: trustees' annual report

Regulation	SORP 2000	Requirement	Yes / N/A / Ref
7(3)		The financial year to which the report relates.	________
7(3)(a)		**A brief summary of the main activities and achievements of the charity during the year in relation to the charity's objects.**	________
7(4)(a)	30a	The name of the charity as it appears in the register of charities and any other name by which it makes itself known.	________

> *Note: Excepted charities which are not registered should provide the name as set out in their governing document and any other name by which they are known.*

Regulation	SORP 2000	Requirement	Yes / N/A / Ref
7(4)(b)	30b	The number assigned to the charity in the register and, in the case of a charitable company, the number with which it is registered as a company.	________

> *Note: Excepted charities which are not registered do not have a charity registration number.*

Regulation	SORP 2000	Requirement	Yes / N/A / Ref
7(4)(c) 7(5)	30d	The principal address of the charity and, in the case of a charitable company, the address of its registered office.	________

> *Note: The Charity Commission may dispense with the requirement to disclose the address of the charity if it could lead to any person being placed in any personal danger.*

Regulation	SORP 2000	Requirement	Yes / N/A / Ref
7(4)(d)	30b	Particulars, including the date if known, of any deed or other document containing provisions which regulate the purposes and administration of the charity.	________
7(4)(e)	31a	A description of the objects of the charity.	________
	30f	Where applicable, details of any specific restrictions imposed by the governing document concerning the way in which the charity can operate.	________
	30e	The names and addresses of other relevant organisations or persons including those acting as bankers, solicitors, auditor (or independent examiner or reporting accountant) or other principal advisers.	________
7(4)(f)	30ciii/civ	The names of any person or body of persons entitled by the trusts of the charity to appoint one or more new charity trustees, and a description of the method provided by those trusts for such appointment.	________
7(4)(g)	30ci	The name of any person who is a charity trustee of the charity on the date when the report is signed, and, where any charity trustee on that date is a body corporate, the name of any person who is a director of the body corporate on that date.	________
7(4)(h)	30 cii	The name of any other person who has, at any time during the financial year in question, been a charity trustee of the charity.	________
7(5)			

> *Note: The Charity Commission may dispense with the requirement to disclose the names of charity trustee(s) if it could lead to that person/(those people) being placed in any personal danger.*

Table 2.1 Charity accounts compliance checklist: trustees' annual report *(cont.)*

Regulation	SORP 2000	Requirement	Yes / N/A / Ref
7(6)		If the charity has more than 50 trustees then the names of not less than 50 trustees must be disclosed.	________
7(4)(i)		The name of any person who is a trustee for the charity (that is those holding property on behalf of the charity) on the date the report is signed.	________
7(4)(j)		**The name of any other person who has, at any time during the financial year in question, been a trustee for the charity (that is those holding property on behalf of the charity).**	________
7(4)(k)	31e	A description of the policies (if any) which have been adopted by the charity trustees:	
		(i) for the purpose of determining the level of income reserves which it is appropriate for the charity to maintain in order to meet effectively the needs designated by its trusts;	________
		(ii) for the selection of investments for the charity; and...........	________
		(iii) for the selection of individuals and institutions who are to receive grants out of the assets of the charity.	________
	30g	Details of any specific investment powers and their authority. ..	________
	31c	A statement regarding the relationships between the charity and related parties and with any other charities and organisations with which it co-operates in pursuit of its charitable objects.	________
7(3)(c)	28	The report shall be dated and signed by one or more of the charity trustees, each of whom has been authorised to do so...	________

Additional requirements for charities with gross income of more than £250,000 per annum

Regulation	SORP 2000	Requirement	Yes / N/A / Ref
7(3)(b)	31d	*Instead of a brief summary of achievements and activities there should be:*	
		A review of all activities, including:	
		• material transactions, significant developments and achievements of the charity during the year in relation to its objects;	________
		• any significant changes in those activities during the year;....	________
		• any important events affecting those activities which have occurred since the end of the year and any likely future developments in those activities;	________
	31f	• where any fund of the charity was in deficit at the beginning of the financial year, the steps taken by the charity trustees to eliminate the deficit.	________
7(3)(b)(ii)	31g	A statement as to whether the charity trustees have given consideration to:	
		• the major risks to which the charity is exposed; and.............	________
		• systems designed to mitigate those risks.	________

Regulation	SORP 2000	Requirement	Yes / N/A / Ref
7(4)(1)	31e	A statement regarding the performance during the financial year of the investments belonging to the charity (if any)............	________
7(4)(m)	31b	A description of the organisational structure of the charity.	________
7(4)(n)	32	A description of any assets held by the charity or by any charity trustee of, or trustee for, the charity, on behalf of another charity. In particular, of any special arrangements made with respect to the safe custody of such assets and their segregation from assets of the charity not so held and a description of the objects of the charity on whose behalf the assets are held.	________

Chapter 3 Statement of Financial Activities (SOFA)

3.1 Introduction

Historically, accounting by charities has been based on a business-type profit and loss presentation, where a surplus or a deficit in the income and expenditure account did not necessarily or fairly reflect the actual true position of the charity. The traditional income and expenditure account did not always fully explain all of the charity's activities.

Charities often receive significant amounts of restricted income which can affect the types and level of service they provide and it is important to consider changes in the amounts of all the resources of the charity. The SOFA is a single accounting statement with the objective of:

- showing all incoming resources and resources expended by the charity in the year on all its funds;
- demonstrating how the charity has used its resources in furtherance of its objects for the provision of benefit to its beneficiaries;
- indicating whether there has been a net inflow or outflow of resources including capital gains and losses; and
- providing a reconciliation of all movements in the charity's funds.

Where statutory requirements, accounting and reporting standards or the requirements of a charity's governing document, make it necessary to prepare a separate primary statement of income and expenditure, a summary income and expenditure account should be prepared. This summary statement and any relevant notes should be appropriately cross-referenced to the statement of financial activities from which the summary amounts would have been derived so that the relevant requirements are met. SORP 2000 has sought to clarify the instances in which such a statement is required.

Charities, except those that are effectively trading, are not usually in the business of directly matching income and expenditure. The normal rules in respect of profit and loss accounts therefore do not apply. Charities are not bottom-line driven and income and expenditure may often be in respect of different periods or not directly linked. For example, grants received this year may be for projects to be carried out in the following year or indeed over a number of years.

Unfortunately, the traditional income and expenditure account with its distinction between revenue and capital does not always adequately explain a charity's activities and in any particular year a charity may use part of its income to purchase fixed assets for its charitable activities. This could therefore lead to a surplus on the income and expenditure account and may give a misleading impression. The SOFA does not include capital expenditure, whether of a charitable or any other nature, and therefore judging the charity on the bottom line criteria will continue to be misleading in these circumstances, where there is significant charitable objective spending of a capital nature.

3.2 Disclosures

The Statement of Financial Activities (SOFA) was introduced in the 1995 SORP. This statement has not been fundamentally altered by SORP 2000. The SOFA still shows in summary form for the period under review:

- all the charity's funds;
- all its incoming resources;
- all its revenue expenditure;
- all transfers between funds;
- gains and losses on investments; and
- how the fund balances have changed since the last balance sheet date.

The SOFA is effectively divided into two parts, a statement of operations and a statement of other changes in net assets. The SOFA has moved away from giving undue emphasis to the bottom line and dropped the use of the words 'surplus' and 'deficit'. It focuses instead on the periodic measurement of the changes in both the nature and amounts of all the net resources of the charity.

3.3 Format

A columnar format is scheduled in the regulations so there is no choice but to comply. For example, for some charities the minimum required will be four columns with the following headings:

- Unrestricted funds;
- Restricted funds;
- Permanent endowment funds; and
- The total for the year.

For many charities, following SORP 1995, this meant the separation of income and expenditure streams between the different types of fund for the first time. There must also be a further column showing the comparative total for the previous year, but it is not a legal requirement to show comparatives for each type of fund.

Where there have been no movements in any particular fund or the charity does not have that type of fund, then it will not be necessary to include that column. Funds may be summarised within their fund type but, as set out in the later section on fund accounting, details of each individual restricted fund and movements on that fund in the year must be given by way of a note to the accounts. Each column should be totalled to show the net incoming/outgoing resources before transfers.

The new format has also introduced standard headings for each row (i.e. line) such as:

- Incoming resources;
- Charitable resources expended;
- Costs of generating funds etc.,

which should help to make the accounts more comparable. The SORP makes clear this information will always be required but, if there has been no movement on a particular heading in the year or previous year, that heading need not be included.

Functional classification of expenditure means that instead of disclosing expenditure by type – such as rent, rates, light and heat – expenditure is described by its nature in terms of charitable expenditure, grants payable, management and administration. Following the incoming resources and resources expended in the year, a total for each fund should be made before gross transfers between funds are shown. Each fund is totalled to show 'net incoming resources before revaluations and investment income disposals'. Gains and losses on revaluations of fixed assets for the charity's own use are then shown. This is followed by the now combined gains and losses on revaluations and disposals of investment assets. This is discussed further in Chapter 13, which deals with investments.

The funds on the face of the SOFA should be reconciled. The net movement in the year should be shown together with the opening total funds per fund type. The combined figure should be shown as total funds carried forward.

To comply with FRS 3, the SOFA should distinguish between continuing, discontinued and acquired operations. This normally applies to the whole of a distinctive type of activity of a charity but not the development or cessation of new projects within that activity (para 67).

In instances where there have been substantial changes in fixed assets for the charity's use, this should be explained in the notes to the accounts to help the reader to understand the effect on liquid funds. Where this is material, the note should follow directly after the reconciliation of funds. Paragraph 86 goes on to say the format should then show:

- net movements in funds for the year;
- resources used for net acquisitions of fixed assets for charity use;
- net movement in funds available for future activities.

Individual charities can expand on these headings where necessary to enable them to give a true and fair view and convey a proper understanding of the nature of all their activities. It is recommended that the charity's aim should be to have a clear link between the incoming and outgoing resources and in particular the functional split of activities.

The examples given in the SORP consider a charity running a care home. This charity could use the sub-heading 'Residential Care Income' and 'Residential Care Costs'. Those charities fundraising through a shop could use the sub-heading 'Shops' in activities for generating funds and costs of generating funds.

3.4 Fund accounting

Trust law requires charities to separately account for all incoming resources, not just monies received which have a restriction imposed by the donor. These amounts are pulled together and accounted for either as restricted or endowment funds, dependent upon their precise nature.

Fund accounting is fundamental to most charities' accounts when funds are received or used for different purposes. Fund accounting, although not a requirement with a separate column for each type of fund, is now enshrined in law through the regulations. The subject is dealt with in greater detail in Chapter 11.

3.5 Incoming resources

3.5.1 Recognition

As the SORP makes clear, all incoming resources that become available to the charity during the year should be recognised in the statement of financial activities (SOFA). This would include all income belonging to the charity regardless of its source or of the purpose to which it is to be or has been put (para 75).

Example 3.1 The ABC Charity

CONSOLIDATED STATEMENT OF FINANCIAL ACTIVITIES
(incorporating an Income and Expenditure Account) for the year ended 31 March 2001

	Notes	Unrestricted Funds £'000	Restricted Funds £'000	Totals 2001 £'000	Totals 2000 £'000
Incoming resources					
Donations and gifts	2	4,130	3,200	**7,330**	6,000
Legacies	3	2,150	–	**2,150**	1,330
Building appeal	17	–	400	**400**	900
Activities in furtherance of the charity's objects:					
Government grants for residential care	17	–	700	**700**	400
Fees for residential care		1,200	–	**1,200**	1,000
Activities for generating funds:					
Merchandising income	4	1,140	–	**1,140**	900
Investment income	5	350	50	**400**	475
Net gain on disposal of fixed assets		20	–	**20**	30
Total incoming resources		8,990	4,350	**13,340**	11,035
Resources expended:					
Cost of generating funds:					
Fund-raising costs		480	210	**690**	550
Building appeal costs	17	–	45	**45**	110
Merchandising costs	4	870	–	**870**	710
Investment management fees		80	10	**90**	110
		1,430	265	**1,695**	1,480
Charitable expenditure:					
Costs of activities in furtherance of charity's objects:					
Residential care costs		1,400	1,030	**2,430**	2,545
Childcare		1,000	2,400	**3,400**	3,150
Emergency services		1,800	1,300	**3,100**	2,800
Information and Education		90	10	**100**	300
Support costs		110	80	**190**	180
Management and administration		210	60	**270**	230
		4,610	4,880	**9,490**	9,405
Total resources expended	6	6,040	5,145	**11,185**	10,885
Net incoming resources/(resources expended) before transfers		2,950	(795)	**2,155**	150
Transfers between funds	17	15	(15)	–	–
Net incoming resources/(resources expended)		2,965	(810)	**2,155**	150
Net gains on investment assets	11	100	–	**100**	250
Net movement in funds		3,065	(810)	**2,255**	400
Fund balances brought forward at 1 April	17	6,300	3,900	**10,200**	9,800
Fund balances carried forward at 31 March	17	9,365	3,090	**12,455**	10,200

All of the above results are derived from continuing activities. All gains and losses recognised in the year are included above. The surplus for the year for Companies Act purposes comprises the net incoming resources for the year plus realised gains on investments and was £2,225,000 (2000: £230,000). Page 10 gives details of changes in resources applied for fixed assets for charity use.

The value of all resources accruing to a charity should be recorded in its SOFA provided it is prudent to do so. The practicality of this needs to be assessed and income should not be recognised until any and all conditions relating to its receipt have been met. Legal enforceability is of paramount importance and charities using the accruals basis should not include income where there is uncertainty as to their entitlement (para 75).

3.5.2 Recognition

All income should be treated in a similar manner and recognised in the SOFA regardless of the source of the income or the use to which it is to be or has been put. Income should be recognised when the following three factors have been met:

- entitlement;
- certainty;
- measurement.

All charities with a gross income in excess of £100,000 will have to account for income on a receivable basis, i.e. by accruing. Only those charities with an income below this amount may use a receipts and payments method. Therefore, once the charity has become entitled to the income, it must account for it.

3.5.3 Regulations

Part 1 dealing with a SOFA at para 3 (1995 regulations) makes it clear that incoming resources should be analysed as:

- incoming resources from donors;
- income from investment;
- income from trading activities:
  - which are in furtherance of the objects of the charity; and
  - which are for commercial or fundraising purposes; and
- any other material incoming resources.

These regulations remain unchanged in the 2000 version.

3.5.4 SORP

The SORP goes somewhat further in its analysis requirements than the regulations and most charities are attempting to follow these recommendations, and certainly by so doing they will ensure that they comply with the regulations as well.

Paragraph 59 highlights items which should be shown as separate lines in the SOFA, where the income is derived from a particular source and is material:

- donations, legacies and similar incoming resources;
- incoming resources from the operating activities of the charity distinguishing between:
  - activities in furtherance of the charity's objects; and
  - activities for generating funds;
- investment income;
- other incoming resources (e.g. net gains on disposals of fixed assets for use by the charity);
- the total of the above resources arising in the year.

3.5.5 Accounting for incoming resources

All incoming resources accruing to the charity, whether capital or income, should be included in the SOFA as soon as they are receivable or entitlement becomes legally enforceable. In the past, income has been carried forward on the balance sheet as a liability, particularly in respect of legacies, however where the trustees can spend such funds whenever they wish it is not right to defer their recognition as income. It is not the restriction that prevents their use, and any restricted income received but unspent at the year end should be carried forward in the relevant restricted income fund.

The situation of a restriction imposed on the use of income must be distinguished from a condition attached to a grant, which must be fulfilled prior to its receipt or use. Income should normally be shown when it is receivable. Income can only be deferred when the donor has imposed restrictions on the expenditure of resources. An example could be where a charity is receiving restricted grant funding from a local authority with a March year end. If the charity had a December year end there could be a case for deferring three months' expenditure. A clear explanation should be given in the notes to the accounts.

As soon as income is recognised as receivable it should be identified as to whether it is restricted or unrestricted and, if restricted, to which particular fund it belongs. With the continuing growth of the so-called 'contract culture', the important issue that has emerged is the consideration of whether contract income under the community care regime is restricted or unrestricted income. Careful attention should be paid to the wording of each individual contract to determine whether the funds are restricted or unrestricted.

3.5.6 Restricted income

The columnar design of the SOFA means that there is even more need to identify and account for restricted income separately. Such income is defined by the SORP as monies subject to specific conditions imposed either by the donor or by the nature of an appeal, for example for a particular purpose or project. The fact that income carries a restriction should not affect the timing of its recognition in the SOFA. However, if conditions must be met before the income can be recognised, then the accounts should not reflect this income either in the SOFA or the balance sheet. A contingent asset may exist.

Funds received for the purchase of restricted assets should be recognised immediately.

Care needs to be exercised in determining the distinction between restrictions relating to the purposes for which a particular resource may be used and those conditions which must be fulfilled prior to its receipt or use by the charity. Standard restrictions on the use to which a resource may be put, however, will not result in the recognition being deferred, as they will not amount to a precondition to be overcome.

It should also be borne in mind that unless a donor specified otherwise, income received on restricted income funds that have been invested must be included within the relevant restricted funds and used for that same purpose. However, income received from the investment of restricted capital funds is unrestricted and available for the general purposes of the charity unless the donor has specified otherwise.

3.5.7 Donations, legacies and similar incoming resources

This part of the SOFA shows all voluntary income sources and will include core-funding grants. It may also include membership subscriptions, gifts in kind, intangible income and sponsorship income where not for goods or services.

The accounts should show the material components of each type of income under this heading either on the face of the SOFA or in the notes to the accounts.

3.5.8 Legacies

The accounting treatment for legacies has in the past often caused difficulties and, therefore, has been reflected in a variety of ways. Following the introduction of the SORP in 1995 it was no longer possible:

- to take legacies 'below the line'; or
- to take legacies straight to reserves; or
- to use an apportionment method.

SORP 2000 has sought to clarify the issues surrounding legacy recognition. Legacies should be monitored from the point of notification. When the legacy is received or the charity is certain of receipt, the legacy should be recognised in the SOFA. This notification may take the form of a letter from the personal representatives advising of payment, but it should not be recognised as income if there are conditions in respect of receipt. Legacies must also be capable of financial measurement.

When a payment is received on account or a letter is received advising that payment will be made, the payment or intended payment should be treated as receivable.

The main issues with legacies tend to arise around the charity's year end. The question of which year the legacy income should be recognised in is considered in para 93 of SORP 2000. When a payment is received or notified as receivable after the accounting year end but it is clear that the personal representatives had agreed it before the year end, then it should be accrued in the SOFA and the balance sheet.

In cases where the charity has been notified of material legacies that are not included in the SOFA, this fact and an estimate, if possible, of the amounts receivable should be disclosed in the notes to the accounts.

3.5.9 Gifts in kind

The Charities SORP recommends that gifts in kind should be included in the SOFA in the following ways:

In the case of charities with shops, such as Oxfam, that are in receipt of donated goods, for example clothes, the income should only be recognised when the clothes are sold. This confirmed that charities do not need to include stocks of donated goods held by a charity at the balance sheet date in the accounts of the charity for that year. Recognition is only on sale.

In other instances where the charity is given an asset for its use, for example a computer, the charity should recognise this as an incoming resource as soon as the gift is available. It should be shown as a donation in the SOFA. To complete the double entry the value attributed will then be capitalised if that is the policy of the charity involved as far as fixed assets are concerned, or written off in the same period as revenue expenditure, e.g. resources expended under the relevant heading.

In cases where the policy of the charity is to capitalise fixed assets, the asset should be identifiable within the reserves of the charity and then written off in line with the normal depreciation policy for a similar asset held by the charity.

3.5.10 Donated assets

'Donated assets are capitalised at a value equivalent to market value at the date of donation.'

Assets given for distribution by the charity should be recognised as income for the year only when distributed (para 95c). This would cover instances where, for example, a charity is perhaps distributing blankets or medicines to Somalia. The charity is receiving donated blankets but the distribution and the entry in the accounts should only be recognised when those blankets or medicines, for example, are passed on to Somalia. At that point it will be shown both as an incoming resource and a charitable resource expended in the same period. A reasonable estimate of their gross value to the charity or the amount actually realised should be given.

The SORP requires that where there are undistributed assets at the year end, a description of the items involved and an estimate of their value should be given by way of a note to the accounts. The basis of any valuation should be disclosed. Where material, an adjustment should be made to the original valuation upon subsequent receipt of the gift.

3.5.11 Intangible income

Paragraph 99 of the Charities SORP 2000 defines intangible income as receipt of assistance in the form of donated facilities or beneficial loan arrangements. It goes on to say that such intangible income should only be included in the SOFA if the charity would otherwise have to purchase the donated facilities and the benefit is quantifiable and material, i.e., the donor is bearing the financial cost of the resources supplied. The value placed on them should be the financial cost to the third party of providing them. An equivalent amount should be included in the SOFA as expenditure under the appropriate heading. Detailed amounts falling under this heading should be disclosed in the notes to the accounts.

Some charities receive substantial amounts of voluntary help (SORP para 99). The SORP states that this should not be accounted for in the SOFA, due mainly to the problems with valuation, but should be dealt with in the notes to the accounts or in the trustees' annual report. This is the case for those organisations that are almost entirely dependent on voluntary help.

Some charities are starting to reflect the value of their volunteers. A major issue with this is the fact that it is very difficult to actually assess the value of a volunteer. Do you value them by the minimum wage (now £4.10 an hour), do you value them by the average wage, or do you value them by those of an equivalent member of staff? The SORP does not recommend that you put a value on the volunteers' help but in practice some charities are starting to put a value through their accounts to account for voluntary help.

3.5.12 Incoming resources from operating activities

This is a new name for an income analysis, previously shown as 'trading', to be included within SORP 2000. The income under this heading falls into two categories:

1. Activities in furtherance of the charity's objects;
2. Activities for generating funds.

These headings can be expanded as required and if necessary further subdivisions can be given in the notes to the accounts. All incoming resources that are in the nature of a payment for the provision of goods or services should be combined together under the relevant activity.

3.5.13 Activities in furtherance of the charity's objects

These activities may include (para 104) sale of goods and services as part of the direct charitable objects, sale of goods and services made by or provided by beneficiaries of the charity, and incoming resources from government or public authorities received in the normal course of trading.

3.5.14 Activities for generating funds

These activities do not form part of direct charitable activities but are carried on in order to generate incoming resources as a way of supporting those activities, for example jumble sales, lotteries etc.

The realisation of donated assets should be included within this section together with sales of bought in goods and licensing income. Ancillary trades should also be included within this category.

3.5.15 Disclosure

An analysis of the charity's activities should be shown in the notes to the accounts to supplement the summarised disclosure on the face of the SOFA. It should give sufficient detail to enable the user of the accounts to be able to understand all of the activities in which the charity is involved.

3.5.16 Subsidiary undertakings

All payments from subsidiary undertakings should be shown separately in the SOFA (for example gift aid payments) and appropriately disclosed. On consolidation the charity will only recognise the operating results of the subsidiary undertaking. Further disclosures required are considered in Chapter 15.

3.5.17 Investment income

Income from investment assets including dividends and interest, but excluding capital returns, should be included as investment income in the SOFA. The notes to the accounts should show gross investment income from each category of investment as follows:

- investment properties;
- investments listed on a recognised Stock Exchange shown gross;
- investments in subsidiary or associated undertakings or in companies which are connected persons;
- other unlisted securities;
- cash deposits held as part of the investment portfolio;
- any other investments.

These items should also be further analysed between investment assets in the UK and those outside the UK.

3.5.18 Incoming resources from government and other bodies

These include income from the European Union and the National Lottery and will normally be included in the SOFA under 'donations, legacies and similar incoming resources' or 'activities in furtherance of the charity's objects'.

The specific terms of the income need to be considered to determine whether it should be included within restricted income. The test tends to be whether, on completion of the project, any surplus income has to be repaid to the funder. If so, then a restriction can be assumed.

The notes should give a full description of the sources of any material incoming resources by category.

3.5.19 Other incoming resources

This will include all items that the charity cannot categorise and which do not conform to any of the above mentioned categories.The most common type of income under this heading will be profit on disposal of a fixed asset for the charity's own use.

3.6 Resources expended

3.6.1 Introduction

Generally as a basic accounting rule, expenditure is not incurred until consideration for the expenditure has passed and something is received in exchange. However, charities are often at odds with this rule.

3.6.2 Accounting for expenditure

Expenditure will be shown in the SOFA under a functional analysis rather than by type. This will help explain the charity's activities so the heading should be chosen with care to reflect the activities and objects of the charity. It should be consistent with the annual report. This functional analysis is the aggregation of costs incurred in pursuit of a defined purpose, for example provision of assistance to the elderly. It is achieved by adding together all costs relating to that specific activity and it is, therefore, likely to include an allocation exercise as well as addition since it summarises expenditure according to the purpose for which costs are incurred.

SORP 2000 has altered the way in which costs are stated in the accounts. Costs fall into two main categories – those for generating funds and those for charitable activities. This alters the disclosure recommended in the previous SORP, which showed expenditure on major charitable activities and the costs of supporting those activities (charitable expenditure) separately from expenditure on fundraising and publicity, management and administration of the charity (other expenditure).

Fundraising and publicity costs now need to be reconsidered as to whether they fall into the category of costs of generating funds. Management and administration costs are now shown under charitable expenditure.

The SOFA presentation can also be altered if this is thought to be more informative for readers of the accounts. A sub-total can be added under the costs of generating funds, which gives the 'net incoming resources available for charitable application'.

3.6.3 Recognition of expenditure and liabilities

All expenditure should be included in the SOFA under the accruals concept. A liability arises as soon as there is legal or constructive obligation committing the charity to the expenditure. As charities often do not receive anything in exchange for expenditure, particularly in respect of grants, the charity's liability has been redefined in SORP 2000 in terms of obligations to a third party. To quote:

> 'A liability will arise when a charity is under obligation to make a transfer of value to a third party.' (para 122)

Liabilities can arise out of a constructive obligation. If a valid expectation has been placed in the mind of the recipient, then in accordance with FRS 12 a commitment may have been created. This may also be influenced by the charity's policy or public commitment to the amount payable. However, if the charity has imposed conditions to be met before the payment is due, a liability has not been created. The commitment should be treated as a contingent liability. The trustees may wish to set up a designated fund in respect of the commitments that they have made. If the commitment cannot be met or is no longer required, the provision should be cancelled against the relevant expenditure heading in the SOFA.

When committing the charity to expenditure over a number of years the best estimate of the cost involved should be included in the SOFA, for example research funding. Where the commitment is over a number of years, it may be necessary to use Discount tables.

This is undoubtedly a grey area. The definition of a liability would certainly not cover the attitude adopted by many charities in the past of treating internal commitments or decisions about future spending as liabilities (see Chapter 16).

The accounting policy for the recognition of different categories should be disclosed in the accounts. If designated funds have been set up in respect of the commitments, the notes to the accounts should give a clear explanation as to why the fund has been set up. If provisions have been cancelled, the notes should give a clear explanation of the reversed amounts and the reasons for them.

3.6.4 Costs of generating funds

SORP 1995 defined fundraising and publicity costs as costs actually incurred by a charity (or by their agent) in helping and inducing others to make voluntary contributions and donations to it. SORP 2000 has developed this cost category further. The costs of generating funds (para 132) are the costs 'which are associated with raising funds from all the possible sources of incoming resources.'

The costs involved will still mainly include fundraising costs, but the definition has been expanded further to include investment managers' fees and the costs of negotiating for contracts/applying for grants. The costs of publicity should also still be included, however the costs should not include an education element. Distinctions should be drawn in line with the charity's circumstances.

However, one problem that frequently arises is that in many cases a charity's publicity will have a two-fold purpose, both that of educating about the objectives and seeking to raise funds. In promoting their confidential telephone facility, the charity ChildLine is both urging the public to send money via a tear-off slip on the advert whilst at the same time encouraging individuals to report cases of abuse. Where both elements are significant, costs should be allocated accordingly.

Where material, the different categories of the costs of generating funds should be shown separately or in the notes to the accounts. An analysis of the major items of expenditure should be shown in the notes to the accounts and linked where possible to the respective incoming resource.

3.6.5 Charitable expenditure

All expenditure should be included in the SOFA as soon as it is incurred. Charitable expenditure comprises all of the costs incurred by the charity in meeting its charitable expenditure. This heading now also includes management and administration costs.

Under SORP 2000 the sub-headings within this cost category include:

- grants payable in furtherance of the charity's objects;
- costs of activities in furtherance of the charity's objects;
- support costs of (a) and (b) where material; and
- costs of management and administration of the charity.

Costs in respect of fixed assets such as depreciation and impairment should be included in the respective cost category.

3.6.6 Charitable objective criteria

It is vitally important that charities carefully consider whether the grants they are making fall within their charitable objectives. A grant made for any other purpose may not be permitted by the charity's governing instrument. Furthermore, if the grant is for a purpose that is not charitable in law then it will not be allowed as 'qualifying expenditure' for tax purposes and the special concessions may, therefore, be restricted or even withdrawn totally.

Charities often make grants overseas and the Inland Revenue takes the view that such payments will only be treated as 'qualifying expenditure' if the charity has taken reasonable steps and can show that the payments will actually be applied for charitable purposes. The burden of proof rests with the charity and it will require forms of internal control to be able to provide this. If grants are being made to a reputable foreign charity, written confirmation that the grant will be properly applied is usually acceptable by the Inland Revenue.

3.6.7 Grants payable

In the case of grant expenditure relating directly to charitable activity, no exchange is involved. This contrasts with the business world as expenditure is treated as not incurred until consideration for the expenditure has passed and something is received in exchange for the expenditure. This creates problems for the charity since it is not possible to match the expenditure with the receipt of goods or services, as there are none.

The issue of dealing with grants payable is a problem area for many charities and this area is addressed in detail later (see Chapter 16).

3.6.8 Cost allocation

Expenditure relating to just one activity or cost category should be directly allocated. Other overheads should be apportioned on a reasonable, justifiable and consistent basis to the relevant cost categories. A number of methods could be used, such as:

- time spent (possibly recorded by time sheet or just estimated on a percentage basis);
- the proportional number of people carrying out each activity; or
- their salary costs for area occupied etc.

The important point to remember is to derive a reasonable method based on the existing information available and apply it consistently over the succeeding years. It will be necessary to disclose the basis used in the accounting policies so that the accounts are fully transparent (para 153). However, it is not possible to define precisely what should be included under each heading.

Where costs do not fall into the categories of costs of generating funds, grants payable, costs of operating activities and support costs they should be included within management and administration of the charity.

Cost allocation is only legally required once a year in order to support the accounts. On an ongoing basis throughout the year accounting records will need to be kept showing 'natural classification' of expense items. This is required in order to support normal budget functions and comparisons of budget with actual (see Chapter 18).

3.6.9 Costs of activities in furtherance of the charity's objects and support costs

The notes to the accounts should analyse the costs by appropriate activity of the charity to assist in the user's understanding of the charity's activities. Where applicable, and the amount is material, the support costs should be shown separately on the face of the SOFA. An analysis of all the major items included in support costs should be given in the notes to the accounts.

The accounts should have appropriate analysis of all material expenditure. Where possible this should be tied into the corresponding incoming resource.

SORP 2000 has tried to move away from the 'good costs/bad costs' of SORP 1995, i.e. everything that was directly charitable was good cost and everything else was bad cost. This led to the increasing misuse of support costs. It is hoped that, with the SORP 2000 moving management and administration into the charitable category, the misuse of support costs will lessen.

3.6.10 Management and administration

Management and administration of a charity is something that arouses a lot of interest, both from the public and the media. There will always remain costs which are incurred in connection with the management of the charity's assets. These are organisational as opposed to project administration costs and include compliance with constitutional and statutory requirements. Such costs should be separately identified and examples include:

- expenditure on trustees, management and annual general meetings;
- compliance with constitutional and statutory requirements, for example:
  - annual audit fee;
  - most legal fees;
  - valuation fees;
- management of the charity's assets.

The allocation of costs to management and administration will continue to be an issue for charities as there is no prescribed format. SORP 2000 indicates that there are indirect and direct costs. The direct costs are as listed above. Indirect costs will be apportioned costs representing costs involved in managing and administering the charity. Those will include both staff and office overhead costs.

A clear analysis of the main items of expenditure on management and administration should be given in the accounts.

3.7 Transfers

Transfers between different funds and gains and losses arising from revaluations, and from the disposal of investment assets should not be included in the incoming resources summary, but shown in a separate section after the expenditure section of the SOFA (para 62). In particular, any transfers included in the SOFA must be explained, where material, in detail in the notes to the account.

In particular, material transfers should be shown separately and not included in the netting off. Transfers should be explained in detail in the notes to the accounts.

3.7.1 Netting off

SORP 2000 states that, as far as practicable, all incoming resources should be reported gross. This means, in particular, that expenditure on fundraising should not be netted off against the funds raised, but should be disclosed separately. Netting off is only permissible for small fundraising events which will not materially understate gross income and expenditure. The costs of the charity's own staff should never be offset against fundraising activities. Material transfers between funds and allocations to designated funds should not be netted off but explained.

Where a capital grant is provided towards the cost of acquiring a fixed asset, the cost of the asset should always be shown gross.

3.8 Gains/(losses) on fixed assets

Gains and losses arising on the disposal, revaluation or impairment of fixed assets will form part of the particular fund in which the asset – investment or other – was held at the time of the disposal, revaluation or impairment.

Impairments should be recognised as an additional depreciation charge against the impaired asset and reflected in the appropriate section in the SOFA.

Gains on disposals of fixed assets should be included within income under 'other incoming resources'. Losses should be treated as an additional depreciation charge and shown under the respective cost category in the SOFA.

Revaluation gains or losses on assets held for the charity's own use should be shown in the section on gains and losses on revaluations of fixed assets for the charity's own use.

Gains and losses on investments, whether they are realised or unrealised, should be shown under the gains and losses on the revaluation and disposal of investment assets.

3.9 Conclusion

The SORP in 1995 introduced some important changes in the basic concepts underlying charity accounts. The income and expenditure account previously used was based on the profit and loss account, which aims to measure the profitability of business enterprises, and is bottom-line driven. SORP 1995 asserted that this was generally unsuitable for charities because they are 'not for profit' bodies. One of the more important things for a charity to consider is its expenditure and whether it is meeting its objects.

The surplus or deficit on an income and expenditure account can be very misleading, as often a surplus may represent funds which are committed (for example, for capital expenditure) but the normal accounting rules do not allow charities to show that committed expenditure. Alternatively, a deficit for the year may be due to responsible trustees ensuring that they use up excess reserves that they have built up previously. The SOFA also incorporates movements in values of investments.

Example 3.2 The Rosanna Grant Trust

STATEMENT OF FINANCIAL ACTIVITIES
for the year ended 30 September 2001

	Notes	Unrestricted Funds £'000	Restricted Funds £'000	Endowment Funds £,000	Totals 2001 £'000	Totals 2000 £'000
Incoming resources						
Investment income	2	634	103	–	**737**	680
Resources expended						
Costs of generating funds	3	14	20	90	**124**	112
Charitable expenditure:						
Grants payable	4	458	85	–	**543**	421
Support costs	5	105	5	–	**110**	81
Management and administration	6	48	3	15	**66**	63
Total incoming resources		625	113	105	**843**	677
Net incoming resources/ (resources expended)		9	(10)	(105)	**(106)**	3
Other recognised gains and losses:						
Gain/(loss) on investments	10	8	12	447	**467**	(103)
Net movements in funds		17	2	342	**361**	(100)
Balance at 1 October 2000		378	5,982	20,223	**26,583**	26,683
Balance at 30 September 2001	14	395	5,984	20,565	**26,944**	26,583

Example 3.3 Aid Overseas

CONSOLIDATED STATEMENT OF FINANCIAL ACTIVITIES
for the year ended 30 September 2001

	Notes	Unrestricted Funds £'000	Restricted Funds £'000	2001 Total £'000	2000 Total £'000
Incoming resources					
Donations legacies and similar incoming resources	2	**6,897**	3,797	**10,694**	10,991
Activities in furtherance of the charity's objects:					
Contracts for operational programme	3	**–**	4,746	**4,746**	4,567
Activities for generating funds:					
Shop income	4	**8,573**	–	**8,573**	6,596
Investment income and interest	5	**190**	39	**229**	202
Total incoming resources		**15,660**	**8,582**	**24,242**	**22,356**
Less: Cost of generating funds					
Shop expenditure	4	**6,494**	–	**6,494**	6,029
Fund-raising costs	6	**1,646**	113	**1,759**	1,584
		8,140	**113**	**8,253**	**7,613**
Net incoming resources available for charitable application		**7,520**	**8,469**	**15,989**	**14,743**
Charitable expenditure					
Costs of activities in furtherance of the objects of the charity:	7				
Grants payable to partner organisations	7, 8	**1,286**	2,239	**3,525**	3,829
Operational programmes	7	**1,032**	4,578	**5,610**	5,892
Gifts in kind	7	**239**	1,092	**1,331**	1,296
Information, campaigning & education	7	**984**	9	**993**	917
Support costs	9	**1,502**	404	**1,906**	1,845
Managing and administering the charity	10	**470**	2	**472**	466
Total charitable expenditure		**5,513**	**8,324**	**13,837**	**14,245**
Total resources expended		**13,653**	**8,437**	**22,090**	**21,858**
Net incoming resources	11	**2,007**	**145**	**2,152**	**498**
Total funds brought forward		**4,006**	2,695	**6,701**	6,203
Total funds carried forward	21, 22	**6,013**	**2,840**	**8,853**	**6,701**

The statement of financial activities includes all gains and losses recognised in the year.

All incoming resources expended derive from continuing activities.

Chapter 4 Balance sheet

A charity's balance sheet is required to give a true and fair view of the state of affairs of the charity at the end of the financial period. The balance sheet provides a picture of the charity's assets and liabilities at one moment in time. As distinct from profit-making entities, SORP 2000 requires the net asset position of a charity to be split between its various types of funds. The funds of a charity should be shown in the balance sheet according to their type. For example, funds should be distinguished between:

- Unrestricted – general;
  – designated;
- Restricted funds
- Endowments – permanent;
  – expendable.

This split between funds, which is based on the principles of trust law, should enable the user of the accounts to be in a clearer position to understand what level of resources are available to the charity.

4.1 Balance sheet presentation

Paragraph 184 provides the headings under which the assets and liabilities of a charity should be disclosed. They are as follows:

- fixed assets, sub-divided between:
  - intangible assets;
  - tangible assets;
  - inalienable and historic assets;
  - investments.
- current assets, sub-divided between:
  - stocks and work in progress;
  - debtors;
  - investments;
  - cash at bank and in hand.
- creditors: amounts falling due within one year;
- net current assets or liabilities;
- total assets less current liabilities;
- creditors: amounts falling due after more than one year;
- provisions for liabilities and charges;
- net assets;
- funds of a charity split between:
  - unrestricted income funds;
  - restricted income funds;
  - endowment funds.

Paragraph 186 states the underlying principle for balance sheet disclosure is that assets and liabilities should be analysed in the manner that enables the reader of the accounts 'to gain a proper appreciation of their spread and character'.

4.2 Intangible fixed assets

SORP 2000 states that intangible fixed assets should be shown in the charity's balance sheet in accordance with the principles of FRS 10 *Goodwill and Intangible Assets*. This requires such assets to be capitalised and amortised over their useful economic life.

4.3 Tangible fixed assets

SORP 2000 updates the previous SORP to include the principles of FRS 15 *Tangible Fixed Assets*. FRS 15 does not apply to those reporting entities applying the Financial Reporting Standard for Smaller Entities (FRSSE) or to investment properties which are covered by SSAP 19. FRS 15 effects tangible fixed assets in the following areas:

- initial measurement;
- depreciation;
- valuation.

4.3.1 Initial measurement

FRS 15 states that all tangible fixed assets should be capitalised in the balance sheet when initially acquired by a charity. These assets should be brought into the balance sheet at their cost of acquisition. Both SORP 2000 and FRS 15 require tangible fixed assets to be measured at the cost which includes all those costs that are directly attributable to bring the assets into a working condition for their intended use (para 192). For example, this includes interest on loans taken out to finance the construction of assets which bring them into working use. However, once the asset has been constructed, even if it is not at full working capacity, no further interest charges should be capitalised. Subsequent expenditure on tangible fixed assets should generally be written off to the SOFA but can be capitalised where it replaces or restores a specifically identified component within the fixed asset or enhances the fixed asset. Circumstances where subsequent expenditure may be capitalised would include:

- where there is an enhancement of the economic benefit – e.g. results in increased capacity;
- where there has been a major refit or refurbishment of the tangible fixed asset;
- inspections and overhauls that may be required for legal reasons.

The following points are also relevant when considering how to account for the initial measurement of a tangible fixed asset:

- any fixed assets acquired via a grant should still have their costs shown as a gross figure in the accounts;
- donated fixed assets should be valued at a reasonable estimate of the gross value to the charity. Where these items were not originally capitalised but the charity now wishes to do so, they can be included in the accounts, at either their original cost or at the original value of the gift, less an amount for depreciation. Where this is not possible, a reasonable estimate of this can be used by the charity instead and this valuation will not be regarded as a revaluation of the fixed asset;
- charities need to distinguish between land and buildings used for functional purposes and land and buildings used for investment purposes. This is an important distinction because investment fixed assets will be governed by SSAP 19. If only a small part of the asset is used for investment purposes, or the commercially leased part is only for a short duration, then the fixed asset can still be treated as a functional fixed asset provided its primary purpose is a functional one for charity use.

4.3.2 Depreciation

FRS 15 did not change any basic principles regarding depreciation but it did tighten up some of the interpretations, which will result in less incidences of non-depreciation being permitted. Depreciation is required in the accounts to reflect the economic benefit of the asset which is consumed over a period of time. Even when an asset has increased in value, there will still be a requirement to depreciate it. The consumption of economic benefits in a period occurs because assets wear out or have a reduced useful economic life. This may be due to the age or obsolescence of the tangible fixed asset. Previously, it had been argued that because certain properties were maintained to such high standards, depreciation would be inappropriate. This high standard may have been achieved by subsequent expenditure on the asset. Although it is acknowledged that subsequent expenditure may extend the useful life of the tangible fixed asset, this does not negate the need for depreciation. Paragraph 200 states the specific conditions under which depreciation may not be applied:

- if the asset is freehold land which is considered to have an indefinitely long useful life;
- if both the depreciation charge *and* the accumulated depreciation are not material because:
  (a) the asset has a very long useful life; or
  (b) the residual value is not materially different from the carrying value of the asset.
  In this situation an impairment review, in accordance with FRS 11, will be required for individual assets or groups of assets that form part of the income generating units. Once the first period of impairment review has been undertaken, only subsequent reviews are needed to update any previous reviews. However, charities preparing accounts under the FRSSE will not only be able to avoid a depreciation charge if they meet the above criteria, but also will not have to conduct an annual impairment review.
- if the assets are inalienable or historic and have not been included in the balance sheet.

4.3.3 Valuation

In line with FRS 15, SORP 2000 provides that charities do not need to revalue their tangible fixed assets but where they do so, then this revaluation needs to apply to the entire class of that fixed asset. FRS 15 aims to stop reporting entities from cherry picking which individual assets they choose to revalue which may result in a biased balance sheet position. This will now apply equally to charities. Classes of tangible fixed assets may be considered under the following headings (narrower headings may be considered):

- Freehold interest in land and buildings;
- Leasehold and other interest in land and buildings;
- Plant and machinery (including motor vehicles);
- Fixtures, fittings and equipment;
- Payments on account and assets in the course of construction.

A revaluation of tangible fixed assets will not be considered to have taken place in the following situations:

- for the initial valuation when the asset was originally donated and capitalised;
- capitalisation of the tangible fixed asset following a change of accounting policy;
- the incorporation into the accounts of previously revalued assets at the date of commencement of the SORP 2000 i.e. the initial carrying value is treated as if it were the cost.

Where fixed assets are revalued, their revaluation should be updated regularly but not necessarily annually. Trustees are required to take a reasonable approach to valuations. At least every five years a suitably qualified person should conduct the valuation with interim reviews conducted if there is evidence of a material change in the value. SORP 2000 allows charities more flexibility than the stricter valuation rules as stipulated in FRS 15 for commercial entities, which need to carry out independent full property valuations every five years. Although FRS 15 requires valuations to be conducted by qualified experts, both it and SORP 2000 acknowledge that there will be limited benefits to charities to this full property valuation process.

For properties, FRS 15 provides the following valuation approaches which charities may adopt. They are as follows:

- **non-specialist properties** (e.g. residential properties, shops or offices)
  – existing use basis (e.g. best price at which the sale of the property would have been completed unconditionally for cash consideration at the date of valuation);
- **specialist properties** (e.g. hospitals or museums)
  – depreciated replacement cost (e.g. realistic estimate of the current cost of constructing an identical or substantially similar new asset with similar service capacity);
- **properties surplus to requirements**
  – open market value (e.g. the net realisable value basis);
- **other fixed assets**
  – open market value or depreciated replacement cost.

For certain assets, a second-hand market or appropriate indexes may be used to conduct the valuation. In this situation, the valuation should be updated on an annual basis.

Where functional fixed assets have been revalued, the notes to the accounts should disclose the following (para 223):

- the name and qualification of the valuer and whether they are a member of staff, a trustee or external to the charity;
- the basis of the valuation;
- the historical cost, less depreciation of the tangible fixed asset;
- the date of the previous valuation;
- where no valuation has been updated, a statement by the trustees that they are not aware of any material changes since the previous valuation.

In addition, where there is a significant difference between the carrying value and the market value in land and buildings, the trustees should make reference to this in the notes to the accounts.

4.3.4 Impairment reviews

SORP 2000 updates the previous SORP for FRS 11 *Impairment of Tangible Fixed Assets*. SORP 2000 acknowledges that it will only be in exceptional situations that a functional fixed asset of a charity will become impaired. Impairment tests will only be required when there has been some indication that an impairment has actually occurred. In this rare situation for a charity, the net book value of a tangible fixed asset will be greater than its recoverable amount and an adjustment will need to be made to write down the value of this asset to its recoverable amount.

A recoverable amount is defined as the higher of the net realisable value and the value in use. Value in use is defined as the present value of the future cash flows from using the asset. However, the fixed assets of charities are not generally held for producing surplus cash flows. Therefore, for a charity to measure the value in use of a fixed asset, SORP 2000 offers the intrinsic worth of the service delivery or the replacement cost of the asset as a measure of its service potential. Each charity is allowed to be subjective in measuring its own service delivery but the basis should still be reasonable, justifiable and consistent. Provided there are no indications that there have been any reductions in the recoverable amount of the asset below its net book value, then the impairment review is not required. Paragraph 226 provides circumstances which may be indicative of impairment. These are as follows:

- physical deterioration, change or obsolescence of the fixed asset;
- social, demographic or environmental changes resulting in a reduction of beneficiaries for a charity;
- changes in the law, other regulations or standards which adversely affect the activities of a charity;
- management commitments to undertake significant reorganisation;
- major loss of key employees associated with particular activities of a charity;
- operating losses on activities using fixed assets primarily to generate incoming resources.

4.4 Inalienable and historical fixed assets

The general principle of FRS 15 is that all tangible fixed assets should be capitalised, including both historic and inalienable assets. An historic asset is defined as being of acknowledged historic, scientific or artistic importance. Charities will need to retain and use their historic assets because this will be in direct furtherance of the charity's objects. Such assets are considered to be held for their lifetime and as they normally form part of a charity's permanent endowment their disposal will only occur in very rare circumstances.

Where these assets are included in a charity's balance sheet, they should be sub-divided in the notes to the accounts. SORP 2000 acknowledges that it may be problematic to attribute cost or value to inalienable and historic assets. Paragraph 211 allows these assets to be excluded from the balance sheet provided that:

- no reliable cost information is readily available and also there are no suitable valuation techniques that are reliable; or
- there are significant costs involved in obtaining a cost or valuation which outweigh any benefits derived by including these assets in the accounts.

SORP 2000 acknowledges it can be particularly problematic to attribute a cost or valuation to donated inalienable and historic assets. However, where these assets are purchased either directly by the charity or by third parties who then shortly after donate the asset to a charity, then the purchase price can be used as a reliable cost basis. Therefore, newly acquired assets will have a value and should be included in the balance sheet. This may lead to potential inconsistencies where previously donated historic or inalienable assets are omitted from the balance sheet but newly acquired assets are included.

In para 214, SORP 2000 provides examples where it envisages the cost of obtaining suitable information may not outweigh the benefit of this information. This will include:

- museum and gallery collections, including the national archives;
- archaeological sites, burial mounds, ruins, monuments and statues.

Where inalienable and historic fixed assets are included as a separate item in the balance sheet, the notes to the accounts may need to be further divided into appropriate classes as applicable to each charity.

Regardless of whether inalienable or historic assets have been capitalised in the accounts, the notes to the accounts, or a separate publication (which is referred to in the notes), the charity should provide the following information on these assets:

- why the assets are considered to be inalienable or historic;
- age and details of the assets;
- use made of the assets.

These details can only be omitted if publication of the information would have a prejudicial effect on the working of the charity. A statement should be made in the notes to the accounts to make reference to those inalienable or historic assets that have not been capitalised.

4.5 Investments

Paragraph 232 requires all investment assets to be shown in the balance sheet at either market value or the trustees' best estimate of market value. Trustees are required to administer the charity's assets on a prudent basis. By valuing investments at market value, a reader of the accounts is in a better position to gauge to what extent the trustees have made appropriate use of the charity's assets. No depreciation need be applied to investment assets. The following bases of valuation apply:

- Listed shares – value on recognised Stock Exchange;
- Unlisted shares – trustees should adopt a reasonable approach with reference to the net assets, earning potential, or dividend history of the company. Where the cost of obtaining a valuation outweighs the benefits to the users of the accounts, the asset may be included in the accounts at cost;
- Investment properties – trustees should adopt a reasonable approach to valuation. This must be carried out at least every five years. In the interim period, the trustees should obtain advice as to the possibility of any material movements between the valuations. Where several assets are involved, it is permissible for valuations to be carried out on a rolling basis over the five-year period.

Where the second or third basis of valuation, referred to above, has been applied, the notes to the accounts should disclose:

- who has carried out the valuation (name, qualification and position); and
- how the valuation has been performed.

The notes to the accounts should show all movements in investment assets and should disclose them between:

- investment properties;
- investments listed on a recognised Stock Exchange;
- investments in subsidiary or associates;
- other unlisted securities;
- cash balances; and
- any other investments.

With the exception of 'any other investments', further disclosure of these investment assets should be given for those assets held in the UK and those held outside the UK. The notes to the accounts should disclose details of:

- portfolio mix, distinguishing between direct and indirect investments;
- any investments that comprise over 5 per cent of the value of the holding;
- those investments where material restrictions apply; and
- analysis of the investments by the type of fund.

4.6 Current assets

In line with standard accounting convention, a current asset should be shown in the balance sheet at the lower of cost and net realisable value. However, current asset investments should be shown at their market value or at the trustees' best estimate of the market value. Debtors may be further analysed in the notes to the accounts between short-term and long-term (over one year) in the following manner:

- trade debtors;
- amounts due from subsidiary and associated undertakings;
- other debtors;
- prepayments; and
- accrued income.

Where investments are held as a current asset, the same disclosure requirements apply as for those investments held as a fixed asset.

4.7 Liabilities

Liabilities should be shown at their settlement value. Where amounts are to be paid over several years, it may be necessary to discount the amount shown in the balance sheet to its present value. Short-term and long-term creditors should be analysed in the notes to the accounts as follows:

- loans and overdrafts;
- trade creditors;
- amounts due to subsidiary and associated undertakings;
- other creditors;
- accruals; and
- deferred income.

Where a charity is acting as an intermediary agent for another charity, it should provide details of this in the notes to the accounts and the intermediary charity does not need to include the related assets and liabilities in the balance sheet. The same details are required where the charity is acting as principal in such a transaction but, in this instance, the assets and liabilities *will* be included in the balance sheet.

4.8 Contingent assets and liabilities

A contingent asset/contingent liability is a potential asset/potential liability that:

- is derived from past events; and
- its existence is determined by the occurrence of one or more uncertain future events which are not necessarily within the charity's control.

A contingent liability also may be a current obligation that is derived from past events but is not included in the accounts because:

- either it is not likely there will be a transfer of economic benefits to settle the obligation; or,
- the amount of the obligation cannot be easily measured.

Both contingent assets and liabilities should be shown in the notes to the accounts and neither the incoming or outgoing resources that relate to them, are reflected in the SOFA or balance sheet. In the notes to the accounts, the amount of a contingent liability should be disclosed at the date the accounts are approved. Similarly, all material guarantees and the circumstances under which such liabilities may occur, should be disclosed in the notes to the accounts. Where the probability of the future transfer of economic benefits is extremely remote, then no disclosure is required of either the contingent asset or liability. Where disclosure is made, then the notes to the accounts should show:

- the nature of each contingency;
- the uncertainties that effect the outcome; and
- an estimate of the financial effect of the contingency, or where no estimate is possible, a note explaining why this is so.

4.9 Loan liabilities

In the situation where certain assets are used as security for a mortgage or charge in order for the charity to receive a loan or other liability, there should be a note in the accounts which discloses:

- details of the assets which are charged;
- the amount of the loan or liability; and
- the proportion of the loan to the value of the assets charged.

Disclosure of inter-fund loans should include:

- the amount of the loan;
- the interest rate used; and
- repayment terms.

Loans to trading subsidiaries should disclose the above information together with details of any security given.

Table 4.1 Charity accounts compliance checklist

Balance sheet

1 General

Yes / N/A / Ref

> *Note: The balance sheet must show the state of affairs of the charity at the end of the financial year. [Sch 1 Pt II 1, para 181], Reg 3(5)b*

		Yes / N/A / Ref
1.1	Are the assets of the charity divided between fixed assets and current assets [para 184]?	
1.2	Have the fixed assets been sub-divided into:	
	1 intangible assets [para 184(i)a]?	
	2 tangible assets for the charity's use [para 184(i)b]?	
	3 inalienable and historic assets [para 184(i)c]?	
	4 investments (including investment properties) [para 184(i)d]?	
1.3	Have current assets been divided between:	
	1 stocks and work in progress [para 184(ii)a]?	
	2 debtors [para 184(ii)b]?	
	3 investments [para 184(ii)c]?	
	4 cash at bank and in hand [para 184(ii)d]?	
1.4	Are the liabilities divided between current and long-term liabilities [para 247]?	
1.5	Is there a heading for net current assets or liabilities [para 184(iv)]?	
1.6	Have the assets and liabilities been analysed in a way that enables a proper appreciation of their spread and character [para 186]?	
1.7	Is there a heading for total assets less current liabilities [para 184(v)]?	
1.8	Is there a heading for provisions for liabilities and charges [para 184(vii)]?	
1.9	Has the figure for net assets been given [para 184(viii)]?	
1.10	Have the charity's funds been divided into:	
	1 unrestricted income funds [para 184(ix)a]	
	2 income funds which are restricted by law as to their use [para 184(ix)b]	
	3 capital funds (i.e. endowments) [para 184(ix)c]	
1.11	Where there are material negative balances on restricted funds, ensure that these have not been netted off on the balance sheet but disclosed separately [para188]	
1.12	Have all fixed assets been capitalised and shown in the balance sheet [para 190]?	
1.13	Are all tangible fixed assets (other than investments) depreciated? If not, do they meet the conditions stipulated in para 200 e.g. asset is freehold land or both depreciation charge and accumulated depreciation are immaterial, or asset is historic or inalienable and has not been included in the balance sheet?	
1.14	Where inalienable and historic fixed assets are included in the balance sheet, are they separately disclosed in the notes to the accounts [para 208]?	
1.15	Where inalienable and historic assets are not shown in the balance sheet, ensure that this is because:	
	(a) no reliable information can be gathered to produce cost or value; or	
	(b) where this information can be gathered, the cost of gathering this information outweighs any additional benefits of disclosing the assets in the accounts [para 211]	

Table 4.1 Charity accounts compliance checklist *(cont.)*

		Yes / N/A / Ref
1.16	Is sufficient detail given on the inalienable or historic fixed assets in the notes to the accounts or in a separate publication e.g. nature and use of asset [para 215]?	
1.17	Where a charity has decided to revalue a fixed asset, ensure that the entire class of that fixed asset is revalued [para 218]	
1.18	Has a reasonable approach to the valuation been adopted e.g. at least every 5 years use of suitable qualified person [para 221]?	
1.19	Is there any evidence to suggest that the recoverable amount of a functional fixed asset is below its carrying amount [para 226]?	
1.20	If there is evidence, has the charity conducted an impairment review by comparing its net realisable value to the value in use for that category of fixed asset [para 227]?	
1.21	When determining the value in use, has the charity adequately measured its own value of service delivery of the asset [para 225]?	
1.22	Where there is an impairment loss, has this been correctly treated as additional depreciation in the SOFA [para 229]?	
1.23	For investment assets for which there is no readily identifiable market price has a reasonable approach to valuation/revaluation been adopted [para 233]?	
1.24	Have current assets other than investments been shown at the lower of cost and net realisable value [para 242]?	
1.25	Are liabilities shown at their settlement value [para 243]?	
1.26	Have liabilities been correctly identified and recognised, differentiating between amounts payable within the next year and amounts payable after more than one year [para 247]?	
1.27	Where there is an asset related to the liability, has this been shown [para 270]?	
1.28	Has the balance sheet been approved by the trustees, as a body, and signed by one of them on their behalf [Reg 3(11), para 28]?	
1.29	Has the date of approval been stated [Reg 3(11), para 28]?	

Chapter 5 Cash flow statements

SORP 2000 expands on the previous guidance provided in the 1995 SORP. Charities still need to follow Financial Reporting Standard 1 (revised in 1996) when preparing a cash flow statement. A cash flow statement should be prepared as part of the charity's primary financial statements if in either its present or its previous financial year the charity met two or more of the following size criteria:

- gross income in excess of £2.8m;
- balance sheet total (gross assets) in excess of £1.4m;
- has more than 50 employees.

The objective stated in SORP 2000 is to show how cash is received and used by the charity in the financial year (para 272). Charities are required to follow the requirements of FRS1 (revised 1996) in preparing their cash flow statement, subject to the following modifications:

- any details given for cash movements should be in accordance with the narrative detail as stated in the Statement of Financial Activities;
- the cash flow statement should begin with net incoming/(outgoing) resources before valuations and investment asset disposals.

SORP 2000 provides further guidance on how to treat movements on endowment funds (para 275). It states these should not be considered as cash flows from operating activities but should be treated as increases or decreases in the financing section of the cash flow statement. Therefore donations to endowments should be treated as additions to the endowment in the financing section. This is because SORP 2000 does not view endowments as part of the charity's ongoing activities. Where there have been receipts and payments following the acquisition and disposal of investments, then these should be shown gross in the 'capital expenditure and financial investment' section of the cash flow statement. Included in this section, and also to be included in the financing section for the same but opposite amount, is the net movement in cash flows attributable to these endowment investments i.e: proceeds minus cost of endowment investments.

In terms of disclosure, the following points should be included (para 276):

- any major items which do not result in cash movements should be disclosed in the notes to the accounts;
- a reconciliation is required of the opening and closing balance sheet amounts for cash and financing movements.

there should also be a reconciliation of cash flow from operating activities to net incoming resources/expenditure as shown in the Statement of Financial Activities.

Table 5.1 Charity accounts compliance checklist: cash flow statement (FRS 1)

Cash flow statement (FRS 1)

0 Overview

Yes / N/A / Ref

0.1 Has a cash flow statement been prepared where the charity has two or more of the following size qualifications:

1 gross resources in excess of £2.8m [para 272 & App 2] .... ________

2 a balance sheet total greater than £1.4m [para 272 & App 2] .... ________

3 more than 50 employees [para 272 & App 2] .... ________

Note: attention should be paid to the governing instrument of the charity, in case it requires a cash flow statement.

0.2 Does it comply with the FRS 1 requirements [para 273]?... ________

Note: Para 276 notes specifically that:
(a) major transactions not resulting in cash movements should be disclosed in the notes, if necessary for an understanding of the underlying transactions;
(b) cash (and any financing) movements should be reconciled to the appropriate opening and closing Balance Sheet amounts; and
(c) the reconciliation of the cash flows from 'operating activities' in the cash flow statement to net incoming resources/expenditure in the SOFA.

0.3 Is the analysis of cash movements in accordance with the charity's operations (para 274)? e.g. does the analysis begin with 'net incoming/outgoing resources before revaluations and investment asset disposals?' .... ________

0.4 Ensure endowment movements are included in 'financing' section of the cash flow statement by (para 275):

- adding donations to endowment funds in 'financing' section; .... ________
- showing gross and separately acquisition and disposal of endowment investments 'capital and financial investment' section;..................................... ________
- disclosing net cash flow movement on these investments as a single line entry in: .... ________
    - in 'capital and financial investment' section; .... ________
    - with corresponding entry in 'financing' section. .... ________
- showing distributions from endowments as a decrease in the 'financing' section.. ________
- not reporting in the cash flow statement, those transactions which do not result in any cash flow (e.g. depreciation, re-valuation and accruals). .... ________

Table 5.1 Charity accounts compliance checklist: cash flow statement (FRS 1) *(cont.)*

Yes / N/A / Ref

Cash flow statement (for company accounts)
Headings in the cash flow statement will normally be revised to accord with the activities of the charity.

> *Note: This section details the requirements of FRS 1 'Cash flow statements' (Revised 1996) (FRS 1(R96)). It is effective for accounting periods ending on or after 23 March 1997. Early adoption is encouraged. The disclosures contained in FRS 1(R96) are required for all company accounts intended to give a true and fair view, except for:*
> - *small companies or groups as defined by Sections 247 to 249 Companies Act 1985 (or entities which would satisfy the definition were they companies);*
> - *subsidiary undertakings where at least 90% of the voting rights are controlled within the group, provided that consolidated financial statements in which the subsidiary undertakings are included are publicly available;*
> - *mutual life assurance companies;*
> - *pension funds;*
> - *open-ended investment funds that meet all the following conditions:*
>   - *substantially all of the entity's investments are highly liquid;*
>   - *substantially all of the entity's investments are carried at market value;*
>   - *the entity provides a statement of changes in net assets;*
>   - *building societies required to prepare a statement of source and application of funds (this exemption is only available until 23 March 1999).*

1 General

> *Note: All cash flows should be classified according to the substance of the transactions which gave rise to them. [FRS 1(R96) p10]*

1.1 Operating cash flows may be reported by either direct or indirect method [FRS 1(R96) p7] .... ______

> *Note: The direct method shows the relevant constituent cash flows; the indirect method calculates operating cash flows by adjustment to the operating profit reported in the profit and loss account.*

1.2 Comparative figures for cash flow statement and notes (except note analysing changes in balance sheet amounts making up net debt and note of material effects of acquisitions and disposals of subsidiary undertakings on each standard heading) [FRS 1(R96) p48] .... ______

1.3 If statement in group accounts – eliminate cash flows internal to group [FRS 1(R96) p43] .... ______

> *Note: Only actual cash flows between entity and group to be included for equity accounted entity. [FRS 1(R96) p44]*

1.4 If subsidiary undertaking has joined or left group – consolidated cash flow should include cash flows of that subsidiary for same period as group's profit and loss account includes its results [FRS 1(R96) p43] .... ______

1.5 If results from an equity accounted entity included as part of operating profit – include dividends received as operating cash flows [FRS 1(R96) p11] .... ______

1.6 Cash flows relating to interest paid to be classified under 'returns on investments and servicing of finance' regardless of whether interest has been capitalised in other primary statements [FRS 1(R96) p10] .... ______

Table 5.1 Charity accounts compliance checklist: cash flow statement (FRS 1) *(cont.)*

Yes / N/A / Ref

2 The statement

2.1 List of cash inflows and outflows classified under standard headings in order specified [FRS 1(R96) p7] .... ______

Note: The standard headings are: 'operating activities', 'returns on investments and servicing of finance', 'taxation', 'capital expenditure and financial investment', 'acquisitions and disposals', 'equity dividends paid', 'management of liquid resources' and 'financing'.

2.2 Total for each standard heading [FRS 1(R96) p7] .... ______

Note: The cash flows relating to the management of liquid resources and financing can be combined under a single heading provided that the cash flows relating to each are shown separately and separate subtotals are given. [FRS 1(R96) p7]

2.3 Separately, where material, under each standard heading, individual categories of cash inflows and outflows as set out below [FRS 1(R96) p8, FRS 6 p33] .... ______

Note: The requirement to show cash inflows and outflows separately does not apply to cash flows relating to operating activities. [FRS 1(R96) p9]
Cash inflows and outflows within the management of liquid resources or financing may also be netted against each other if they either:
(a) relate in substance to a single financing transaction (which is one that fulfils the conditions in para 35 of FRS 4 'Capital Instruments'), or [FRS 1(R96) p9(a)]
(b) are due to short maturities and high turnover occurring from rollover or reissue (for example, short-term deposits or a commercial paper programme). [FRS 1(R96) p9(b)]

Returns on investments and servicing of finance	
Interest received, including any related tax recovered	Interest paid (whether capitalised or not) including any tax deducted and paid to taxing authority
Dividends received net of any tax credits (separately for equity accounted entities)	Cash flows treated as finance costs under FRS 4 (including debt and non-equity share issue costs)
	The interest element of finance lease payments
	Dividends paid on non-equity shares of the entity
	Dividends paid to minority interests

Taxation (excludes tax cash flows not related to revenue or capital profits, e.g., VAT)	
Cash receipts including tax rebates, claims or returns of overpayments	Cash payments including ACT
For a subsidiary, cash receipts from other members of the group for group relief	For a subsidiary, payments made to other members of the group for group relief

Table 5.1 Charity accounts compliance checklist: cash flow statement (FRS 1) *(cont.)*

Yes / N/A / Ref

Capital expenditure and financial investment	
Receipts from sales or disposals of property, plant or equipment	Payments to acquire property, plant or equipment
Receipts from the repayment of the reporting entity's loans to other entities or sales of debt instruments of other entities other than receipts forming part of an acquisition or disposal or a movement in liquid resources	Loans made by the reporting entity and payments to acquire debt instruments of other entities other than payments forming part of an acquisition or disposal or a movement in liquid resources

Acquisitions and disposals	
Receipts from sales of investments in subsidiary undertakings, showing separately any balances of cash and overdrafts transferred as part of the sale	Payments to acquire investments in subsidiary undertakings, showing separately any balances of cash and overdrafts acquired
Receipts from sales of investments in other entities associates or joint ventures	Payments to acquire investments in associates and joint ventures
Receipts from sales of trades or businesses	Payments to acquire trades or businesses

Equity dividends paid	
	Dividends paid on the reporting entity's, or, in a group, the parent's, equity shares, excluding ACT

Management of liquid resources	
Withdrawals from short-term deposits not qualifying as cash in so far as not netted off	Payments into short-term deposits not qualifying as cash in so far as not netted off
Inflows from disposal or redemption of any other investments held as liquid resources	Outflows to acquire any other investments held as liquid resources

Financing (any financing cash flows received from or paid to equity accounted entities should be disclosed separately)	
Receipts from issuing shares or other equity instruments	Repayments of amounts borrowed (other than overdrafts)
Receipts from issuing debentures, loan notes, bonds, notes, and other long bonds and from other long-term and short-term borrowings (other than overdrafts)	The capital element of finance lease rental payments
	Payments to reacquire or redeem the entity's shares
	Payments of expenses or commissions on any issue of equity shares

2.4 Cash flows not specified in categories set out under 2.3, shown under most appropriate standard heading [FRS 1(R96) p10] .... ______

2.5 Cash flows relating to exceptional or extraordinary items:

1 shown under appropriate standard heading .... ______

2 identified in cash flow statement or note [FRS 1(R96) p37] .... ______

Table 5.1 Charity accounts compliance checklist: cash flow statement (FRS 1) *(cont.)*

Yes / N/A / Ref

2.6 Cash flows to be shown net of any attributable VAT or other sales tax unless irrecoverable [FRS 1(R96) p39] .... ________

2.7 Net cash flow to or from taxing authority of VAT or other sales tax to be allocated to cash flows from operating activities (unless different treatment is more appropriate in circumstances) [FRS 1(R96) p39] .... ________

2.8 If restrictions apply to recoverability of taxes – irrecoverable amount to be allocated to those expenditures affected [FRS 1(R96) p39] .... ________

> *Note: If this is impracticable, the irrecoverable tax should be included under the most appropriate standard heading. [FRS 1(R96) p39]*

2.9 Taxation cash flows, excluding those related to revenue or capital profits and VAT or other sales tax, to be included under same standard heading as cash flow that gave rise to taxation cash flow (unless a different treatment is more appropriate in circumstances) [FRS 1(R96) p40] .... ________

2.10 If portion of business undertaken by foreign entity – cash flows of that entity to be included in statement on basis used for translating results of those activities in profit and loss account [FRS 1(R96) p41] .... ________

2.11 If hedging transactions – report associated cash flows under same standard heading as transaction that is subject of hedge [FRS 1(R96) p42] .... ________

3 Notes to the statement

3.1 Reconciliation between operating profit and net cash flow from operating activities showing separately:

1 movements in stocks, debtors and creditors related to operating activities .... ________

2 other differences between cash flows and profits .... ________

3 difference between dividends received and results taken into account for equity accounted entities [FRS 1(R96) p12] .... ________

> *Note: The reconciliation may be given either adjoining the cash flow statement or as a note. The reconciliation is not part of the cash flow statement: if adjoining the cash flow statement, it should be clearly labelled and kept separate. [FRS 1(R96) p12]*

3.2 Reconciliation between movement of cash in year with movement in net debt [FRS 1(R96) p33] .... ________

> *Note: The reconciliation may be given either adjoining the cash flow statement or as a note. The reconciliation is not part of the cash flow statement: if adjoining the cash flow statement, it should be clearly labelled and kept separate. [FRS 1(R96) p33]. The note to the statement that analyses changes in the balance sheet amounts making up net debt does not require comparative figures [FRS 1(R96) p48].*

3.3 Changes in net debt analysed from opening to closing component amounts showing separately, where material, changes resulting from:

1 cash flows of entity .... ________

2 acquisition or disposal of subsidiary undertakings .... ________

3 other non-cash changes .... ________

4 recognition of changes in market value and exchange rate movements [FRS 1(R96) p33] .... ________

Table 5.1 Charity accounts compliance checklist: cash flow statement (FRS 1) *(cont.)*

		Yes / N/A / Ref
3.4	If several balance sheet amounts combined to form components of opening and closing net debt – sufficient detail to enable cash and other components of net debt to be respectively traced back to amounts shown under equivalent captions in balance sheet [FRS 1(R96) p33]	______
3.5	If portion of business undertaken by foreign entity – basis used for translating results of those activities in profit and loss account to be used in presenting movements in stocks, debtors and creditors in reconciliation between operating profit and cash from operating activities [FRS 1(R96) p41]	______
3.6	If rate used to translate intragroup cash flows is not actual rate – exchange rate differences arising included in effect of exchange rate movements shown as part of reconciliation to net debt [FRS 1(R96) p41]	______
3.7	For cash flows relating to exceptional or extraordinary items – explanation of relationship between cash flows and originating exceptional or extraordinary item [FRS 1(R96) p37]	______
3.8	If cash flows exceptional because of size or incidence but not related to items treated as exceptional or extraordinary in profit and loss account – sufficient disclosure to explain cause and nature [FRS 1(R96) p38]	______
3.9	If subsidiary undertaking acquired or disposed of in year:	
	1 summary of effects indicating how much of the consideration comprised cash	______
	2 as far as practicable, material effects on amounts reported under each standard headings [FRS 1(R96) p45, FRS 6 p33]	______

> *Note: The note of the material effects of acquisitions and disposals of subsidiary undertakings on each of the standard headings does not require comparative figures. [FRS 1(R96) p48]*

3.10	If material transactions not resulting in movement of cash or cash equivalents and if disclosure necessary for an understanding of underlying transaction – disclose [FRS 1(R96) p46]	______
3.11	If restrictions prevent transfer of cash from one part of business or group to another – identify amounts and explain circumstances [FRS 1(R96) p47]	______

Chapter 6 Accounting policies and notes to the accounts

6.1 Basis of preparation of accounts

It is essential that the accounts are accompanied by an explanation of the basis on which they have been prepared. The accounting policies adopted for dealing with material items should therefore be explained in the notes to the accounts. These explanations should be clear, fair and as brief as is consistent with clarity (para 282). In the transition period between SORP 1995 and SORP 2000 the relevant SORP complied with should be stated. Effectively, the approach taken in both the regulations and the SORP that the accounts should include an explanation of the accounting policies used to prepare them follows very closely the requirements of both the Companies Act 1985 and FRS 18 *Accounting Policies*, which has replaced SSAP 2. It is quite clear that the statement of accounting policies must be detailed enough to cover all material items. Indeed FRS 18 promotes the adoption and review of the accounting policies most appropriate to the particular circumstances of each entity for the purposes of giving a true and fair view.

In some respects SORP 2000 has increased the number of notes that could possibly be included in the accounts particularly in respect of income and expenditure. Provision to remove some of the income disclosure from the face of the SOFA does not mean that the disclosure is no longer required, and this should be included within the notes to the accounts.

6.2 Fundamental accounting concepts

The accounting policies adopted must be sufficiently disclosed for users to understand the policies adopted and how they have been applied. A distinction is drawn between the principles on which the accounts are prepared and estimation techniques used for valuation purposes. Of the four fundamental accounting concepts in SSAP 2 – consistency, prudence, going concern and accruals – only the last two remain within FRS 18. FRS 18 continues the appropriateness of accounting policies and estimation techniques for each entity. The objectives should be judged against each other and the cost of providing the information. Trustees will need to consider on an annual basis whether their accounting policies are appropriate, relevant, reliable, comparable (the combination of consistency and disclosure) and understandable. Those charities preparing receipts and payments accounts need only consider the objective of comparability.

6.3 Accounting standards

True and fair view accounts should follow the standards laid down in SSAPs and FRSs which have been issued, or adopted by the Accounting Standards Board, SORP 2000, the relevant legislation and the historical cost basis of accounting. They should be in accordance with terms relevant to the charity's circumstances and accounts. Any departures must be justified with a full explanation; otherwise it may be deemed that the accounts do not provide a true and fair view (para 280).

6.4 Accounting policies

It is necessary for trustees to explain in the notes to the accounts the accounting policies they have adopted to deal with material items and specifically to state whether the accounts have been drawn up in accordance with the SORP. Examples and matters on which the accounting policies should be explained where the amounts involved are material, include:

- donations, legacies and other forms of voluntary income or benefit (particularly when legacies are considered to be receivable);
- whether incoming resources are deferred;
- recognition of gifts in kind;
- grants payable and receivable;
- direct charitable expenditure and support costs;
- costs of generating funds;
- the cost of management and administration;
- the basis of allocation or apportionment between cost headings;
- investment assets and the income arising therefrom;
- gains and losses on investment assets;
- valuation, capitalisation and depreciation of fixed assets;
- netted off expenses and related income;
- commitments not yet met; and
- the use of designated funds.

The notes to the accounts should give a description of the sources of any material incoming resources. Trustees should only include those notes that are relevant to the charity. The opening statement to the SORP makes it clear that the Charity Commission expects the accounts of charities and their accounting practices to comply fully with the SORP. Insofar as a charity does not comply with the SORP in material respects, then the accounts should identify that fact clearly and provide a full explanation. If no explanation is given or the Charity Commission deems the explanation unsatisfactory, then it will decide whether or not to raise the matter with the charity concerned and, if circumstances in their view warrant it, to institute an inquiry.

6.5 Other notes

Notes to the accounts are covered in considerable detail in Pt IV of the regs (SI 1995/2724) on pages 11–13. These should now be read in conjunction with reg 3(10) Notes to the Accounts (SI 2000/2868). References to the notes to the accounts are included throughout the SORP. There is in addition a separate section looking at additional notes to the accounts. In some instances the SORP 2000 goes further in its requirements than the regulations require.

Charities are required to prepare notes to their accounts. In a number of instances the requirements are no different to those prepared under the Companies Act formats, e.g., debtors and creditors. Commentary is given on the more specific notes to the accounts below.

6.5.1 Trustee remuneration

Trustees cannot normally benefit from their position. This is only permissible in certain circumstances and where the charity's constitution includes an appropriate charging clause. Any transaction should be disclosed, as there is no materiality in respect of such costs. Each transaction must be separately disclosed, together with trustee name, a description of the payment and the amount. This includes any pension arrangements made. The legal authority by which the payment is made should also be given. Where none of the trustees or any persons connected have received any such remuneration, this should be stated.

Example 6.1 The ABC Charity

Notes forming part of the financial statements for the year ended 31 March 2001

1 Accounting policies

(a) **Basis of preparation**
The financial statements have been prepared under the historical cost convention, with the exception of investments which are included at market value. The financial statements have been prepared in accordance with the Statement of Recommended Practice (SORP), "Accounting and Reporting by Charities" published in October 2000 and applicable accounting standards.

The statement of financial activities (SOFA) and balance sheet consolidate the financial statements of the charity and its subsidiary undertaking. The results of the subsidiary are consolidated on a line by line basis.

The charity has availed itself of Paragraph 3 (3) of Schedule 4 of the Companies Act and adapted the Companies Act formats to reflect the special nature of the charity's activities. No separate SOFA has been presented for the charity alone as permitted by Section 230 of the Companies Act 1985 and paragraph 304 of the SORP.

(b) **Company status**
The charity is a company limited by guarantee. The members of the company are the trustees named on page 1. In the event of the charity being wound up, the liability in respect of the guarantee is limited to £1 per member of the charity.

(c) **Fund accounting**
General funds are unrestricted funds which are available for use at the discretion of the trustees in furtherance of the general objectives of the charity and which have not been designated for other purposes.

Designated funds comprise unrestricted funds that have been set aside by the trustees for particular purposes. The aim and use of each designated fund is set out in the notes to the financial statements. Restricted funds are funds which are to be used in accordance with specific restrictions imposed by donors or which have been raised by the charity for particular purposes. The cost of raising and administering such funds are charged against the specific fund. The aim and use of each restricted fund is set out in the notes to the financial statements.

Investment income and gains are allocated to the appropriate fund.

(d) **Incoming resources**
All incoming resources are included in the SOFA when the charity is legally entitled to the income and the amount can be quantified with reasonable accuracy. For legacies, entitlement is the earlier of the charity being notified of an impending distribution or the legacy being received.

Gifts in kind donated for distribution are included at valuation and recognised as income when they are distributed to the projects. Gifts donated for resale are included as income when they are sold. Donated facilities are included at the value to the charity where this can be quantified and a third party is bearing the cost. No amounts are included in the financial statements for services donated by volunteers.

(e) **Resources expended**
All expenditure is accounted for on an accruals basis and has been classified under headings that aggregate all costs related to the category. Where costs cannot be directly attributed to particular headings they have been allocated to activities on a basis consistent with use of the resources. Premises overheads have been allocated on a floor area basis and other overheads have been allocated on the basis of the head count.

Fund-raising costs are those incurred in seeking voluntary contributions and do not include the costs of disseminating information in support of the charitable activities. Support costs are those costs incurred directly in support of expenditure on the objects of the charity and include project management carried out at Headquarters. Management and administration costs are those incurred in connection with administration of the charity and compliance with constitutional and statutory requirements.

Example 6.1 The ABC Charity *(cont.)*

(f) **Tangible fixed assets and depreciation**
Tangible fixed assets costing more than £1,000 are capitalised and included at cost including any incidental expenses of acquisition.

Depreciation is provided on all tangible fixed assets at rates calculated to write off the cost on a straight line basis over their expected useful economic lives as follows:

Freehold land	nil
Freehold buildings	over 50 years
Project and office equipment	over 5 years
Computer equipment	over 3 years
Motor vehicles	over 4 years
Equipment held under finance leases	over the life of the lease

(g) **Investments**
Investments are stated at market value at the balance sheet date. The SOFA includes the net gains and losses arising on revaluations and disposals throughout the year.

(h) **Stock**
Stock consists of purchased goods for resale. Stocks are valued at the lower of cost and net realisable value. Items donated for resale or distribution are not included in the financial statements until they are sold or distributed.

(i) **Pension costs**
The cost of providing pension and related benefits is charged to the SOFA over the employees' service lives on the basis of a constant percentage of earnings which is an estimate of the regular cost. Variations from regular cost, arising from periodic actuarial valuations are allocated over the expected remaining service lives of current employees on the basis of a constant percentage of current and estimated future earnings. Any difference between the charge to the statement of financial activities and the contributions payable to the scheme is shown as an asset or a liability in the balance sheet.

(j) **Finance and operating leases**
Rentals applicable to operating leases are charged to the SOFA over the period in which the cost is incurred. Assets purchased under finance lease are capitalised as fixed assets. Obligations under such agreements are included in creditors. The difference between the capitalised cost and the total obligation under the lease represents the finance charges. Finance charges are written-off to the SOFA over the period of the lease so as to produce a constant periodic rate of charge.

(k) **Foreign currencies**
Transactions in foreign currencies are recorded at the rate ruling at the date of the transaction. Monetary assets and liabilities are retranslated at the rate of exchange ruling at the balance sheet date. All differences are taken to the SOFA.

6.5.2 Related party transactions

SORP 2000 has considered at length related party transactions (paras 157–168). Appendix 1 Glossary section 26 deals with the definition of the terms 'Institution connected with a charity', 'Related to the charity' and 'connected with a charity trustee or to a person related to the charity'.

Related parties include trustees and someone who is related to the charity as well as someone connected with the trustee or person related to the charity.

Any transactions entered into by a charity should be for the best interest of the charity – only the charity's interests should be considered. Transparency is important especially where a transaction could be questioned due to the relationship. Related party transactions could affect the reported financial transactions and results.

According to para 161 of the Charity SORP, transactions should include:

(a) purchases, sales, leases and donations of goods, property, money or other assets;
(b) supply of services by the related party to the charity or vice versa; and
(c) any other payments or benefits made to the trustees in accordance with the governing document of the charity.

The required disclosure is:

(a) the name of the transacting related party or parties;
(b) description of the relationship;
(c) description of the transaction;
(d) amounts involved;
(e) outstanding balances at the balance sheet date and any provisions for doubtful debts;
(f) any amounts written off from such balances during the accounting year; and
(g) any other elements of the transaction necessary for an understanding.

In para 165 of SORP 2000 guidance is given on the types of transaction that are unlikely to influence the pursuance of the separate independent interests of the charity. Disclosure would not be necessary for those unless there is evidence to the contrary. The problems of related party transactions are dealt with later (see Chapter 14).

6.5.3 Trustees' expenses

Under the SORP, reimbursements made to trustees in respect of services rendered or expense incurred in performance of their duties needs to be disclosed. The amount of the reimbursement, together with a description of the nature of the reimbursement and the number of trustees reimbursed, needs to be given in the notes to the accounts. Paragraph 168 of the SORP deals with occasions where the charity acts as agent. Where trustees have received no expenses, this should be stated.

6.5.4 Indemnity insurance

This is often a particularly contentious subject and many charities are now taking out indemnity insurance, details of which need to be shown in the notes to the accounts (para 170). Where funds belonging to the charity have been used in the purchase of insurance either:

- to protect the charity from loss arising from the negligence or defaults of its trustees, employees or agents; or
- to indemnify the trustees or other officers against the consequences of any neglect or default on their part,

these facts, and the cost involved in providing such insurance, should be disclosed in detail in the notes to the accounts.

Example 6.2 The ABC Charity

6. Total resources expended

	Staff Costs £'000	Other Direct Costs £'000	Other Allocated Costs £'000	Total 2001 £'000	Total 2000 £'000
Fund-raising costs	210	360	120	**690**	550
Building appeal costs	25	5	15	**45**	110
Merchandising costs	80	560	230	**870**	1,040
Investment management fees	–	90	–	**90**	110
Residential care costs	2,000	330	100	**2,430**	2,545
Childcare	2,800	345	255	**3,400**	3,150
Emergency services	1,980	870	250	**3,100**	2,800
Information and education	25	65	10	**100**	300
Support costs	45	110	35	**190**	50
Management and administration	85	145	40	**270**	230
Total resources expended	7,250	2,880	1,055	**11,185**	10,885

Other direct costs include:	2001 £'000	2000 £'000
Auditors' remuneration:		
Audit fee	**14**	13
Accountancy, taxation and other services	**6**	9
Operating lease rentals – Land and buildings	**110**	110
– Plant and equipment	**70**	70
Depreciation	**380**	270
Finance lease interest	**12**	14

7. Trustees' remuneration

The trustees neither received nor waived any emoluments during the year (2000: £Nil).

Out of pocket expenses were reimbursed to trustees as follows.

	2001 Number	2000 Number	2001 £'000	2000 £'000
Travel	2	3	**640**	530
Visit to Sudan Project	1	–	**1,200**	–
Other	1	1	**40**	65
	4	4	**1,880**	595

During the year payments of £2,500 were made to the Harvey Print Company for the printing of the Annual Report. Mrs W. Williams, a trustee of this charity, is a director of that company. Mr H. Singh, a trustee, is also a trustee of the Packwood Foundation that provided free accommodation to the charity during the year valued at £24,000.

Example 6.3 YHA (England and Wales) Limited

NOTES TO THE FINANCIAL STATEMENTS
for the year ended 29 February 2000

22. **INDEMNITY INSURANCE**
The charity has purchased insurance for the trustees and officers of the charity against liability arising for wrongful acts in relation to the charity. The cost of this insurance amounts to £4,160.

6.6 Branches

If any branches are omitted from the accounts, the reason for the omission must be given, although individual branches do not need to be named.

6.7 Trading subsidiaries

The treatment of trading subsidiaries and consolidation is considered later (see Chapter 15).

6.8 Investments

Investments are dealt with later (see Chapter 13) in commentary and guidance on specific problem areas. Charities have to account for their investments at market value and show movements in gains and losses within the SOFA.

6.9 Grants

Grants are considered later (see Chapter 16). Material grants made by a charity to one or more institutions should be appropriately analysed and explained either in the statement of financial activities, or in the notes to the accounts, or by means of a separate publication referred to in the notes and reconciled to the total amount charged in the accounts. Material is considered to be expenditure constituting more than five per cent of total resources expended. Disclosure should consist of:

- the name of the recipient institution; and
- the aggregate amount of the grants made to that recipient in the accounting period.

The note should reconcile to the amount disclosed in the statement of financial activities and distinguish whether grants are individual or institutional. There is no requirement to disclose those grants that are below £1,000 (however they should be totalled), and only the 50 largest grants need to be disclosed within the financial statements. Nor do grants to individuals have to be disclosed in detail, but the total must be disclosed.

When the trustees feel that disclosure of material grants will seriously prejudice either the recipient or the charity, they need not disclose individual details of any such grant but they must show in the accounts the total amount of all such grants. However, the full details of these grants, which have not been disclosed, must be reported separately in writing to either the Charity Commission or other appropriate regulatory body, setting out the reasons for the non-disclosure. The trustees' report should confirm that this has been done.

6.10 Management and administration costs of the charity

There needs to be a clear analysis of all major components of the total cost of management and administration in the notes to the accounts. Such expenditure includes both direct and indirect costs.

6.11 Staff costs

It is important that staff costs are disclosed in charity accounts. This includes seconded and agency staff. Any staff provided and paid for by a third party should be separately disclosed.

Total staff costs should be given together with a split between gross wages and salaries, employer's National Insurance costs and pension contributions. The number of full time staff equivalents should also be given.

SORP 2000 has increased the disclosure limits for higher paid staff. In future, staff earning more than £50,000 should be disclosed in bands of £10,000. Where none of the staff earn more than £50,000, this fact should be stated. In an extension to SORP 1995, pension details must be disclosed for higher paid staff.

6.12 Cost of audit, independent examination/reporting accountant services and other financial services

Notes to the accounts should disclose total amounts paid to the respective scrutiniser. These costs should be analysed between costs of external scrutiny and provision of other financial services.

6.13 *Ex-gratia* payments

When a charity makes payments, gives a non-monetary benefit, makes other expenditure of any kind, or waives rights to property to which the charity is entitled for a purpose which is not in accord with the furtherance of the charity's activities but fulfilling a moral obligation, this should be disclosed in the accounts together with the authority by which this payment is made.

If payments have been made which the trustees reasonably consider to be in the interests of the charity, they should not be treated as *ex-gratia* – even though there may be no legal obligations to make them, e.g., redundancy payments in excess of the statutory payments.

6.14 Fixed assets

As we have seen (see Chapter 4), the SORP 2000 makes it clear that fixed assets held for the charity's use should be shown in the balance sheet at cost (or valuation) net of depreciation.

6.15 Accounting for separate funds

Although fund accounting is dealt with later (see Chapter 11), charities have to give details in the notes to their accounts of the funds they hold. They need to account for the proper administration of the individual funds in accordance with their respective terms of trust. To discharge this obligation, details concerning individual funds may be given in the notes, differentiating in particular between the restricted and unrestricted funds.

Example 6.4 The Higher Education Charity

7. Analysis of total resources expended

	Staff costs £'000	Other costs £'000	Depreciation £'000	Total £'000
Charitable activities				
Teaching	3,068	250	62	**3,380**
Welfare	997	746	54	**1,797**
Premises	567	1,671	264	**2,502**
Support costs	310	408	11	**729**
Grants, awards and prizes	–	251	–	**251**
Management and administration	–	45	–	**45**
	4,942	3,371	391	**8,704**
Costs of generating funds:				
Financing costs	–	217	–	**217**
Investment management	–	10	–	**10**
Fund-raising	49	41	–	**90**
Total for charity	**4,991**	**3,639**	**391**	**9,021**
Trading costs of the subsidiary	240	1,225	1	**1,446**
Total for group	**5,231**	**4,864**	**392**	**10,487**

8. Management and administration

	2001 £'000	2000 £'000
Auditors' remuneration (see note 6)	**16**	21
Governors' liability insurance	**1**	–
Staff costs	**20**	18
Office costs	**8**	2
	45	41

9. Tangible fixed assets

	Freehold land £'000	Freehold buildings £'000	Motor vehicles £'000	Furniture & equipment £'000	Charity total £'000	Subsidiary: furniture & equipment £'000	Group total £'000
Cost							
1 September 2000	6,000	4,403	40	1,500	**11,943**	58	**12,001**
Additions	–	490	14	142	**646**	–	**646**
Disposals	–	(69)	(9)	(21)	**(99)**	(6)	**(105)**
31 August 2001	6,000	4,824	45	1,621	**12,490**	52	**12,542**
Depreciation							
1 September 2000	–	1,331	35	1,203	**2,569**	46	**2,615**
Charge for year	–	232	5	154	**391**	1	**392**
Disposals	–	(10)	(9)	(13)	**(32)**	(3)	**(35)**
31 August 2001	–	1,553	31	1,344	**2,928**	44	**2,972**
Net book values							
31 August 2001	6,000	3,271	14	277	**9,562**	8	**9,570**
31 August 2001	*6,000*	*3,072*	*5*	*297*	***9,374***	*12*	***9,386***

Notes should cover the following areas:

- the assets and liabilities representing the various funds of the charity should be clearly analysed between those funds. The notes should indicate whether or not sufficient resources are held in an appropriate form to enable each fund to be applied in accordance with the restrictions imposed;
- the gains and losses on assets held in a particular fund form part of that fund. Similarly, provisions for depreciation or for a permanent fall in value form part of the fund in which the asset is held;
- restricted funds may be restricted as to the use of income or capital or both. Income generated from assets held in a restricted fund will be restricted income and will need to be shown as such within the notes to the accounts; and
- similarly, designated funds should be analysed within the notes to the accounts together with the policy for determining them. These are discussed later but form part of the charity's unrestricted funds and notes should show the assets and liabilities represented by these funds.

6.16 Transfers between funds

In disclosing details of movements of funds, transfers affecting restricted funds should be shown separately from allocations to designated unrestricted funds. Material transfers out of unallocated to designated funds should be separately disclosed without netting off and should be accompanied by a narrative explanation of the nature of the transfer or allocation and the reason for it (para 44).

Example 6.5 Arts Theatre Trust Limited

6. Managing and administering the charity

	2001 £'000	2000 £'000
Salaries and wages	**86**	73
Meeting costs	**22**	6
Legal and professional expenses	**19**	12
Office costs	**25**	22
	152	113

7. Staff costs and trustees' remuneration

	2001 £'000	2000 £'000
Wages and salaries	**620**	603
Social security costs	**41**	39
Pension costs	**19**	11
Ex-gratia payments	**16**	–
	696	653

The ex-gratia payment was made to a former chief executive for whom no pension provision had been made. The Charity Commission approved payment on 15 December 2000.

No employee earned more than £50,000 per annum (2000 – nil).

The trustees were not paid or reimbursed for expenses during the year.

8. Staff numbers

The average number of full-time equivalent employees (including casual and part-time staff) during the year was made up as follows:

	2001 No	2000 No
Arts department	**11**	11
Administration, marketing and commercial	**14**	13
Technical	**11**	10
Bars and coffee shop	**21**	17
Front of house, box office, cleaning	**20**	21
Course tutors, models	**31**	30
	108	102

9. Movement in total funds for the year

	2001 £'000	2000 £'000
This is stated after charging:		
Operating leases – equipment	**13**	13
Depreciation	**66**	60
Auditors' remuneration		
external audit	**8**	6
other services	**2**	6

Chapter 7 Accruals and accounting for the smaller charity

The guidance issued by the Charity Commission in October 1995, *Accruals – Accounting for the Smaller Charity*, is a guide to the Charities SORP for unincorporated charities with an annual income of up to £100,000 and with no branches or investment assets. This was updated in September 1999 by the issue of CC55 *Accruals – Accounting for the Smaller Charity* and there is further guidance in CC65 SORP 2000 *Accruals Accounts Pack*, published in 2001.

7.1 Unincorporated charities with income under £100,000

Unincorporated charities with income under £100,000 have the option to choose how to show their accounts. They can show their accounts either under the accruals method or under the receipts and payments method (see Chapter 8).

7.2 Incorporated charities

The incorporated charity has to account under the accruals method. It does not have the option to show its accounts under the receipts and payments method, irrespective of its level of income.

The smaller charity, unless preparing its accounts under the receipts and payments method, can also follow the Financial Reporting Standard for Smaller Charities (FRSSE), except where it conflicts with SORP 2000, in which case SORP 2000 should be followed. The incorporated charity must follow the SORP 2000. A charity with branches or investment assets is not entitled to prepare its accounts under the method of accruals accounting for the smaller charity. The guidance issued on this was based on the lengthier statement of recommended practice *Accounting by Charities*, the original SORP published in 1995.

The regulations oblige larger charities to disclose in the notes to the accounts particulars of any material departure from accounting and reporting standards and the SORP. These requirements apply only where the gross income of the charity exceeds £100,000 for the year.

The trustees remain responsible for the preparation of their trustees' report, although the work of preparing the accounts may be delegated under the accruals accounting for the smaller charity method. The trustees must however see copies of the accounts before approval.

7.2.1 Accounts structure

The accounts structure follows the normal structure of accounts under the accruals accounting method and would include a statement of financial activities, a balance sheet and notes to the accounts. Guidance is given elsewhere in this publication regarding their respective presentation.

The statement of financial activities in most cases will be the same as a traditional income and expenditure account with the addition of the balance brought forward from the previous year.

The balance sheet should explain in general terms how the funds may, or because of restrictions imposed by donors, must, be utilised.

According to the regulations, charities with an annual gross income that does not exceed £250,000 do not have to give details of the cost of trustee indemnity insurance, or costs of insuring against trustee negligence against losses arising. Also, charities do not need to state whether the accounts have been prepared in accordance with any applicable accounting standards and statements of recommended practice, or give particulars of any material departure from those standards and statements of practice and the reasons for doing so.

Emoluments of employees earning more than £50,000 in bands of £10,000 need to be disclosed. Transactions with trustees and other connected persons need to be disclosed, together with details of any indemnity insurance taken out on their behalf.

The accruals method for SORP accounting for charities with income under £100,000 does not differ materially from the treatment of larger charities preparing their accounts under the SORP accounting method.

7.2.2 Materiality

This concept needs to be considered, and in particular if there is doubt as to whether or not something is 'material' it should be included.

7.2.3 Accounting policies

Accounting policies should be appropriate to the charity (see Chapter 6 for further guidance).

7.2.4 Fund accounting

The principles of fund accounting as set out in Chapter 11 should be followed in preparing accruals accounts.

Chapter 8 Receipts and payments accounts

The Charity Commission issued in October 1995 *Guidance on Accounting for the Smaller Charity*, which contains simplified extracts from the SORP, as it was the Charity Commission's opinion that many of the SORP's recommendations were suitable mainly for large charities, or those with complicated finances. Charity SORP 2000 also discusses the applicable use of receipts and payments accounts. The receipts and payments account is a relatively simple form of account suitable for smaller charities and consists of a summary of money received and paid during the financial year concerned. The statement of assets and liabilities is a straightforward schedule of information, which does not require the accountancy knowledge needed to prepare a balance sheet. (Incorporated charities, however, cannot benefit from this and must produce accrual accounts.)

In September 1999 CC54 *Accounting for the Smaller Charity* updated the requirements for those producing receipts and payments accounts. This guidance is sufficient and does not need to be supplemented by knowledge of the Charities SORP. The Commission also published a booklet this year (2001), CC64 SORP 2000 *Receipts and Payments Accounts Pack*.

The practices described in this guide for preparing accounts and annual reports of small charities are recommendations, not legal requirements. Charities are advised to follow the recommendations, since they represent best practice, but are not obliged by law to do so. The accounts do not claim to show a true and fair view of the charity's financial activities and state of affairs. Accounting standards do not generally apply to such accounts.

8.1 What are the legal requirements?

In England and Wales, s42 (3) of the Charities Act 1993 applies. This allows a charity to prepare a 'receipts and payments account' for the year and a 'statement of assets and liabilities' at the year end, instead of preparing full accounts for a particular financial year. This is on condition that in that financial year the charity's gross recorded income from all sources was £100,000 or less, and it is not a company. There are no statutory requirements as to what must be contained in the receipts and payments account or the statements of assets and liabilities.

In Scotland, the Charities Accounts (Scotland) Regulations 1992 apply. This allows a recognised body to prepare a 'receipts and payments account' for a particular financial year and a 'statement of balances' as at the year end if in that financial year the charity's gross receipts amounted to £25,000 or less. The receipts and payments account and statement of balances must contain the information listed in Pt 2 of Sch I to the Charities Accounts (Scotland) Regulations 1992 and Pt 2 of Sch II to those regulations, information which must be given in notes to the accounts.

In Northern Ireland and in the Republic of Ireland there are no regulations governing either the form or the contents of charity accounts.

8.2 Annual report

The trustees of all registered charities in England and Wales are required by s45 of the Charities Act 1993 to prepare an annual report containing the information required by the Charities (Accounts and Reports) Regulations 1995. In Scotland, each recognised body must produce a report containing the information specified in Pt 3 of Sch I to the Charities Accounts (Scotland) Regulations 1992. In Northern Ireland and the Republic of Ireland there are no legal requirements to prepare annual reports.

8.3 Trustees' responsibility for annual report and accounts

The trustees of a charity are responsible for preparing the accounts and annual report. Whether or not trustees delegate the preparation of accounts to others (perhaps to their accountant or treasurer or to employees of the charity), the trustees themselves remain responsible for ensuring that the accounts and report comply with the law. The legal requirements for producing and laying accounts before the Annual General Meeting and for allowing other trustees access to the accounts with a reasonable amount of time before the accounts are approved, hold for both the smaller charity and the larger charity. The accounts have to be approved in the same way as for a larger charity and accounts must be delivered to the Charity Commission. The accounts of an unincorporated charity not exceeding £10,000 gross income and total expenditure for the year will not normally be required to be audited or independently examined, nor will they need to be submitted to the Charity Commission. Members of the public can request copies of the accounts.

8.4 Charity Commission annual accounts form

For England and Wales, the Charity Commission has prepared a standard form for use in preparing a charity's receipts and payments accounts and statement of assets and liabilities. No charity is obliged to use this form but its use or adaptation for use is recommended by the Charity Commission as an alternative. The form contains notes and instructions for trustees on how to complete the form in accordance with the law. Copies are available without charge from the Charity Commission. The format is readily adaptable by umbrella bodies to suit their particular needs.

8.5 General principles

Disclosure of accounting basis
A receipts and payments account is a factual record of money received and paid during the financial year. A statement of assets and liabilities is a list of significant possessions and outstanding financial obligations as at the end of the financial year. Because a receipts and payments account and a statement of assets and liabilities differ from other forms of annual accounts in important ways, the trustees should always mention in a note attached to the accounts the fact that they have been prepared on the 'receipts and payments' basis. In the same note, the trustees should confirm that the accounts comply with the appropriate legal requirements.

Accounting for branches
A charity may have branches or local groups which raise funds in the name of the charity and on its behalf. Funds raised in this way should be included in the charity's accounts in the same way as for a larger charity; the trustees will need to obtain accurate returns from branches and groups. The figures from the branch/group returns should be added to the receipts and payments and assets and liabilities in the charity's own accounts. In doing so, transactions within the same fund which are internal to the charity (e.g. a donation received by a branch

or a group and then paid over to the headquarters unit) should be eliminated in order to avoid double counting of those items in the charity's receipts and payments account.

Materiality
An item should be regarded as material unless the trustees of a charity can justify its omission from the accounts or annual report on the grounds that it would be too trivial to influence the reader. In cases of doubt, the item should be regarded as material and should be included in the accounts or report.

Consistency
The annual accounts should be 'consistent'. This is the only accounting convention always applicable to receipts and payments accounts.

8.6 Accounting for restricted funds

Where a charity holds both restricted and unrestricted funds, either a separate receipts and payments accounts should be prepared for each fund or columnar receipts and payments accounts should be produced. If a single receipts and payments account is prepared covering all funds, both restricted and unrestricted, the account must still distinguish clearly which funds are restricted and which are unrestricted. If this is not done, it will appear to the reader of the accounts that all funds are held on exactly the same basis. It may also increase the risk that the trustees of the charity will begin to regard all funds as unrestricted. This must be avoided, since to spend restricted funds as if they were unrestricted funds may lead to a breach of trust. The income from assets held as part of a restricted fund is itself subject to the same restriction and must be accounted for as part of the same restricted fund. The only exceptions to this are:

- where the donor has expressly provided for some other use for the income; or
- where the asset is part of a permanent endowment held for the general purposes of the charity, in which case the income is unrestricted since it can be spent for the charity's general purposes (unless the charity's trusts provide otherwise).

When assets or investments held within a restricted fund are sold, the proceeds of sale are held within the same restricted fund.

8.7 The receipts and payments account

8.7.1 Income and expenditure

The receipts and payments account recognises only money received and paid in the year and excludes the value of all other assets received in kind unless, and until, converted into money. Any such assets retained at the year end should therefore be shown in the statement of assets and liabilities. When calculating the figure of 'gross' income, for statutory purposes, certain miscellaneous receipts may also need to be included, for example a transfer from endowment of capital converted into income for spending, or a refund of an expenditure payment made in a previous year.

On the other hand, if the charity receives a loan that is to be repaid later, then that receipt would not normally count as part of its income. Similarly, if the charity makes the repayment of a charitable loan, the payment would not normally count as expenditure. Expenditure on the receipts and payments basis means the payment of charitable grants and other costs of the charity's activities as recorded in the receipts and payments account of each of its funds. This does not include charitable loans, which are expected to be repaid to the charity, nor does it include the purchase of investments or fixed assets used by the charity, nor any loss on disposal of such assets.

However, when calculating the figure of 'total expenditure' for the year, for statutory purposes certain miscellaneous payments may also need to be taken into account (e.g. a refund of income received in a previous year).

8.7.2 Donations, gifts and legacies

All cash receipts from donations, gifts, legacies and other voluntary sources should be included in the receipts and payments account at the same time as the cash is actually received. This also applies to grants. A donation, gift or legacy which is received in the form of assets other than cash cannot be shown in the receipts and payments account until the trustees convert it into cash by selling it. In that event, the cash receipt should be entered in the accounts at the time the property is sold. If the asset has not been sold by the end of the year and is still in the trustees' possession, it should be included in the list of assets and liabilities with a note of the fund of which it forms part. If the asset is sold for cash in the following year, the cash receipt should be shown in the following year's receipts and payments account. If the asset is sold before the accounts preparation is completed, details of the sale together with the proceeds should be given. In cases where the charity is in receipt of a donation in kind, which it subsequently distributes without recognising any income or expenditure, it should not be shown in the receipts and payments account. Instead, the receipt of the gift and its subsequent distribution should be described in the annual report.

In cases where the trustees are notified that they are the beneficiary of a legacy and the cash is not received before the year end, but they are certain that they have a legally enforceable right to receive it in future, it should be included in the statement of assets and liabilities. A legacy should be described as the right to the property and not as the property itself because at that stage the trustees owned the right to the property but not the property itself.

8.7.3 Other benefits received by the charity

In instances where the charity is in receipt of an intangible benefit, such as printing appeal leaflets or the provision of an interest free loan, this cannot be reflected in the receipts and payments account since the benefit was non-monetary. Instead, the benefit should be described in the annual report in a way that properly illustrates its value and importance to the charity.

8.7.4 Trading receipts and payments

Any receipts from trading should be shown gross in the receipts and payments account. It is not acceptable simply to show the profit received, or loss, from the trading. In the case of a fundraising event, the proceeds of the event should be shown as receipts with the costs of organising the event shown as payments. This applies to any form of trading whether directly connected with the charity's purposes or whether carried out purely in order to raise funds. It is also applicable where the trading is regular or permanent and where the trading is occasional. If the charity has a non-charitable company for the purposes of carrying out permanent trading activities, which the charity itself may not carry out, profits derived from this should be shown in the receipts and payments account separately from other receipts.

8.7.5 Recovery of tax

If the charity is entitled to recover tax credits on dividends that it has received, the tax recovered should be shown under a separate heading in the accounts from the income on which the tax was recovered. The same applies to tax recovered on covenanted payments, or on gift aid payments where the tax is recovered separately from the payments. If trustees are entitled to recover tax but have not received the tax repayment by the end of the tax year, the tax repayment cannot be shown in the receipts and payments account. The tax repayment should be shown in the statement of assets and liabilities with the explanation that it has been claimed but not yet received. When the tax refund is received it should then be shown in the receipts and payments account.

8.7.6 Classification of receipts

All amounts received of the same type should be added together and the totals should be shown under appropriate headings in the accounts. Appropriate headings are: donations; gifts, legacies and similar receipts; dividends and interest from investments other than shares in a trading subsidiary set up by the charity; gift aid payments from shares in a trading company set up by the charity; rents and property held as an investment; and interest on deposits of cash etc. All charities are different, and classifications will differ from charity to charity. However, income should be classified in order to show the charity's cash receipts without unnecessary detail, and the corresponding figures for the previous financial year should be given for each item in the list for comparison. Trustees are free to devise their own headings; the same applies to the classification of payments.

8.7.7 Classification of payments

All payments of the same type should be added together and totals shown under appropriate headings. The corresponding figures for the previous financial year should be given for each item in the list of payments for comparison.

Appropriate headings are: grants of money made to beneficiaries; money spent in publicising the charity and educating the public about its work; costs of goods or services provided to the charity's beneficiaries; fundraising and publicity costs; and the costs of management and administration of the charity. Payments to acquire fixed assets, either outright or under hire purchase arrangements, will also be included here.

8.7.8 Staff and trustee costs

The emoluments of employees earning more than £50,000 – in bands of £10,000 – still need to be disclosed. Transactions with trustees and related parties, including their reimbursements for expenses, need to be disclosed, together with details of indemnity insurance taken out on their behalf.

8.8 Statement of assets and liabilities

This should be adequate to show the readers of the accounts what assets the trustees control.

8.8.1 Cash and bank deposits

These are the cash resources of the charity, which are immediately available to the trustees, and they should be listed as the first item in the statement of assets and liabilities. A separate figure will need to be given for each of the charity's restricted and unrestricted funds. Deposits, which must be left for a fixed period, should not be included here since trustees do not have immediate access to the cash, but they should be included in the list of investments.

Bank balances must be reconciled for unpaid cheques and deposits before the accounts are drawn up. Unpresented cheques must not be counted as creditors.

8.8.2 Other monetary assets

All debts and money owed to the charity should be listed under this heading. This includes sums owed to the charity as repayments for loans made by it, and tax recovery claims made but not yet received. Small sums of the same type should be added together as one item. A note should be added to each item to show the fund to which the item belongs.

8.8.3 Investment assets

Any asset or property held by the charity, as an investment either to generate income or to increase capital, should be shown under this heading. This includes any stocks and shares that can be bought or sold, any cash deposits that must be left for a fixed term, and land with or without buildings and any interest in land such as a rent charge. There is no requirement to show investment assets at market value, unless an evaluation is essential to a meaningful description of the asset. If a charity has set up its own non-charitable trading company, any shares which the charity owns in that company should also be included.

The list should show to which of the charity's restricted or unrestricted funds the asset belongs. Its value to the charity should be shown in a note. If an asset is difficult or expensive to value, the note should include the estimated market value or the insured value of the asset on the last day of the financial year. If any asset is land, the note should include the address and a brief description of the property. It would also be helpful to include the original cost of the land to the charity and briefly to describe the age and condition of any buildings.

8.8.4 Fixed assets used by the charity

Assets held by the charity mainly for its own use should be listed in a category of their own. If the charity has set up a separate non-charitable company to provide charitable services, the charity's shares in this company should be included here. Assets of this sort should be included in the list whether they are owned outright or on hire purchase terms. Even an asset that cannot be sold because the charity's governing document prohibits a sale should be included.

The list of assets held for use by the charity should include notes that allow the reader to gain a clear picture of the value of these assets to the charity. The notes should indicate the age, condition and estimated market value (or insured value) of each major asset. If an asset has no major market value because either the law or the charity's governing document prohibits its sale, or because the asset is not saleable in practice (such as a statue or monument), this fact should be disclosed.

8.8.5 Liabilities

Liabilities should be considered in two categories. A current liability is one that is due to be settled by the charity during the course of the next financial year, while a future liability is one falling due for payment at any time after the end of the next financial year. For major liabilities, the actual date on which the liability falls due should be given if it is known. Liabilities of different types should be listed separately, although several liabilities of the same type may be added together and shown as a single figure.

Where a liability relates directly to an asset mentioned in the list of assets, the relationship between the asset and the liability should be disclosed. For instance, a motor vehicle purchased by the charity under a finance lease should be shown in the list of assets. The related liability is the commitment by the charity to pay all the future instalments of the finance lease. The number and frequency of the instalments should be shown here as a liability, together with the amount of each instalment.

Similarly, where the charity is committed to making rental payments over a number of years, the extent of the obligation should be noted, e.g. 'the charity is committed to paying rent of £1,000 per annum for a further seven years under the existing lease on its premises.

If a charity has undertaken to make a charitable payment on some date in the future, this should be shown as a liability only if the charity is now bound to make the payment. If the commitment to make the payment is neither legally binding nor unavoidable in the interests of the charity, then the commitment does not amount to a liability. Similarly, if the commitment only becomes legally binding in the event that some condition is fulfilled in the future, then it should not be shown as a liability. The trustees should show in a note to which of the charity's restricted or unrestricted funds each liability relates.

8.8.6 Guarantees and other contingent liabilities

All guarantees given by the charity should be identified and the amount of money guaranteed by the charity should be disclosed. The trustees should also explain in a note what it is that they have guaranteed. For instance, one charity may need a loan from the bank but, being a new charity, may not have a good enough credit rating with the bank and a second charity with a good credit rating may offer to guarantee the loan. The trustees of the second charity should disclose the amount of the guarantee, the fact that it is acting as a guarantor for XYZ charity, and give the date on which the guarantee is likely to end.

Any other liability which the trustees think is likely to become payable at some time in the future should also be included under this heading, together with a note explaining how and why the liability arises. A note should be given of any pending litigation and the anticipated outcome (if known).

8.9 The trustees' annual report

The trustees' annual report should follow the same format that a larger charity's trustees' report would take, although it does not need to include as much detailed information as a larger charity's. The annual report should identify the charity, how it is constituted, and its aims and officers, and should provide a brief but comprehensive review of the year's activities and achievements, including the main features of the accounts. Guidance and a checklist for this are the same as a charity preparing accounts under the full SORP.

8.9.1 Legal and administrative information

The full name of the charity should be stated together with its charity number, if registered, and the principal or registered address of the charity. It should give details of the nature of the governing document, together with names of the trustees and names and addresses of the charity's main advisers, e.g. solicitors and independent examiner. A note of any restrictions limiting the charity's activities and any specific investment powers should also be given.

8.9.2 Narrative information

Aims and organisation

The charity should give details on its aims and how it is going about achieving them. It should give a brief summary of the main purposes or objects for which the charity is established, as set out in its governing document, and how the charity is organised, for example: where it operates; whether it has voluntary, seconded or paid staff; whether it has connections with other charities; a brief summary of the main charitable activities undertaken during the year and how these relate to its objects; details of any major changes in aims and organisation since the last report and why these were made.

Review of progress and achievements

It will be from this point of the report that the reader should be able to judge the charity's effectiveness. It should contain:

- a brief summary of the main achievements of the year in relation to the charity's objects;
- a review of financial activities and affairs.

The SORP makes various recommendations which are not required by the regulations. If there is nothing to report the topic should be omitted. The guidance includes a glossary of terms used. The glossary is similar to the glossary included in the SORP with a few exceptions.

Review of financial activities
The review should comment on the following:

- any major cash or non-cash transactions undertaken;
- any important events occurring after the year end but before the date on which the trustees' report was signed;
- figures demonstrating the impact the charity is making;
- the extent to which the charity is relying on volunteer help, gifts in kind or free facilities;
- a review of the performance of any trading subsidiary;
- a review of the adequacy and availability of cash, and non-cash resources available to meet substantial liabilities and obligations;
- a list of any assets mortgaged as security for a loan or other liability;
- brief particulars of any grants of cash or other assets exceeding £1,000, including name of recipient;
- transactions between the charity and any connected charities;
- any payments to trustees made by either the charity or any charity with which it is connected;
- any trustee indemnity premiums paid out of the funds of the charity;
- the total of any *ex gratia* payments made by the charity;
- details of any assets for which the charity is responsible as custodian trustee for another charity.

Only a few charities will have something to report on all of the aspects set out below.

8.10 Change in accounting basis

According to SORP 2000 (para 357), for each year in which the charity changes from accruals accounts to receipts and payments accounting or vice versa, the corresponding amounts for the previous financial year should be restated on the basis of the new accounting policy.

Chapter 9 Audit and independent examination

9.1 Audit

9.1.1 Introduction

Charity audit is an audit of stewardship and there is an overlap between the role of the external auditor and the charity's head of finance. Secrecy is no longer allowed and a greater openness is required with trustees no longer allowed to be unaccountable to anyone. All those with an involvement in a charity, i.e., stakeholders, be they donors, creditors, grantees, trustees, employees, etc., have the right to expect that the resources entrusted to the charity are being used cost-effectively. It must therefore be part of the audit to ensure that this happens.

9.1.2 Legal position

Until the Charities Act 1993, there was no statutory auditing requirement for charities. The Charity Commission did, however, have power under s8 (3) of the Charities Act 1962 'to require that the condition and accounts of a charity for such a period as they think fit shall be investigated and audited by an auditor appointed by them'.

Section 22(4) of the Trustee Act 1925 empowers trustees 'in their absolute discretion from time to time but not more than once in every three years unless the nature of the trust or any special dealings with the trust property make a more frequent exercise of the rights reasonable, cause the accounts of the trust property to be examined or audited by an independent accountant'.

In addition, obviously, certain charities may have to have an audit, for example those of a certain size and incorporated under the Companies Act, those incorporated under the Industrial and Provident Societies Acts, charitable housing associations, all charities for the disabled or charities governed by the War Charities Act 1940, charitable friendly societies and those whose governing instrument, e.g., trust deed, requires it.

Both the Woodfield Report (1987) and the White Paper *Charities – A Framework for the Future* (1989) proposed forms of audit or examination according to the size of charities. There followed a Bill debated in the House of Lords towards the end of 1991 from which emerged the Charities Act 1992, now mainly consolidated into the 1993 Act.

The audit requirements specified in s43 (as amended) that if a charity's gross income or total expenditure in any of the following:

- relevant year;
- financial year of the charity immediately preceding the relevant year; or
- financial year of the charity immediately preceding the year specified in para (b);

exceeded £250,000, then the accounts have to be audited by a person who:

- is in accordance with s25 of the Companies Act 1989 eligible for appointment as a company auditor; or
- is a member of a body for the time being specified in the regulations still to be laid out and is under the rules of that body eligible for appointment as auditor of the charity.

Where the annual gross income or total expenditure is effectively less than £250,000 but more than £10,000 in any of the specified years, then the accounts have to be independently examined by a person who in the opinion of the trustees is reasonably believed to have the requisite ability and practical experience to carry out a competent examination of the accounts.

Alternatively, the trustees can, if they wish, still have the accounts audited and must of course do so if the governing instrument demands it. It is a point worth making that where a charity qualifies for independent examination but its constitution requires an audit, then it may be worth revising the constitution. In cases where the charity is incorporated and has income of less than £250,000, an accountant's report can be included. The statutory threshold for commercial companies was increased from £350,000 to £1,000,000 in 2000. However, the legislation specifically held the level of income at £250,000 for charitable limited companies.

9.1.3 Accounting and financial standards

Accounting systems must reflect the activities of the charity and provide sufficient information to control and manage these activities. Accounting by charities is reflected in SORP 2000 and not primarily driven by FRSs and SSAPs. Therefore, in considering the appropriateness of these financial reporting standards, it must be remembered that they have been prepared to deal with business enterprises where the motive is profit, not with charities where the motive is certainly different.

One example is that of SSAP 4, dealing with the treatment of Government grants, which lays down definite rules about accounting for both capital and revenue grants. From a charity's viewpoint, the difference between capital and revenue grants is often irrelevant and this led to a recommendation under SORP 1995 which many auditors find difficult to understand and follow. Therefore treatments that are quite clearly presenting a true and fair view for a commercial organisation may not be so for a charity. SORP 2000 has however endeavoured to ensure that the SORP and accounting guidelines are harmonised.

9.1.4 Scope

No two charities are the same. The scope of the audit or independent examination can depend on the status of the charity, which will also determine the type of any report that has to be given. It is essential that any auditor or independent examiner should know and understand the legal structure of the organisation and recognise what is included within the scope. Charities are governed in many different ways:

- as an unincorporated association;
- as a company – probably limited by guarantee;
- as a trust;
- by Royal Charter;
- by specific Act of Parliament; or
- under one of the various acts relating to friendly, industrial and provident societies, and housing associations.

The purpose of an audit has to be to provide an independent review of the financial affairs of an organisation. Obviously, therefore, the terms of the auditor's appointment set out in an engagement letter should determine the actual scope of the audit and the nature of the report required. The requirements of a charity audit became clearer, from the auditor's point of view, following the publication (October 1995) of the Auditing Practices Board (APB) guidance note.

Auditors are required to express the opinion that the accounts give a 'true and fair' view. However, unfortunately, there often is an expectation gap between what the trustees or the staff of the charity think they are receiving from the audit, and what the auditors think they are being asked to provide. Therefore, it is vital that the precise scope of the audit is clearly defined in the letter of engagement and it is important that the auditors are willing to discuss this matter with the client.

The auditors should review the trustees' report. They should ensure that the information in this report is consistent with that given in the financial statements. If there are misleading differences between the trustees' report and the underlying financial statements, such that the user of the accounts could be misled, the auditor should disclose this in the audit report.

9.1.5 Guidelines

The audit guidelines, published as Practice Note 11 *The Audit of Charities*, take the form of commentary on points to be considered by auditors in order to meet the requirements of the Auditing Practices Board's auditing standards. The Note provides background information on the regulatory and legal framework relating to charities in the UK. This Practice Note is currently being revised. At the time of writing (April 2001) the consultation note has not been issued.

The Practice Note sets out special considerations relating to the audit of charities which arise from individual Statements of Auditing Standards, and where no special considerations apply no comment is made.

The purpose of this Practice Note is to provide guidance on the application of auditing standards when auditing a charity rather than giving a general commentary on such audits. It then seeks to incorporate all the significant issues which are likely to need particular attention by a charity's auditors. The five key areas covered are:

1. factors of relevant law and regulations;
2. factors affecting auditor's assessment of risk;
3. controls over key aspects of a charity's income and assets;
4. content of report on financial statements;
5. matters to be reported directly to the Charity Commission.

Whilst charity auditors must have a clear understanding of the organisation as there is a clear public expectation that charities are properly run and managed, responsibility for achieving this aim lies with the trustees of the charity, and for England and Wales, with the Charity Commission and not with the auditors.

The review of the Practice Note has been brought because:

- there have been changes in tax legislation – charities are now able to include an amount of taxable trading within their records;
- a number of new FRSs were issued which affect the guidance given in the existing Practice Note 11;
- the APB has issued further guidance such as SAS 480;
- the references to the Charity Commission publications are out of date; and
- SORP 2000 was issued in October 2000.

9.1.6 Reports

There is no common report to suit all charities because of the way in which they may be constituted and governed by many different rules and laws. The auditor's report on the financial statements of a charity registered under the Companies Act will continue to be determined in accordance with the provisions of that Act, and addressed to the members of the charity. However, auditors' reports on the financial statements of a charity registered under the Acts relating to friendly, industrial and provident societies will be in a different form and addressed to the charity itself.

The current APB Practice Note includes 12 examples of auditors' reports on charities' financial statements, taking account of the different circumstances and the different legislative requirements that apply not only in England and Wales where the Charity Commission has jurisdiction, but also in Scotland.

9.1.7 Management letter

The annual return that charities are required to fill in and return to the Charity Commission asks questions regarding the audit management letter. The initial question is in respect of whether the charity has received a management letter and in cases where it has done so, the Commission goes on to ask whether the charity has acted upon the recommendations made in this letter.

The auditor is ideally placed to make recommendations to improve systems of control within the charity itself. The report should not just list what is wrong, with solely negative criticism, it should be constructive, suggesting ideas for building on the strengths, whilst pointing out the weaknesses and providing ways of overcoming them. The charity's attention should be drawn to departures from best practice within the charity sector.

9.2 Independent examination

9.2.1 Introduction

Whether a charity needs an audit or independent examination depends on its size. To meet the requirements of the Charities Act 1993, all charities with an income in excess of £250,000 will require audit – whether independent examination is required or not depends on the legal status of the charity, i.e., whether it is incorporated or unincorporated. Those unincorporated charities with an income between £10,000 and £250,000 will require as a basic minimum an independent examination. Incorporated charities fall under the auspices of the Companies Act 1985 in respect of the requirement to audit and the preparation of an accountant's report.

9.2.2 What is independent examination?

This is a less onerous form of scrutiny than audit although the level of assurance given by independent examination is higher than that given under the exemption report regulations for companies. It is primarily based on a review of the accounts and consideration of any unusual items or disclosures identified. It indicates whether certain matters have been brought to the reviewer's attention. The examination must be carried out in accordance with the directions issued by the Charity Commission.

The level of assurance provided by independent examination may be lower than that provided by audit, but it can be a very attractive option. This is true particularly where a charity's accounts have traditionally been 'audited' to satisfy members or the terms of a charity's trust by an individual without formal auditing qualifications.

If the accounts are prepared on an accruals basis, then the independent examiner must check them for compliance with the regulations in terms of format and content, review accounting policies, and enquire about post balance sheet events. The examiner must also compare the accounts with the trustees' report to make sure the two are consistent.

9.2.3 Who can do an independent examination?

An independent examiner is defined as 'an independent person who is reasonably believed by the trustees to have the requisite ability and practical experience to carry out competent examination of the accounts'. The Charities Act 1993 went on to define 'independent' as having 'no connection with a charity's trustees which might inhibit the impartial conduct of the examination'.

Example 9.1 Dorsetshire Drugs Advice Centre

Report of the auditors
To the members of Dorsetshire Drugs Advice Centre

We have audited the financial statements on pages 6 to 12 which have been prepared on the basis of the accounting policies set out on page 8.

Respective responsibilities of the management committee and auditors
As described on page 3, the members of the management committee, who are directors for the purpose of company law and trustees for the purpose of charity law, are responsible for the preparation of financial statements. It is our responsibility to form an independent opinion, based on our audit, on those statements and to report our opinion to you.

Basis of opinion
We conducted our audit in accordance with Auditing Standards issued by the Auditing Practices Board. An audit includes examination, on a test basis, of evidence relevant to the amounts and disclosures in the financial statements. It also includes an assessment of the judgements made by the management committee in the preparation of the financial statements, and of whether the accounting policies are appropriate to the charitable company's circumstances, consistently applied and adequately disclosed.

We planned and performed our audit so as to obtain all the information and explanations which we considered necessary in order to provide us with sufficient evidence to give reasonable assurance that the financial statements are free from material misstatement, whether caused by fraud or other irregularity or error. In forming our opinion we also evaluated the overall adequacy of the presentation of information in the financial statements.

Opinion
In our opinion the financial statements give a true and fair view of the charitable company's state of affairs as at 31 March 2002 and of the incoming resources and application of resources, including its income and expenditure, for the year then ended and have been properly prepared in accordance with the Companies Act 1985.

Fred Bloggs & Co

Registered Auditors
Birmingham

14 September 2002

Example 9.2 The Rosanna Grant Trust

Report of the auditors
To the trustees of The Rosanna Grant Trust

We have audited the financial statements on pages 5 to 11 which have been prepared under the accounting policies set out on page 7.

Respective responsibilities of the trustees and auditors
As described on page 3 the charity's trustees are responsible for the preparation of financial statements. It is our responsibility to form an independent opinion, based on our audit, on those statements and to report our opinion to you. We have been appointed auditors under section 43 of the Charities Act 1993 and report in accordance with regulations made under section 44 of that Act.

Basis of opinion
We conducted our audit in accordance with Auditing Standards issued by the Auditing Practices Board. An audit includes examination, on a test basis, of evidence relevant to the amounts and disclosures in the financial statements. It also includes an assessment of the significant estimates and judgements made by the trustees in the preparation of the financial statements, and of whether the accounting policies are appropriate to the charity's circumstances, consistently applied and adequately disclosed.

We planned and performed our audit so as to obtain all the information and explanations which we considered necessary in order to provide us with sufficient evidence to give reasonable assurance that the financial statements are free from material misstatement, whether caused by fraud or other irregularity or error. In forming our opinion we also evaluated the overall adequacy of information in the financial statements.

Opinion
In our opinion the financial statements give a true and fair view of the state of affairs of the charity as at 30 September 2001 and of its incoming resources and application of resources in the year then ended and have been properly prepared in accordance with the Companies Act 1993.

A Charity Auditor

Registered Auditors
London

12 January 2002

Example 9.3 The ABC Charity

Report of the auditors
To the members of The ABC Charity

We have audited the financial statements on pages 8 to 20 which have been prepared on the basis of the accounting policies set out on pages 11 and 12.

Respective responsibilities of the trustees and auditors
As described on pages 4 and 5, the trustees are responsible for the preparation of the financial statements in accordance with United Kingdom law and accounting standards. Our responsibilities, as independent auditors, are established in the United Kingdom by statute, the Auditing Practices Board and by our profession's ethical guidance.

Basis of opinion
We conducted our audit in accordance with Auditing Standards issued by the Auditing Practices Board. An audit includes examination, on a test basis, of evidence relevant to the amounts and disclosures in the financial statements. It also includes an assessment of the significant estimates and judgements made by the trustees in the preparation of the financial statements, and of whether the accounting policies are appropriate to the group's circumstances consistently applied and adequately disclosed.

We planned and performed our audit so as to obtain all the information and explanations which we considered necessary in order to provide us with sufficient evidence to give reasonable assurance that the financial statements are free from material misstatement, whether caused by fraud or other irregularity or error. In forming our opinion we also evaluated the overall adequacy of the presentation of information in the financial statements.

Opinion
In our opinion the financial statements give a true and fair view of the state of affairs of the charity and group at 31 March 2001 and of the group's incoming resources and resources expended, including its income and expenditure, for the year then ended and have been properly prepared in accordance with the Companies Act 1985.

An Auditor

Registered Auditors
London

16 June 2001

The independent examiner will need to have good analytical and communication skills to be able to raise questions and to interpret and challenge responses. Also, the individual chosen should have practical experience, which should be indicated by involvement with the financial administration or independent examination of similar charities.

Although the independent examiner should be familiar with accountancy methods, the examiner need not be a practising accountant. Someone with a professional qualification, especially a qualified accountant, however, is strongly recommended by the Charity Commission, particularly for a larger charity or cases where accruals accounting is adopted.

9.2.4 Independent examination report

The content of this report is determined by the regulations and it should be signed by the independent examiner personally, not on behalf of his/her firm, and must state any relevant professional qualifications or professional body of which he/she is a member. Examiners should avoid making positive statements of opinion or belief that could only be substantiated by carrying out an audit. The examiner should report clearly and unambiguously where the charity's accounts appear to be in order.

9.2.5 The carrying out of an independent examination – directions and guidance notes

In March 1996, the Charity Commission issued guidance on the carrying out of an independent examination. The guidance covers examination requirements, the question 'what is an examination?', the selection of examiners and the examiner's report. This is also under review by the Charity Commission and will be published as CC63 *Independent Examination of Accounts under SORP 2000: Directions and Guidance Notes.*

9.3 Whistle-blowing

This additional role, given to the auditor or independent examiner of an unincorporated charity of reporting certain facts directly to the Charity Commission, is designed to increase public confidence. However, a similar right does not exist where the charity is incorporated. This duty occurs where the auditor or independent examiner finds evidence of deliberate or reckless misconduct by one or more trustees which puts the funds of the charity at risk.

Auditors and independent examiners should not have to change the scope of their work to discover whether or not reportable issues exist. A duty arises if something is discovered whilst carrying out the audit/independent examination which in their opinion is judged to be of 'material significance'.

The APB Practice Note currently sets out the three particular types of issues likely to be reportable:

1. significant inadequacy in the arrangements made by trustees for the discretion and management of a charity's affairs;
2. a significant breach of the legislative requirement or of the charity's trusts;
3. circumstances indicating a probable deliberate misuse of charity property.

The APB requires that the auditors discuss concerns with trustees as part of the process of forming a judgement as to whether a particular issue needs to be reported directly to the Charity Commission. It is not intended that the auditor/examiner should report on insignificant issues, particularly where such issues have been satisfactorily resolved.

The regulations provide rights of access to all documents relating to the charity and which the auditor/independent examiner properly considers it necessary to inspect. This includes the right to require information from past or present trustees, officers or employees.

It is likely that the revised Practice Note 11 will extend the requirement to 'whistle-blow'. The Charity Commission considers that there are far more cases where auditors should be whistle-blowing than is currently the case. In the future the Commission will expect to see more cases reported.

Part III
Commentary and guidance on specific problem areas, guidelines and definitions

Chapter 10 Charitable companies

Charitable companies are required to meet the reporting requirements of the Companies Act 1985 in addition to SORP 2000. Company legislation requires annual financial statements to give a true and fair view of the state of the affairs of the company at the end of the year and of its profit or loss for that year. However, it is important to note that directors should modify the headings within the balance sheet and profit and loss account where the special nature of the company's activities dictate this. Therefore, charitable companies will need to comply with SORP 2000 in order to meet the requirements of company law to show a true and fair view and to adapt the accounts to the special nature of being a charity. Paragraph 334 clearly states that any material departure from SORP 2000 needs to be disclosed but will not be justified 'simply because it gives the reader a more appealing picture of the financial position or results of the charity'. As far as charitable companies are concerned, following SORP 2000 is a minimal requirement and there may indeed be further additional requirements as laid down in company legislation.

There is a particular requirement under Companies Act 1985 for all companies to include an 'income and expenditure account' within their accounts. The Statement of Financial Activities (SOFA) has been constructed to show separately all the gains and losses of a charity in the income and expenditure account with a separate section within the SOFA to show the statement of total recognised gains and losses as required by Financial Reporting Standard 3.

In order for a separate summary income and expenditure account to be avoided, the headings within the SOFA need to be adapted to include a title of income and expenditure account and statement of total recognised gains and losses, together with a subtotal of 'net income/(expenditure) for the year' which should take the place of the heading 'net incoming/(outgoing) resources for the year'. In stating the possible need for a separate summary income and expenditure account, SORP 2000 does not make any reference to unincorporated charities.

For incorporated charities, a summary income and expenditure account may still be required where (para 335):

(a) there is a movement on endowment (capital) funds during the year; and
(b) unrealised gains and losses arose during the year.

Company legislation does not allow capital items to be shown in an income and expenditure account. Hence, if there is a movement of such funds, a separate summary income and expenditure account needs to be produced.

SORP 2000 allows both unrealised and realised gains and losses on investments to be shown in one line in the statement of total recognised gains and losses. Therefore, a company's accounts need to reflect in the notes, the total net income/(expenditure) for the year including any realised gains or losses arising. Unrealised gains and losses can not form part of a company's income/(expenditure) for the year as a company needs to report only its historic cost profits/(losses) per FRS 3.

Where a summary income and expenditure account is produced, it should be derived from and cross referenced to the corresponding figures in the SOFA. The summary statement should distinguish between continuing operations, acquisitions and discontinued operations.

The summary income and expenditure account should include:

- gross income;
- net gains or losses from disposals of fixed assets;
- transfers from endowment funds;
- total income;
- total expenditure; and
- net income or expenditure for the year.

There is a difference between the original depreciated cost or valuation of an asset and the revalued amount. This difference will result in a revaluation reserve within a company's accounts which company law requires to be disclosed separately. This reserve does not have a significant impact for charities as they do not distribute their profits. Charitable companies must nevertheless separately disclose the revaluation reserve within the fund section either on the face of the balance sheet or by use of a prominent insert.

There still remains an inconsistency within the regulatory framework for the reporting requirements for incorporated and unincorporated charities. An unincorporated charity with an annual income between £10,000 and £90,000 will require an independent examination which is a form of external scrutiny of the charity's accounts. An incorporated charity whose annual income is between £10,000 and £90,000 requires no such external scrutiny of their accounts.

Within the reporting framework of companies itself there are further differences in reporting requirements. For example, an incorporated charity with an income between £90,000 to £250,000 per annum, requires a reporting accountants' report under s249A(2) of the Companies Act 1985. For incorporated charities whose income is over £250,000 per annum, a full audit is required. However, for commercial companies, no form of external examination (of either a reporting accountants' report or a full audit) is required until the income is in excess of £1m in the year. This extra external scrutiny for charitable companies is due to the public accountability and range of stakeholder interest that exists within the charity sector.

Table 10.1 Charity accounts compliance checklist: summary income and expenditure account (only applies to charitable companies)

1 General

		Yes / N/A / Ref
1.1.1	Is the charity incorporated?	
1.2.1	Does this summary have to be prepared [para 335]?	________

> *Note: Where the charity has no endowment fund movements, both for the current and the previous year, the summary income and expenditure account may be omitted. In such cases, the SOFA should show the amount of the net revaluation gains/losses for the year in a separate section, after prominent sub-totals entitled 'net income/expenditure for the year'. Therefore, the SOFA would consist of two parts, the account of income and expenditure for the year to comply with FRS 3, and the statement of total recognised gains and losses together with the reconciliation of funds.*

1.2.2	Have there been movements on endowment (capital) funds during the year [para 335a]?	________
1.2.3	Have there been any unrealised gains and losses arising during the year [para 335b]?	________
1.2.4	Where no summary income and expenditure is required, has the SOFA been appropriately modified [para 336]?	________
1.3	Is this account derived from and cross referenced to, the corresponding figures of the SOFA [para 337]?	________
1.4	Has the following information been given:	
	(a) Gross income from all sources [para 337a]?	________
	(b) Net gains/losses from disposals of all fixed assets belonging to the charity's income funds [para 337b]?	________
	(c) Transfers from endowment funds of capital resources converted into income [para 337c]?	________
	(d) Total income [para 337d]?	________
	(e) Total expenditure [para 337e]?	________
	(f) Net income or expenditure for the year [para 337f]?	________

Chapter 11 Fund accounting

There is a common misconception that the SORP introduced fund accounting in 1995. This is not the case. Fund accounting has been in existence for some considerable time, but prior to the implementation of the SORP few charities complied with the requirement.

A fund is defined in SORP 2000 as a pool of unexpended resources held in and maintained separately from other pools because of the circumstances in which the resources were originally received or the way in which they have subsequently been treated. A charity's funds are distinct from its reserves. Reserves are the part of the charity's funds which are freely available for its general purposes (see Chapter 2).

All charities have funds. These may be unrestricted, designated, restricted or endowed. They may have different labels, such as capital funds, but in law fall under one of these headings. Funds are defined in Appendix 3 of SORP 2000. Where charities have more than one type of fund under their control there are additional requirements. SORP 2000 requires accounting for the proper administration of the individual funds in accordance with the respective terms of the trust. To discharge this obligation details concerning individual funds may be given in the notes, but the accounts should provide a summary of main funds, differentiating in particular between the restricted and unrestricted funds. The definitions of the individual types of funds are detailed below.

11.1 Unrestricted funds

Unrestricted funds are expendable at the discretion of the trustees in furtherance of the objects of the charity. These funds must be free from any restriction imposed by either a donor, legacy or contract. Some trustees have power to declare specific trusts over unrestricted funds. If such a power is available, and is exercised, the assets affected will form a restricted fund and the trustees' discretion to apply the fund will be legally restricted. Designated funds form part of unrestricted funds and are considered in more detail below.

11.2 Designated funds

Designated funds are unrestricted funds earmarked for a particular project. Designation has an administrative purpose only and does not legally restrict the trustees' discretion to apply the fund. These funds should be accounted for within unrestricted funds. They can be used, as for example, anticipated repairs and maintenance following a health and safety review. The precise purpose of all designated funds should be stated in the notes to the accounts.

In cases where assets are donated as a gift in kind, SORP 2000 recommends capitalising the asset and treating the asset and its subsequent depreciation through a designated fund.

11.3 Restricted funds

Restricted funds are funds subject to specific trusts, which may be declared by the donor or with the donor's authority, but are still within the objects of the charity or determined by the type of appeal the charity has mounted. Restricted funds may be restricted income funds, which are expendable at the discretion of the trustees in furtherance of some particular aspect of the objects of the charity, or they may be capital funds where the assets are required to be invested or retained for actual use rather than expended. Distinction should be drawn between income and capital funds. Any income arising from the restricted assets of a fund will be treated as restricted unless the donor has specified otherwise or the income is distributable at the discretion of the trustees. Any funds in deficit should always be separately disclosed and an explanation should be given in the trustees' report. Trustees should be able to account for each individual restricted fund.

Notes to the accounts should analyse movements on individual restricted funds showing opening and closing balances, together with income, expenditure and any gains or losses, unrealised or realised, arising in the year.

If income is received with restrictions or conditions which cannot be met then the income should not be shown in the statement of financial activities, but treated as a creditor in the balance sheet. This would be true also of income received for which the charity, under its objects, does not have the power to engage in.

11.4 Endowment funds

Permanent endowment funds exist where there is a capital fund with no power to convert the capital into income. These funds must generally be held indefinitely. The concept of permanence does not mean the assets held in the endowment fund cannot be exchanged, nor does it mean that they are incapable of depreciation or loss, for example if the fund is represented by investments and the value of the investments fall. However, the permanent endowment fund cannot be used as if it were income.

Where assets held in a permanent endowment fund are exchanged, their place in the fund must be taken by the assets received in exchange. This may be a change of investment, but can mean the application of the proceeds from the sale of freehold land and buildings. This initial gift and subsequent increases and decreases in the amount of any endowment funds should be distinguished in the SOFA as part of these funds. Certain payments must be made out of the endowments funds, for example investment manager's fees in relation to investments held within the endowment fund.

The notes to the accounts should show how they have arisen and analyse the endowments between permanent and expendable. The example of The Higher Education College accounts for the year ended 31 August 2000 is shown as Example 11.1.

Income earned from permanent endowment funds will generally be unrestricted unless a specific purpose has been declared by the donor in which case the income will be restricted. Any income unspent at the end of the year should be carried in the appropriate restricted or unrestricted fund.

Expendable endowments are those funds which at the discretion of the trustees may be applied as income. As already mentioned, all income from these funds should be included in the SOFA. If the application of the income is restricted to a particular purpose, the income and expenditure should be appropriately identified in the restricted fund and any not spent at the year end should be carried forward as a restricted fund.

Example 11.1 The Higher College Charity

Notes forming part of the financial statements for the year ended 31 August 2001

1 Principal accounting policies

The financial statements of the Charity are prepared in accordance with The Charities (Accounts and Reports) Regulations 2000 and the Statement of Recommended Practice "Accounting and Reporting by Charities" issued in October 2000 ("SORP"), and with applicable accounting standards. These financial statements are drawn up on the historical cost accounting basis except that investment assets are carried at market value.

(a) **Group accounts**
These financial statements consolidate the results of the charity and its wholly-owned subsidiary HC Enterprises Limited on a line by line basis. A separate statement of financial activities for the charity itself is not presented because the charity has taken advantage of the exemptions afforded by paragraph 304 of SORP.

(b) **Fees and similar income**
Fees receivable and charges for services and use of premises are accounted for in the period in which the service is provided. Fees receivable are stated after deducting allowances, scholarships and other remissions granted by the school from its unrestricted funds, but include contributions received from Restricted Funds for Scholarships, Bursaries and other grants.

(c) **Donations and fund accounting**
Donations received for the general purposes of the Charity are included as unrestricted funds. Donations for activities restricted by the wishes of the donor are taken to "restricted funds" where these wishes are legally binding on the Governors. Donations required to be retained as capital in accordance with the donor's wishes are accounted for as "endowments" – permanent or expendable according to the nature of the restriction.

(d) **Resources expended**
Resources expended are accounted for on an accruals basis. Certain expenditure is apportioned to cost categories based on the estimated amount attributable to that activity in the year. These estimates are based on staff time or the floor area as appropriate. The irrecoverable element of VAT is included with the item of expense to which it relates.

Fuel supplied to the schools by a subsidiary company is treated as a cost of the schools, and the sale proceeds and associated costs are excluded from trading income and trading expenditure. Likewise, construction and repair costs, supplied to the Charity by its subsidiary, are capitalised or expensed and excluded from trading income and expenditure.

(e) **Operating leases**
Rentals payable are charged on a time basis over the lease term.

(f) **Pension schemes**
The Charity contributes to the Teachers' Superannuation Scheme at rates set by the Scheme Actuary and advised to the Board by the Scheme Administrator. The Charity also contributes to a defined contribution scheme for non-teaching staff.

(g) **Financing costs**
Financing costs include amounts accrued in accordance with the terms of the Advance Fee contracts.

***Example 11.1 The Higher College Charity** (cont.)*

14. Net assets of the group's funds

The group's net assets belong to the various funds (including Advance Fees) as follows:

	Fixed assets £'000	Investments £'000	Net current assets £'000	Long-term liabilities £'000	Fund balances £'000
Endowment funds	–	4,033	–	–	**4,033**
Restricted funds	–	811	275	–	**1,086**
Unrestricted funds					
Designated funds					
Advance fees	–	1,939	185	(1,831)	**293**
Tangible fixed assets fund	9,562	–	(2,000)	–	**7,562**
Heritage fund	–	250	2	–	**252**
Non-charitable trading funds	8	–	–	–	**8**
General Reserve	–	–	1,190	(44)	**1,146**
	9,570	7,033	(348)	(1,875)	**14,380**

Net current assets for Advance Fees comprised:	
Cash	**397**
Advance fees due within one year	**(505)**
	(108)

14A. Endowed funds: movements in the year

	Balance at 1 September 2000 £'000	Incoming endowments £'000	Amounts expended £'000	Transfers and investments gains/(losses) £'000	Balance at 31 August 2001 £'000
Permanent endowments:					
Foundation capital	563	–	–	15	**578**
Other Special Trusts:					
Grants and allowances	1,772	8	–	66	**1,846**
Scholarships, bursaries	1,460	–	–	(17)	**1,443**
Prize and other funds	168	–	–	(2)	**166**
	3,963	**8**	**–**	**62**	**4,033**

The Foundation Capital represents the original endowment to provide free education. The income of this fund contributes to the free education of pupils whose parents live in Newshire.

The other Special Trusts consist of a number of individual trusts and prize funds set up by individual donors.

Each fund is allocated its proportion of investment income and gains and losses and bears its own expenses.

11.5 Investment gains or losses

If a gain is made on the disposal of an asset, the gain will form part of the fund in which the asset was held. An unrealised gain on an asset will also form part of the fund in which the asset is held. Similarly, unrealised losses and provision for depreciation and for the permanent diminution in value of an asset will reduce the fund in which the asset is or was held (as in the case of a realised loss).

Detailed record-keeping for each individual fund is essential to ensure gains, losses and provisions are added to or deducted from the correct fund.

11.5.1 Fixed assets acquired

Fixed assets are to be accounted within the fund from which they were acquired. For example, in the case of the Disabled Drivers Association, the National Lotteries Charities Board gave funds towards the charity's new headquarters. The building is restricted and any associated depreciation would need to be offset against this fund. A fall in permanent value would need to be accounted for against this fund.

11.6 Separate bank accounts

Historically, the Charity Commission recommended that trustees kept separate bank accounts for each separate fund. They have now accepted that, provided accounting systems are suitable, there is no need for a separate bank account for each individual fund.

However, it will continue to be necessary to distinguish clearly between the separate assets and liabilities for each type of fund. Charities must be able to distinguish between money held on trust for a specific charitable purpose and that held for general purposes.

11.7 Income generated by restricted funds

There is a need to recognise restricted income in the SOFA. However, there may be certain circumstances where recognition may be delayed (because of timing) or not occur at all (because of being unable to meet preconditions).

It is important to recognise that where restricted income is invested temporarily and generates further income, that income is itself restricted unless the donor made clear that the income from the investment could be used for general purposes. Some doubts have been expressed as to whether restricted funds can in fact be spent on items such as fundraising and publicity, or management and administration. This will depend on the type of fund but, for example, where a charity has mounted a specific fundraising appeal to generate funds for a special purpose, e.g., a third-world charity raising funds for the latest famine, then quite clearly the costs of raising those funds, primarily fundraising and publicity, are chargeable against the fund.

Given that the definition in SORP 2000 of management and administration relates to the charity rather than its core activities, it is unlikely that these expenses will be chargeable against restricted funds. However, there are inevitably administration costs in relation to the project which may well be correctly charged to the restricted fund, for example the costs of an accountant based in the third-world country specifically administering the famine relief (see above) would most certainly be a legitimate charge against a restricted fund.

11.8 Funds structure

The trustees need to decide on a format that will tie the necessary disclosures on individual fund balances into a summary statement. In the case of The ABC Charity (CC66), they disclose each fund separately in the restricted fund notes showing brought forward balances, any income and expenditure in the year, realised and unrealised gains and losses and a carried forward amount. Supporting notes then explain the purpose of each fund.

Where funds are consolidated with those of a non-charitable trading subsidiary, an appropriate separate fund heading such as 'non-charitable trading funds' would be shown on the face of the balance sheet. This could normally be treated as an unrestricted fund.

The SOFA should itself analyse restricted and unrestricted funds and the respective movements in the year, together with a brought forward and carried forward position. This should be supported as discussed above by notes analysing the funds and showing the nature and purpose of each fund.

Transfers between funds should also be shown separately on the face of the SOFA. Transfers affecting restricted funds should be shown separately to those affecting unrestricted and designated funds. Material transfers to designated funds should be accompanied by a narrative note explaining the nature of the transfer or allocation and the reason for it.

Any fund in deficit should be separately disclosed and an explanation given in the trustees' report.

11.9 Restricted income and expenditure

The trustees of a charity will be in breach of trust if they expend restricted income otherwise than in the furtherance of that aspect, or those aspects, of the objects of the charity to which expenditure is restricted. It is therefore essential that due care is taken to spend out of a particular restricted income fund only where the trusts so permit.

Expenditure may be charged to a restricted fund which is not at the time in credit, or not in sufficient credit, where there is a genuine anticipation of receipts which can properly be credited to the fund in order to meet the expenditure (this can be where a grant has been agreed but the project must start before funding can be received, or where a decision has been taken to invite donations for that fund).

The fund which is actually drawn upon to finance the expenditure should be held upon trusts which are wide enough to permit the expenditure (in case the expected receipts do not materialise). However, if expenditure has been charged to an unrestricted fund, it should not subsequently be recharged to restricted fund receipts simply in order to increase the fund of unrestricted income. This again increases the need for adequate record-keeping of each individual restricted, designated and endowment fund.

In the case of restricted funds, which can only be used for the purposes for which they are given, cost allocation cannot automatically be applied to these funds as the donor may have specified that only direct costs may be spent – rather than direct costs and apportioned support costs.

Where indirect costs cannot be charged under the specific trusts declared by the donor, a charity may want to show the actual costs of the direct charitable expenditure carried out by applying restricted funds. This can be done by charging the relevant support costs, costs of generating funds and management and administration costs to the restricted fund, and then making a transfer from unrestricted funds to restricted funds to match the amount of these indirect costs; thus ensuring that the restricted fund balance carried forward is in accordance with the specific trusts declared by the donor. Alternatively, a charity may feel that only the total figures accurately reflect the relative costs of the charity and that individual fund columns should not be viewed in isolation.

To illustrate the above point, consider a corporate fundraiser who spends a significant amount of time and resources arranging a big fundraising campaign by a large corporation for a specified charitable project. If the company specifies that only direct costs may be incurred and no management and administration costs are allowed, then the fundraising, management and administration costs incurred in raising and spending this income would have to be charged against unrestricted funds. Looking at the restricted fund column in isolation, the user might be led to believe that restricted funds are far more efficient as they do not incur any fundraising or administration charges – which is not strictly the case.

Charities might consider stating in advance that where restricted funds are being given, a certain percentage of costs (being both direct and apportioned costs) will include management and administration, fundraising and support costs. This would ensure that costs are apportioned consistently across all the charity's activities.

In the extreme case where a large proportion of a charity's activities are supported by restricted funds which do not permit the allocation of management and administration, fundraising and support costs, a charity might find itself unable to fund its overhead costs out of unrestricted funds.

11.10 Income application

This is an area that is causing problems for many charities and many charity auditors. Where restricted income has been temporarily invested prior to application for a suitable charitable purpose, any income gains derived from the investment will be added to, and form part of, the restricted income fund in question. For example, grants received in advance may be placed on deposit at a bank until required. The interest earned on that money will also form part of the specific restricted fund.

Income derived from the investment capital funds may be applied for the general purposes of the charity (unrestricted income), unless a specific purpose has been declared by the donor for the application of the income from the capital fund in question. Such income will be applicable for that purpose and will be restricted income. Gains from the realisation of investments in a capital fund form part of the fund itself. This again increases the requirement for keeping adequate records of each individual fund held by the charity.

11.11 Fund assets and liabilities

The assets and liabilities representing the various funds of the charity should be analysed between these funds.

A note such as the ABC Charity note shown at Example 11.2 should be given. This note should indicate whether the types of assets held within specific funds are appropriate to meet the requirements of that fund.

For example, if the purpose of a fund is to grant income in respect of a salary and this is represented by cash, there is no problem. If, however, the salary which was due in the next year was represented by a fixed asset such as a building or a long-term investment, then there is a clear problem realising that asset to be able to pay the salary in the short term.

The notes should make clear whether or not the assets held in the fund are short-term assets.

Example 11.2 The ABC Charity

18. Analysis of group net assets between funds

	Restricted funds £'000	Designated funds £'000	General funds £'000	Total £'000
Fund balances at 31 March 2001 are represented by:				
Tangible fixed assets	1,270	4,230	–	**5,500**
Investments	–	–	2,000	**2,000**
Current assets	1,820	350	4,385	**6,555**
Current liabilities	–	–	(1,500)	**(1,500)**
Long term liabilities	–	–	(100)	**(100)**
Total net assets	3,090	4,580	4,785	**12,455**

19. Subsidiary company

The charity owns the whole of the issued ordinary share capital of ABC Enterprises Ltd, a company registered in England. The subsidary is used for non-primary purpose trading activities, namely the mail order retail operation and the sale of bought in goods through the charity's shops. In addition corporate sponsorships and non-tax exempt events are often carried out by the subsidiary. All activities have been consolidated on a line by line basis in the SOFA. The total net profit is gifted to the charity. Corporate income is treated as donations. A summary of the results of the subsidiary is shown below:

ABC Enterprises Ltd	**Mail Order 2001 £'000**	**Shops 2001 £'000**	**Corporate 2001 £'000**	**Total 2001 £'000**	**Total 2001 £'000**
Turnover	400	460	350	**1,210**	1,300
Cost of sale	390	310	150	**850**	900
Gross profit	10	150	200	**360**	400
Administrative expenses	30	40	40	**110**	130
Net profit/(loss)	(20)	110	160	**250**	270

The aggregate of the assets, liabilities and funds was:

Assets	**590**	470
Liabilities	**(589)**	(469)
Funds (representing 1000 ordinary shares of £1 each)	**1**	1

11.12 Can restrictions be removed?

It is possible either to remove a restriction entirely, or to at least make the effects less stringent. This is particularly opportune where the objective for which the funds were originally raised is no longer relevant, the project has been completed, or the project is impossible to complete. In the first instance, it would be necessary to attempt to obtain permission from the donor to use the funds left over for some alternative purpose. However, in instances such as an appeal, the problem arises that there are often so many donors that it is impossible to go back to each individual donor and request their permission to use the funds in a different way.

In these situations, the Charity Commission can be appealed to in order that they may introduce a cy prés scheme. The cy prés scheme is a method whereby the Charity Commission can move the funds into the next best means of achieving the same objective.

It is important that charities in their fundraising documentation do not restrict the funds totally, for example, many charities now include in their fundraising documentation the statement that the funds will go towards a specific project, and any surplus may be used in furtherance of other projects of the charity. In law, if the restricted funds have been used for a particular purpose, or cannot be used for a particular purpose, and there are surplus funds, these funds should be returned to the original donor. However, if there are surpluses after completing the project for which the fund was raised, then the charity can retain those funds for future use on a project of exactly the same nature.

11.13 Is project grant income restricted?

This depends on the type of grant, and general grants towards the overall objectives of the charity, often known as 'core funding', will not be restricted, but it is most certain that grants for a specific project will be. The best test is to check what can be done with any surpluses at the end of the project. Do they need to be retained for a further specific purpose similar to the original, returned to the grant giver, or can they be used for an alternative purpose? This will indicate whether the grant is for core funding or is a restricted income source.

In conclusion, charities need to ensure that they have an adequate reporting system with which to report funds. Careful consideration needs to be given to new donations and fundraising campaigns regarding whether they are creating a legal restriction in any way. If this is the case, adequate records to identify income and the associated expenditure need to be set in place. It is far easier to account as you go or to be aware of the need to account than in the future having to look retrospectively on what was received.

Chapter 12 Summary financial information and statements

Many charities publish separate information from the annual report and accounts which often forms part of fundraising or public awareness campaigns. This information may be produced as part of a separate document by the charity, often known as an annual review. Such information may be communicated in graphical or tabular form or as an extract of the accounts. SORP 2000 clarifies the disclosure requirements that should accompany such information but it does not dictate the nature or content of the summary financial information. However SORP 2000, para 294 does state that such summary financial information should:

(a) contain information on the Statement of Financial Activities;
(b) contain information on the balance sheet;
(c) be consistent with the full accounts; and
(d) not be misleading by either omitting information or combining information.

Although it is acknowledged that summary financial information may be contained in annual reviews to convey key financial messages, the full annual report and accounts must nevertheless still be produced by the charity.

Where summarised financial statements are produced, a statement must be signed on behalf of the trustees to include (para 295):

- the fact that the summarised financial statements are not the full statutory accounts but merely a summary of financial information relating to both the Statement of Financial Activities and the balance sheet;
- the nature of external examination applied to the full statutory accounts;
- confirmation that the external examination resulted in an unqualified report;
- if the report was qualified, further details need to be provided as to the nature of the qualification;
- for branch accounts, clarification is required that the summary is only for the branch;
- details of where the full annual report and accounts can be obtained;
- the date on which the full annual accounts were approved; and
- confirmation that the full report and accounts have been sent to the Charity Commission (and to Companies House for incorporated charities).

Where the full accounts have been externally examined, the external examiner should attach a statement providing an opinion confirming whether or not the summary financial information is consistent with the full statutory accounts.

SORP 2000 goes further than the original SORP by requiring a statement signed on behalf of the trustees to be included where any form of summary financial statement is produced which does not include information on either the Statement of Financial Activities or the balance sheet. This statement should include:

- purpose of the information;
- whether or not the statement is from the full accounts;
- whether or not these accounts have been audited, independently examined or subject to a reporting accountants' report; and
- details of how the full statutory accounts, trustees' report and external examiners' report can be obtained.

Table 12.1 Charity accounts compliance checklist

Summary financial information and statement

Note: This section only applies where summarised accounts are prepared.

Yes / N/A / Ref

1 General

1.1 Has the full annual report and accounts also been produced [para 294]? .... ________

1.2 Are the summarised accounts consistent with the full accounts [para 294]?............ ________

1.3 Do they contain information relating both to the SOFA and the balance sheet [para 294]? .... ________

1.4 Are they accompanied by a statement, signed on behalf of the Trustees, which discloses:

- (a) That they are a summary of the information extracted [para 295a]? .... ________
- (b) Whether or not the full accounts have been audited or independently examined [para 295b]? .... ________
- (c) The date on which the annual report and accounts were approved and whether they have been submitted to the Charity Commissioners [para 295g and 295h]? .... ________
- (d) Whether the auditors' or independent examiner's opinion on the full accounts was qualified or not [para 295c]? .... ________
- (e) Where branch accounts are produced, that the summary states it is only for branch accounts [para 295e]? .... ________
- (f) Details of how the full annual accounts, external examiners' report and Trustees' report can be obtained [para 295f]? .... ________

1.5 If the opinion was qualified, does the report given in the summarised accounts provide sufficient information to enable a user to appreciate the significance of the auditors' or independent examiner's reservations [para 295d]? .... ________

1.6 In the case of charitable companies is there a statement indicating whether or not the statutory accounts for the relevant year(s) have been delivered to the Registrar of Companies [para 342]? .... ________

1.7 Is there an external examiner's statement providing an opinion whether or not the summary information is consistent with the full accounts [para 296]? .... ________

1.8 Does other summary information not including a SOFA or balance sheet have an accompanying trustees' statement showing:

- purpose of the information [para 297a]? .... ________
- whether or not it is from full accounts [para 297b]? .... ________
- whether or not full accounts have been externally examined [para 297c]?........ ________
- details of how full accounts, external examiners' report and trustees' report can be obtained [para 297d]? .... ________

Chapter 13 Investments

13.1 Market value versus cost

Investments, since the introduction of SORP 1995, have had to be stated at market value on the balance sheet. Initial adverse reaction to this, one of the most controversial of SORP 1995 recommendations, was caused not only by genuine concerns about the cost of revaluation but also by the realisation of the profound effect that it had on some charities' accounts. It has turned the spotlight on to charities' policies on reserves and investments and also on to the trustees' responsibilities in respect of both. Charities should now have been revaluing their investments at market value for at least the last four years.

The Charities SORP recommends that all fixed asset investments be valued at market value at the balance sheet date or at the trustees' best estimate of value at that date. The note to the accounts should give full details of the movements in the valuation of fixed assets. Fixed asset investments should also include cash held for investment purposes unless the intention is to realise the asset without reinvestment of the proceeds. The proceeds should then be shown within current assets.

Details of historical cost should now be shown by way of note. If the charity has branches and these branches have investments they should also be shown at market value.

There has been concern expressed that the use of market value investments can be misleading. This stems from the often temporary nature of stock market movements; another Black Monday on the Stock Exchange could have a devastating but potentially misleading effect on a charity's balance sheet as share prices subsequently recovered. This could be a serious problem, but if the fluctuations are of a very short-term nature, disclosure of this fact can be made in the accounts. If they do represent a permanent diminution in value or if the fall is of unknown duration then it is prudent to reflect the situation in the accounts and plan accordingly.

Excerpt from Toc H Women's Association Trust Property Accounts for the year ended 31 March 1998:

Example 13.1 Excerpt from Toc H Women's Association Trust Property Accounts for the year ended 31 March 1998

	£	£
8. **FIXED ASSET INVESTMENTS**	49,732	40,849
Investments listed on a recognised stock exchange	4,000	4,000

	Listed Securities £
Valuation at 1 April 1997	40,849
Add: – Net gains on revaluation at 31 March 1998	8,883
Valuation at 31 March 1998	49,732

The investment is in UK Investment Funds.

The stock market value of the investments has fallen following the year end, however, the loss is not considered to be a permanent diminution in value.

As there is a specific requirement in the Charities Act 1993 accounting regulations, the inclusion of investments at market value is mandatory for unincorporated charities. However, care will need to be exercised in the case of incorporated charities as the company accounting requirements have not been amended and so, strictly speaking, incorporated charities have a choice of using cost or market valuation. For the sake of consistency and comparability there is a very strong argument that all charities, whether incorporated or unincorporated, should show long-term investments at market value.

Where there is no readily identifiable market price the trustees should adopt a reasonable approach (para 233). In cases where the cost of obtaining a valuation outweighs the benefit to users of the accounts the asset may be included at cost. Investment assets other than shares or securities can be valued every five years.

13.2 Realised/unrealised gains and losses

The introduction of the revaluation of investments to market value each year therefore has led to the creation of unrealised gains or losses. This is the difference between the market value at the closing balance sheet date and the market value at the opening balance sheet date in cases where there have been no movements in the investment during the year, i.e. no purchase or sales. Where shares have been acquired during the year then the unrealised gain or loss is the difference between the market value at the closing balance sheet date and the cost at acquisition. These gains or losses are dealt with separately in each of the particular funds the charity holds investments in. All changes in the year, whether realised or unrealised, should be reported in the SOFA.

Realised gains and losses made on the disposal of assets were previously shown separately to unrealised gains and losses on the face of the SOFA. SORP 2000 now permits the inclusion as a single line – 'realised and unrealised gains and losses'. However, the note to the accounts should state the basis of the inclusion.

A note of caution: whilst market value may provide a truer and fairer view of the charity's worth than original cost, it does not necessarily reflect the value which will be available in future because market values change. It is now the accepted practice for many charities to show as an investment reserve, i.e., designated fund, the accumulated difference between the historical cost and the market value at the balance sheet date, i.e., the cumulative unrealised gain or loss.

13.3 Investment note

Where investments have been valued other than by reference to readily available market prices, the note should disclose who has made the valuation, giving their name, qualification and position and how the valuation has been carried out.

The note should show all changes in values of investment assets and reconcile the opening and closing book value of the investments.

The note should show all changes in values of investments broken down by type and should include:

- investment properties;
- investments held on a recognised stock exchange;
- investments in subsidiary or associated undertakings;
- other unlisted securities;
- cash; and
- any other investments.

These should also be further broken down as investment assets in the UK and investment assets outside the UK.

Further details should show how the portfolio is structured and include details of any material investments (e.g., over five per cent of portfolio) and any other material restrictions applying on the realisation of those assets.

The fund analysis note should break down the investments held across the different types of funds.

13.4 Accounting policy

The accounting policy for investments should note that investments are stated at market value. However, if investments are not listed on a recognised stock exchange, investment properties or investments in subsidiary undertakings, the note may need to be modified. The basis of inclusion in the SOFA of unrealised gains and losses on investments should be stated (para 287).

13.5 Investment policy

Charities should have an investment policy. This should set out the purposes for holding their investments, for example for income generation or short-term capital growth. The investment policy is now required to be included in the trustees' report and a commentary on performance against policy should be given.

13.6 Short-term investments

Where investments are held as current assets the same disclosure is required as for fixed-asset investments (para 246).

13.7 Costs of generating funds

Following the SORP review cost allocations were considered. Investment management costs have in the past been included within management and administration costs. They are now to be shown within the category – 'costs of generating funds'.

Example 13.2 The Edinburgh Educational Trust

10. Investments

	2001 £'000	2000 £'000
Market value at 1 April 2000	**6,811,833**	4,355,998
Add: Acquisitions at cost	**909,534**	442,837
Less: Disposals at opening book value	**(948,888)**	(428,480)
Net gains on revaluation at 31 March 2001	**239,172**	2,441,478
	7,011,651	6,811,833
Cash at bank awaiting investment	**46,859**	37,348
Market value at 31 March 2001	**7,058,510**	6,849,181
Cost as at 31 March 2001	**3,287,089**	2,610,427

Investments in individual entities held at 31 March 2001 which are over 5% of portfolio by value are:

BP Amoco – Market value £400,000

All investments held are listed UK Securities.

11. Debtors

	2001	2000
Revenue Grants – Scottish Executive	**87,400**	89,162
Local authority fees	**5,200**	46,598
Other debtors	**12,264**	15,781
Prepayments and accrued income	**20,482**	8,785
	125,346	160,326

12. Creditors: Amounts falling due within one year

	2001	2000
Trade creditors	**239,933**	263,534
Other creditors	**233,813**	–
Deferred income (note 13)	**353,564**	389,179
Accruals	**262,093**	49,928
	1,089,403	702,641

13. Deferred income

	2001	2000
Balance at 1 April 2000	**389,179**	352,244
Local authority fees received	**442,454**	605,078
Released to statement of financial activities	**(478,069)**	(568,143)
Balance at 31 March 2001	**353,564**	389,179

Example 13.2 The Edinburgh Educational Trust *(cont.)*

Notes forming part of the financial statements for the year ended 30 September 2001

1 Accounting policies

(a) Basis of accounting

The accounts have been prepared under the historical cost convention as modified by the revaluation of investment assets and are in accordance with applicable accounting standards, the Charities Accounts (Scotland) Regulations 1992 and Accounting and Reporting by Charities: Statement of Recommended Practice (SORP) issued in October 2000.

(b) Donations, legacies and similar incoming resources

Donations, legacies and similar incoming resources are included in the year in which they are receivable, which is when the charity becomes entitled to the resource.

(c) Grants receivable and local authority fees

Grants receivable and local authority fees are credited to the Statement of Financial Activities (SOFA) in the year for which they are received. Deferred income represents amounts received for future periods and is released to incoming resources in the period for which it has been received.

(d) Investment income and rental income

Income from investments and from rental income is included in the SOFA in the year in which it is receivable.

(e) Expenditure

All expenditure is included on an accruals basis and is recognised when there is a legal or constructive obligation to pay for expenditure. All costs have been directly attributed to one of the functional categories of resources expended in the SOFA. The Trust is not registered for VAT and accordingly expenditure is shown gross of irrecoverable VAT.

(f) Tangible fixed assets

Until 31 December 1991 neither the original cost nor improvements to freehold land and buildings were capitalised because the buildings are historic, inalienable and form part of a permanent endowment which means that these cannot be sold but must be held in perpetuity.

The original cost of the assets and improvements thereto is not available. The users of the accounts are principally the trustees, parents of children attending the school and various donors. The trustees consider the cost of carrying out a professional valuation to include these assets at a value in the accounts to be considerable compared to the limited additional benefit derived by the users of the accounts.

Since 1 January 1992, all improvements to land and buildings costing more than £1,000 are capitalised and depreciated. Other tangible fixed assets costing more than £1,500 are capitalised and depreciated over 4 years. At 31 March 2001, all such assets have been fully depreciated and eliminated from these accounts.

(g) Depreciation

Depreciation is charged to write off the cost less estimated residual value of property improvements over 20 years.

(h) Investments

Investments are included at market value at the year end.

Gains and losses on disposal and revaluation of investments are charged or credited to the SOFA.

Example 13.3 The ABC Charity

10. Tangible fixed assets

	Freehold land and buildings £'000	Project and office equipment £'000	Computer equipment £'000	Motor vehicles £'000	Total £'000
Cost					
At 1 April 2000	4,350	400	250	200	**5,200**
Additions	1,700	180	100	10	**1,990**
Disposals	(300)	–	–	–	**(300)**
At 31 March 2001	5,750	580	350	210	**6,890**
Depreciation					
At 1 April 2000	800	200	150	50	**1,200**
Charge for year	90	150	88	52	**380**
Disposals	(190)	–	–	–	**(190)**
At 31 March 2001	700	350	238	102	**1,390**
Net book value					
At 31 March 2001	5,050	230	112	108	**5,500**
At 31 March 2000	3,550	200	100	150	**4,000**

Project and office equipment includes assets with a net book value of £140,000 (2000: £180,000) held under finance leases. Freehold land and buildings includes freehold land of £1.2 million that is not depreciated.

Capital expenditure contracted for, but not provided in the financial statements, was £250,000 (2000: £190,000).

11. Fixed asset investments

	2001 £'000	2000 £'000
Group:		
Market value as at 1 April 2000	**3,000**	2,800
Additions	**1,200**	865
Disposal proceeds	**(2,300)**	(915)
Net investment gains	**100**	250
Market value at 31 March 2001	**2,000**	3,000
Historical cost at 31 March 2001	**1,860**	2,890
UK listed investments are represented by:		
Fixed interest securities	**900**	1,600
Equity shares	**620**	580
Investment trusts and unit trusts	**480**	820
Total	**2,000**	3,000

Investments held by the charity also include an additional £1,000 (2000: £1,000) investment in the subsidiary company at cost (see note 19).

Chapter 14 Related party transactions

14.1 Introduction

SORP 1995 did not have much to say on this topic specifically although there were references to connected charities and to dealings with trustees. Chapter 18 of the first edition of this book looked at the problem area of connected charities. This chapter incorporates a revised version of that as well as expanding further into related parties as a result of FRS 8 *Related Party Disclosure.*

14.2 SORP 2000 definitions

Connected charities are those which have common, parallel or related objects and activities and either:

(a) common control; or
(b) unity of administration.

On the other hand Appendix 1, SORP 2000 *Accounting and Reporting by Charities*, goes on to define related parties in considerably more detail. It sees related parties including all of the following:

- an institution connected with the charity;
- individuals or institutions related to the charity; and
- individuals or institutions connected with a charity trustee or to a person related to the charity.

It goes on to define each of these three categories and gives examples.

An institution is connected with a charity if it is controlled by or if a participating interest in it is beneficially owned by the charity. The following are deemed to be related to the charity:

1. any charity trustee and custodian trustee of the charity;
2. any person or body with the power to appoint or remove a significant proportion of the charity trustees of the charity;
3. any institution connected with the charity and any director of that institution;
4. any other charity with which it is commonly controlled;
5. any pension fund for the benefit of employees of the charity;
6. any officer, agent or employee of the charity having authority or responsibility for directing or controlling the major activities or resources; and
7. any person connected to a person who is related to the charity.

Finally in defining related parties SORP 2000 considers that the following should be treated as connected with a charity trustee or a person related to the charity:

- members of the same family or household of the charity trustee or related person who may be expected to influence, or be influenced by, that person in their dealing with the charity;
- the trustees of any trust not being a charity, the beneficiaries or potential beneficiaries of which include a charity trustee or related person or a person referred to in 1. above;
- any business partner of a charity trustee or related person or any person referred to in 1. or 2. above;

- any body corporate, not being a company which is controlled entirely by one or more charitable institution linked to the charity;
- any person or body who makes available to the charity the services or body as a charity trustee is connected with a charity trustee.

The definition of common control is that it exists if:

- the same person (including family and business relationships) or person have the right to appoint a majority of the trustees of both or all charities; or
- the same person or persons hold a majority of the voting rights in the administration of both or all of the charities (the notion of an umbrella organisation is included here).

14.3 FRS 8 *Related party disclosures*

This financial reporting standard determines who and what are related parties in general terms and the disclosures necessary to draw attention to the possibility that the reported financial position and results may have been affected by the existence of related parties and by material transactions with them. Paragraphs 157–169 of SORP 2000 explain the application of FRS 8 with specific respect to charities.

14.4 Disclosures

To gain more transparency of the accounts and a greater appreciation of the nature of the charity's activities, the trustees' report should include a statement regarding the relationship between the charity and related parties and with any other charities and organisations with which it cooperates in the pursuit of its charitable objectives (otherwise known as connected charities). Where the relationship of one charity with another amounts to direct control then the accounts for the two entities should be accounted for together under the heading of branch accounting. Separate legal entities which may be known as branches but do not fall within the definition of a branch should prepare their own annual report and accounts and where they are connected charities the relationship should be explained in the trustees report.

Where a charity holds resources for a third party and these have not been included in the SOFA or balance sheet, then the notes to the accounts should analyse the movement of those resources during the year relating to each party or type of party where material. If the resources had been held for related parties, third party or otherwise, the required disclosures of paras 163–164 of SORP 2000 should be set out.

It is necessary to show as a note to the accounts any related party transactions. A related party transaction is one where the charity has a relationship with another party or parties which might inhibit it from pursuing its own separate interests. It is paramount that any decision by a charity to enter into a transaction ought to be influenced only by the consideration of the charity's own interests. This requirement is reinforced by legal rules which, in certain circumstances, can invalidate transactions where the charity trustees have a conflict of interest. Transparency is particularly important where the relationship between the charity and the other party or parties to a transaction suggests that the transaction could possibly have been influenced by interest other than the charity's. Only material transactions need to be disclosed in the notes to the accounts, and as SORP 2000 states at para 161, related party transactions potentially include:

'(a) purchases, sales, leases and donations (including donations which are made in furtherance of the charity's objects) of goods, property, money and other assets such as intellectual property rights to or from the related party;

(b) the supply of services by the related party to the charity, and the supply of services by the charity to the related party. Supplying services includes providing the use of goods, property and other assets and finance arrangements such as making loans and giving guarantees and indemnities;

(c) any other payments and other benefits which are made to trustees under express provisions of the governing document of a charity or in fulfilment of its charitable objectives.'

As the SORP continues the required disclosure is:

'(a) the name(s) of the transacting related party or parties;
(b) a description of the relationship between the parties (including the interests of the related party or parties in the transaction);
(c) a description of the transaction;
(d) the amounts involved;
(e) outstanding balances with related parties at the balance sheet date and any provision for doubtful debts from such persons;
(f) any amounts written off from such balances during the accounting year; and
(g) any other elements of the transactions which are necessary for the understanding of the financial statements.'

Where related party transactions are such that they are unlikely to affect the separate independent interests of the charity, or they are not material, then they need not be disclosed unless there is evidence to the contrary. With the exception of trustee remuneration, the disclosures can be given in total for similar transactions and types of related party unless the disclosure of an individual transaction or connected transactions is necessary for an understanding of the impact of the transactions on the accounts of the charity or where it is a legal requirement. Paragraph 165 of SORP 2000 gives some examples of related party transactions that are unlikely to need reporting.

There is only one example of the required disclosure note shown in SORP 2000 *Example Reports and Accounts* (CC66) which is for Arts Theatre Trust Limited. This is note 20, which states:

Example 14.1 Arts Theatre Trust Limited

'The charity has a very close relationship with N Arts which is a charity, BF Borough Council and B Town Council, all of whom nominate the majority of the trustees and provide funding to enable the charity to carry out its charitable objectives. The following is a summary of transactions with those entities:

	2001 £'000	2000 £'000
Revenue funding		
BF Borough Council	405	501
B Town Council	104	100
N Arts Trust	154	150
	663	751

All the above funding was received under contracts with the charity to provide services, e.g., training in drama production, and has been included in the financial statements under the heading *Incoming Resources: from operation of theatre and arts centre.*

The charity also received a donation in kind, from BF Borough Council for the rent of premises, the value of which could not be quantified and therefore has not been included in these financial statements. There were no outstanding balances with the related parties at 31 March 2001 (2000 – £nil).'

Chapter 15 Consolidation of subsidiary undertakings and accounting for associates, joint ventures and joint arrangements

Charities traditionally have accounted for their trading subsidiaries in a variety of ways. In some cases they have consolidated the accounts of the subsidiary on a line by line basis and in other cases on a one-line basis, i.e., net. Many charities have prepared group accounts and even those who have consolidated only a single line in the SOFA have produced a fully consolidated balance sheet.

The purpose of consolidation is to present a true and fair view of the financial position of the group. FRS 2 covers the principles and methods of consolidation. The 1989 Companies Act introduced several significant changes, which considerably reduced the number of reasons for excluding a subsidiary from consolidated accounts. The Companies Act takes precedence over the Charities Act.

As a result, many charities that were incorporated had to reconsider their policy on consolidation where they had previously excluded subsidiaries. In most cases charities will need to prepare group accounts. SORP 2000 lists a number of exceptions where group accounts do not need to be prepared, but in most cases consolidated accounts will be necessary.

Section 229 (2) of the Companies Act allows the exclusion of subsidiaries on consolidation provided that the inclusion of all subsidiaries is not material to giving a true and fair view. Whilst this may be satisfactory for commercial organisations, it is often not the case for charities. This is because their public image, fundraising aspects and the fact that the public's money is involved would make it detrimental to exclude from consolidation these trading subsidiaries even where they are not material. An undertaking is a parent undertaking to a subsidiary undertaking if:

- it holds the majority of the voting rights in the subsidiary undertaking;
- it is a member of the subsidiary undertaking and has the right to appoint or remove a majority of its board of directors;
- it has the right to exercise a dominant influence over the subsidiary undertaking by virtue of:
  - provisions contained in the subsidiary undertaking's memorandum or articles; or
  - a control contract;
- it is a member of the subsidiary undertaking and controls, alone, in accordance with an agreement with other shareholders or members, a majority of the voting rights in the undertaking; or
- it has a participating interest in the undertaking and:
  - it actually exercises a dominant influence over it; or
  - the charity and the subsidiary undertaking are managed on a unified basis.

FRS 2 applies to all parent undertakings and requires compliance so that those preparing accounts in this way will produce consolidated financial statements, which are intended to give a true and fair view of the financial position and profit or loss (or income and expenditure).

The FRS defines an undertaking as a 'body corporate or partnership, or an incorporated association, carrying on a trade or business with or without a view to profit'. Therefore, although only charities that are incorporated will be caught by the Companies Act, FRS 2 will effectively pick up all entities whether incorporated or not if they are preparing true and fair view accounts. It is made clear in FRS 2 that it would be very rare for an organisation with subsidiaries not to consolidate.

Under the Charities Act 1993 the Charity Commission require accounts for group and charity to be filed which include both group and charity Statements of Financial Activities. However, the Charity Commission will accept accounts which separately identify the assets and liabilities of the charity and its subsidiaries and where the turnover and results are clearly stated. The Commission has the right to ask for individual charity accounts, as do members of the public. Accounts should be prepared and approved by the trustees for each entity.

SORP 2000 also gives guidance on the treatment of the non-company charity as a subsidiary (paras 306–308).

15.1 Accounting for subsidiary undertakings

SORP 2000 covers this in considerable detail (paras 309–319). It is a requirement that the trustees' annual report provides information by way of separate comment on the trading performance of any of the charity's subsidiary undertakings, whether those are set up for charitable or non-charitable purposes (para 312).

The notes to the accounts should show the name of each subsidiary undertaking and the full particulars of the charity's shareholding or, if none, the other controlling interest. In those cases where consolidated accounts have not been prepared, the trustees must explain the reasoning behind the non-consolidation and show this in the notes to the accounts (para 316). The details of each subsidiary should be given as follows:

- its name;
- particulars of the charity's shareholding or other controlling interest in it;
- how its activities relate to those of the charity;
- the aggregate amount of its assets, liabilities, capital and reserves as at the end of the year; and
- a summary of its turnover and expenditure, and its profit or loss for the year.

SORP 2000 clearly highlights that it is important whatever the presentation adopted that there is sufficient information to distinguish the assets and liabilities and transactions of the charity from those of its subsidiary(ies), and in addition that the results of the subsidiary(ies) are clearly stated (para 304).

15.2 Method of consolidation

In the past charities have tended to consolidate their subsidiaries on a one-line basis. The result of the trading subsidiary was consolidated into the consolidated Statement of Financial Activities as 'Income from trading subsidiary'.

Under SORP 2000 income and expenditure must now be consolidated on a line by line basis. All income and expenditure should be shown gross after the elimination of any intra-group transactions. Income and expenditure from the trading subsidiary should be combined with comparable activities in the charity. For example, fundraising costs within the subsidiary should be shown within costs of generating funds. If necessary, the appropriate headings within the SOFA should be amended to reflect the activities of the group. In cases where this cannot be shown, segmental analysis should be provided in the accounts. The segmental analysis should be sufficiently detailed to distinguish the key results of the charity from those of its subsidiary undertakings, e.g., management and administration costs.

15.2.1 Disclosure

(a) the trustees' report should include comment on the results of a charity's subsidiary undertaking;
(b) the method of consolidation and extent to which subsidiaries and associated companies have been included or excluded should be stated. In cases where subsidiaries are excluded reasons must be given; and
(c) notes to the consolidated accounts should include the position of both group and parent undertaking.

Where there are a number of subsidiaries, only those subsidiaries whose results materially affect the position of the group need to be disclosed. Full details should, however, be retained and made available to any member of the public on request.

The accounting policy should state that 'a separate statement of financial activities (SOFA) is not presented because the charity has taken advantage of the provisions of paragraph 304 of the SORP'.

Funds or reserves retained by the subsidiary undertaking not for charitable purposes should be separately disclosed in the accounts.

15.3 Accounting for associates, joint ventures and joint arrangements

FRS 9 covers the accounting for associates, joint ventures and joint arrangements. FRS 9 provides detailed guidance on how to determine the relationship.

SORP 2000 makes clear that where a charity holds 20 per cent or more of the voting rights in any form of undertaking, it will be presumed to have a significant influence over the operating and financial policy of the undertaking unless evidence to the contrary is shown. In all these cases the undertaking will then be considered to be an associated undertaking (para 322).

In a joint venture situation a separate entity is controlled by a number of undertakings, all of which have a say in the operation of the venture. More than 20 per cent of the shareholding can be held without it being an associated venture as long as the absence of overall control can be demonstrated.

The trustees should provide, in a note to the charity's accounts, the following information in relation to each such undertaking in which it has a participating interest. This information is to be included even in situations where the charity has no subsidiary undertakings or has not prepared consolidated accounts in accordance with paras 309 and 311 of the SORP. The disclosure should include the following:

- its name;
- particulars of the charity's shareholdings or other interest in it;
- the nature of the activities of the associate or joint venture; and

Example 15.1 Aid Overseas

3. Activities in furtherance of the charity's objectives

	2001 £'000	2000 £'000
Contracts for operational programmes		
UK Government – Department for International Development	**1,415**	1,296
Other UK agencies – National Lottery Charities' Board	**25**	25
European Union	**1,933**	1,901
United Nations agencies	**269**	276
Non-UK governments	**1,020**	991
Other international agencies	**132**	128
Less deferred income	**(48)**	(50)
	4,746	**4,567**

All the income arising under the above contracts is considered to be restricted to particular projects, an outline of which are given in note 7.

4. Shop income and expenditure

	Aid Overseas Trading Ltd £'000	Charitable Trading £'000	2001 Total Shop Activities £'000	2000 Total Shop Activities £'000
Turnover from donated goods	–	6,985	**6,985**	5,366
Turnover from purchased goods	1,588	–	**1,588**	1,230
Total shop income	**1,588**	**6,985**	**8,573**	**6,596**
Operating expenses	(1,012)	(4,626)	**(5,638)**	(5,187)
Management expenses	(452)	(404)	**(856)**	(842)
Shop expenditure	**(1,464)**	**(5,030)**	**(6,494)**	**(6,029)**
Net income from trading	**124**	**1,955**	**2,079**	**567**

This represents income from the sale of donated and bought-in goods through the charity's shops.

The profit of Aid Overseas Trading Limited is gifted to the charity so that there is no liability to Corporation Tax for that entity. Further details are set out in note 15 to the accounts.

5. Investment income and interest

	Unrestricted £'000	Restricted £'000	2001 Total £'000	2000 Total £'000
Deposit interest	182	39	**221**	196
Investment income from quoted investments	8	–	**8**	6
	190	**39**	**229**	**202**

- the charity's interest in the results, showing separately its share in:
  - gross incoming resources by type;
  - costs of generating funds;
  - expenditure on charitable activities;
  - expenditure on management and administration;
  - the net results;
  - ains or losses in investments and the share in unrealised gains on other fixed assets;
  - fixed assets;
  - current assets;
  - liabilities under one year;
  - liabilities over one year;
  - the different funds of the charity;
  - contingent liabilities and other commitments; and
  - particulars of any audit or other qualifications to the accounts.

For joint arrangements the notes should provide appropriate details of the charity's commitments in the arrangement. Joint arrangements are often entered into by charities acting in partnership but without establishing a separate legal entity.

Associates should be included in the accounts under the net equity method. The SOFA should include a line with the net interest in the result after the 'net incoming/(resources expended)' line. The balance sheet should distinguish the net interest in the associate.

Joint ventures should be accounted for on a gross equity method. The share of the income from the venture should be separately identified on the face of the SOFA. Gross incoming resources can be shown on a line by line basis in the SOFA together with the corresponding expenditure. The SOFA must show separately the net results for the year from the joint venture after the 'net incoming/(resources expended)' line. An alternative method is to treat the activities as a joint venture arrangement. Any obligations that the charity is required to meet in respect of the joint venture should be either accrued for or shown as a contingent liability.

Similarly, any gains and losses within the associate or joint venture must be accounted for separately.

In the examples booklet (CC66) issued by the Charity Commission in respect of preparation of accounts under Charity SORP 2000, there are no examples of associates, joint ventures and joint arrangements.

Chapter 16 Accounting for grants receivable

Within the current contract culture, charities receive various types of incoming resources. These may come from Government, Local Authority, European Union or the National Lottery. To the extent the grants, contracts or service agreements provide core funding or are of a general nature, they will be included in the heading within the SOFA of 'donations, legacies and similar incoming resources.' However, should the funding be related to a specific service or activity, e.g., provision of a bed space in a hostel, to be carried out by the charity, then the receipt should be included in the heading 'activities in furtherance of the charity's objects' (para 103).

Paragraph 116 states that if the incoming resources have certain conditional terms attached to them, then a restricted fund will arise. For this to be the case the condition must be more than merely the funder's expectation of a service provision. When the full service has been provided by the charity and there is a surplus which can be clawed back by the funder, then these incoming resources should be included as a restricted fund.

SORP 2000 provides the basic principles for recognition of incoming resources within the SOFA to include the resource when it is both prudent and practicable to do so (para 75). SORP 2000 does not allow incoming resources to be recognised in the SOFA until:

(a) all conditions for the receipt have been met by the charity; and
(b) there is reasonable assurance of receipt.

Paragraph 79 considers the situation where a charity receives incoming resources by way of grant or donation. The purpose of this donation may be for general or specific purposes. The general principle is that charities are entitled to account for the incoming resources when they are receivable. This would even be the case where a charity receives a grant or donation but only spends this money after the year end. SORP 2000 clearly states that in this situation, the incoming resources should be recognised in full in the SOFA and should not be deferred simply because the related expenditure has not been incurred.

SORP 2000 does outline the situation where incoming resources should be deferred and this is where the funder or donor has imposed restrictions on when the expenditure should be made. These restrictions are considered to be preconditions for use and would not meet the previous criteria as outlined in para 75 because conditions for receipt have not been met. This deferral of income would be in the case where a grant has been received which is specifically to be spent in a future accounting period. This is different from the previous case where the incoming resource was recognised in the SOFA because here the charity had within its own jurisdiction the option when to spend the incoming resource and merely made their own decision to spend the related expenditure in the next period.

The second scenario envisaged by SORP 2000 where incoming resources should be deferred is in the case of those charities that charge for goods and services to perform their charitable activities. If the charity does not have sufficient entitlement because they have not delivered the goods or services then deferral of income would be appropriate (para 78).

Many charities receive grants to enable them to buy fixed assets. Once again para 80 states that all incoming resources should only be recognised in the SOFA where the charity is entitled to this income. This also includes the situation where the incoming resource is in relation to a fixed asset. Where the funding has been provided specifically to provide a fixed asset, then the incoming resource should be shown in the SOFA as a restricted fund. The fact that the incoming resource is for a restricted purpose (i.e., a fixed asset) does not amount to a precondition and therefore SORP 2000 reinforces the principle that the grant for a fixed asset should be accounted for in full in the SOFA, albeit within a restricted fund. Where the grant is of a general nature, the trustees may choose to set up a designated fund to reflect the net book value of the fixed asset and charge the depreciation of the fixed asset to that fund over its useful economic life. By accounting for the transaction in this manner, both accounting standards (including SSAP 4) and SORP 2000 will have their requirements met.

All material incoming resources should have an accounting policy within the accounts. Paragraph 283c provides that 'the basis of recognition of all grants receivable, including those for fixed assets, and how the grants are split between the different types of incoming resources' should be stated.

Chapter 17 Recognition of liabilities and commitments

17.1 Grants payable

The issue of how to account for grants payable is directly linked to the correct recognition of liabilities. SORP 2000 updates the previous SORP to include FRSs 5 and 12. This extends the principle of recognition of liabilities to include not only a legal obligation but also a constructive obligation. A charity will have a constructive obligation to meet a liability where there has been an established pattern of practice or policies where the charity has indicated to a third party that it will undertake certain responsibilities and, as a result of these, the charity has created a valid expectation to these third parties that it will discharge these responsibilities.

Accounting for grants payable is made more problematic due to the fact that normally when expenditure has been made, consideration will have been received by the charity in return for that expenditure. This is not the case for grants payable. Paragraph 122 states that any liability and related expenditure should be accounted for in full by the charity as soon as the relevant obligation arises. If a recipient of the grant has a valid expectation, as outlined in FRS 12, then a constructive obligation may well exist. The charity's past and present conduct will help determine whether such a valid expectation can be deemed to have arisen. In this situation, the full amount of the grant over the total number of years it is to be provided may need to be accounted for in year one by the charity.

However, there are cases where charities will only undertake grant commitments when certain preconditions have been met by either the charity itself or the third party. If, for example, a three year grant programme has been promised by a charity to a third party, it may be the case that the second and third year grants are only payable on the condition of a successful completion of the first year's work. In this case, the three year grant has only been given subject to future reviews and it would be incorrect to include the full three year's grant liability in the first year's accounts of the charity as certain preconditions will not have been met at the year end. Nevertheless, where the liability is not accrued because preconditions have not been fulfilled, then a contingent liability will be created.

In the situation where a multi-year grant is to be funded by a charity and this grant meets the conditions for full inclusion in the first year's accounts, the best estimate of the future expenditure should be considered by the charity when accounting for the grant. This will include considering any related uncertainties or risks relating to the settlement of the grant, together with using appropriate discount rates. If the grant does not meet the conditions for full recognition in year one, the trustees may wish to set up a designated fund to meet the future contingent liability.

The original SORP attempted to ensure that grants should not be accounted for in the current year merely because they had been authorised for payment by the respective trustees' subcommittee. SORP 2000 does reinforce this point but has broadened the opportunity for accounting for the whole amount of a multi-year grant in full in year one by adopting FRS 12's definition of a liability which includes the concept of a constructive obligation. In addition to the constructive obligation within FRS 12, FRS 5 states 'whilst most obligations are legally enforceable, a legal obligation is not a necessary condition for a liability. An entity may be commercially obliged to adopt a certain course of action that is in its long-term best interest in the wider sense, even if no third party can enforce that course.' This reinforces FRS 12's definition of a constructive obligation where a valid expectation on the part of the third party has been created.

17.2 Disclosure of grants payable

SORP 2000 states that where a charity makes grants in excess of 5 per cent of its total resources expended, the charity should regard its grant making as material (para 139). Disclosure of grants payable should show how these grants relate to the objects of the charity. The trustees may provide the necessary analysis and explanation of the charity's grant making in either the trustees' annual report or by means of a separate publication. This analysis should distinguish between grants payable to individuals and those to institutions.

For both types of grants the analysis should be sufficient to disclose the total number and total value of grants made for different charitable purposes. For institutional grants, the first 50 grants made should be disclosed. If the charity has made more than 50 institutional grants then the largest 50 should be disclosed. However, there is no requirement to disclose grants which are below £1,000 in total. This disclosure should include the name of the recipient institution and the total number and value of grants made to the institution. This analysis should be reconciled to the grants payable figure shown in the SOFA.

Paragraph 146 outlines the exceptional circumstances where the disclosure of a material institutional grant could seriously prejudice the furtherance of the purposes of either the recipient or the charity itself and therefore non-disclosure of this grant is permitted. In this situation the charity would still need to:

- disclose in the notes the total number, value and purpose of non-disclosed grants;
- provide details of these grants and reason for non-disclosure to the Charity Commission; and
- confirm in the trustees' annual report whether or not details of the non-disclosed grants have been given to the relevant regulatory body.

17.3 Provisions for commitments

SORP 2000 reinforces the principle stated in the previous SORP that there is a distinction between those commitments of a binding nature and those that are a mere intention. The making of a non-contractual promise would not necessitate a binding commitment for accounting purposes. There would be no legal or constructive obligation as per FRS 12. However, where the conditions of FRS 12 and SORP 2000 have been met, a provision should be accounted for in the charity's accounts and it should be split in the balance sheet between those liabilities falling due within one year and those falling due after more than one year. The amount of the liability that should be recognised will be the best estimate of the expenditure that is required to settle the present obligation at the balance sheet date or to transfer it to the third party at that time (para 251).

In determining this best estimate, both the timing of the relevant cash flows and the future events and uncertainties related to the obligation need to be considered. Provisions over several years will need to be discounted to their present value at the balance sheet date where the amount is material. This best estimate of the liability should be reviewed annually. In the situation where trustees have made unenforceable promises which do not amount to binding commitments, they may still wish to set aside designated funds to meet this expenditure as and when it may arise (para 255).

The notes to the accounts should disclose the amount of the provisions and when they are likely to be met. All movements on these provisions should also be included. Paragraph 258 requires a distinction to be made between binding commitments that are shown in the balance sheet as liabilities and those which are mere intentions to spend and have not been included in the balance sheet. In both situations the following details should be disclosed:

- the reason for the commitments;
- total amount of the commitments;
- amount outstanding at the start of the year;
- amount charged in the SOFA for the year;
- amount released during the year; and
- amount of commitment outstanding at the end of the year as between payable within one year and over one year.

Chapter 18 Cost allocation

18.1 Nature of problem

In company accounts the bottom line is the all important figure but this is certainly not true in the case of charities. The way in which costs are disclosed in charity accounts, under functional headings (such as cost of generating funds) compared with costs shown by natural headings (such as salaries, rent, rates, etc.) are of equal importance on the face of the SOFA and will be of primary importance to the user of the accounts. This is particularly true in relation to charitable expenditure.

Costs by function tell the user of the accounts how the charity has applied its resources. The allocation and apportionment of costs to these headings is not a straightforward task and this has resulted in inconsistencies of treatment across charities. SORP 1995 went some way to resolving these problems. However, confusion still remained in relation to what costs to allocate to 'management and administration of the charity' as well as how to use the 'support costs' heading. Under SORP 2000, both cost headings will be shown as 'charitable expenditure'.

The other major problem has been how to allocate costs which are recorded by their natural classification in a charity's accounting records (for example salaries, rent, rates, postage, telephone, etc.) to the functional cost headings. Where it is not immediately obvious what costs should be allocated to what functional cost category, it may be necessary for costs to be apportioned across a number of functional headings.

The end result of the allocation and apportionment of costs is final costs figure by function, which will be reviewed with great interest by the users of the accounts. What costs have been directly allocated to which heading and how costs have been apportioned between headings is therefore of fundamental importance.

The regulations make clear that those charities whose gross income does not exceed £250,000 per annum will not have to provide a functional classification split of costs. Instead they may choose to use a natural classification, e.g. salaries, wages, rent, rates, etc. In other words the preparation of functional classification of costs only applies to those charities whose gross income is in excess of £250,000 per annum.

18.2 Guidelines

Chapter 3, which looks at the SOFA when dealing with expenditure, reviews the main cost headings recommended by the SORP as:

- cost of generating funds; and
- charitable expenditure.

Cost of generating funds includes all those costs previously shown under the heading 'fundraising and publicity costs' but the definition has been expanded considerably (see Chapter 3). As far as charitable expenditure is concerned this functional cost will now include as sub-headings:

- grants payable in furtherance of the charity's objects;
- costs of activities in furtherance of the charity's objects;

- support costs of the two points above where material; and
- costs of management and administration of the charity.

The allocation of costs to the prime headings and sub-headings should follow the principles set out in SORP 2000 at para 153:

> 'It is not practicable to define precisely what should be included under each expenditure heading as each charity's circumstances will be different. Furthermore, charities will often group expenditure under different headings for internal reporting purposes from those which will be disclosed in the annual accounts. In attributing costs, the following principles should be applied:
>
> (a) No part of expenditure incurred on activities falling directly within one cost category should be allocated to any other cost category.
> (b) Items of expenditure which involve more than one cost category, for example the cost of running an office which houses both fundraising and charitable project support functions, should be apportioned on a reasonable, justifiable and consistent basis to the cost categories involved.
> (c) Where costs should not be allocated to categories in para 60(i) (cost of generating funds) and 60(ii) (a–c) (grants payable, cost of operating activities, and support costs) they should be included within 60(ii)(d) management and administration of the charity.'

As SORP 2000 states at para 154 – and this is a point that applies to all charities (AA notification) – the method of allocation and apportionment of costs should be included in the accounting policy note. For example, costs might be apportioned by the following methods:

- staff hours recorded by timesheet or estimated from normal activity; or
- staff numbers – by activity; or
- floor space occupied;

This can be done as a year end exercise using a spreadsheet so does not require any modification to be made to a charity's accounting records which record costs by their natural classification.

18.3 Accounting policy notes

As SORP 2000 states in para 284 (b):

> 'The policy for including items within types of resources expended should be given. In particular the policy for including items within:
>
> (i) costs of generating funds;
> (ii) grants payable in furtherance of the charity's objects, activities in furtherance of the charities objects and support costs;
> (iii) management and administration.
> and in addition
>
> (c) **AA** – The methods and principles for the allocation and apportionment of all costs between the different categories of expenditure in (b). This disclosure should include the underlying principle, i.e. whether based on staff time, staff salaries, space occupied or other. Where the costs apportioned are significant, then further classification on the method of apportionment used is necessary including the proportions used to undertake the calculations.'

18.4 Support costs

Support costs remain probably one of the most under-used expenditure categories recommended in 1995. Appendix 1.29 of SORP 2000 has updated the definition used in SORP 1995 to:

> '"Support costs" of charitable activities comprise costs incurred directly in support of expenditure on the objects of the charity, and can therefore be considered as part of total expenditure directly relating to the objects of the charity. Such costs will include all services (either at headquarters or through a regional network) which are identifiable as wholly or mainly in support of the charity's project work or other charitable expenditure (excluding management and administration costs) if – but only if – they are an integral part of the cost of carrying out the direct charitable objectives of the charity.'

Such costs would include the direct costs of preparing for a project and an appropriate proportion of overhead costs such as central stores, finance department and office accommodation. Support costs are often incorrectly classified as 'management and administration' costs. To assess whether the costs are support costs or management and administration costs, it is necessary to assess whether they are 'organisational' or 'project' overheads and then allocate to management and administration and support costs respectively.

The Cancer Research Campaign's object is the furtherance of research into the causes of cancer. To achieve this objective, it makes grants to universities, institutes, hospitals, etc., where research is being carried out. At its headquarters it has a scientific department whose activities, whilst not engaged directly in research, are to assist those who are carrying out the research. Costs of this activity would therefore be correctly allocated to support costs.

As we have seen, the accounting policy note should inform the user of the method adopted with regards to the allocation and apportionment of costs to the functional cost heading. The examples that follow are taken from SORP 2000 CC66 *Example Reports and Accounts.*

Example 18.1 Arts Theatre Trust Limited

'Certain expenditure is directly attributable to specific activities and has been included in those cost categories. Certain other costs which are attributable to more than one activity, are apportioned across cost categories on the basis of an estimate of the proportion of time spent by staff on those activities.'

Example 18.2 The ABC Charity

'All expenditure is accounted for on an accrual basis and has been classified under headings that aggregate all costs related to the category. Where costs cannot be directly attributed to particular headings they have been allocated to activities on a basis consistent with use of the resources. Premises overheads have been allocated on a floor area basis and other overheads have been allocated on the basis of the head count.

Fundraising costs are those incurred in seeking voluntary contributions and do not include the costs of disseminating information in support of the charitable activities. Support costs are those costs incurred directly in support of expenditure on the objects of the charity and include project management carried out at Headquarters. Management and administration costs are those incurred in connection with administration of the charity and compliance with constitutional and statutory requirements.'

A further understanding as to how central costs have been allocated can be gained by looking at the notes to the accounts. These should show the analysis of major cost items within each functional cost sub-heading on the face of the SOFA. Costs that should be apportioned across functional cost headings include costs that many immediately consider to be management and administrative costs.

The accounting function, for example, may produce information for project managers (carrying out the charitable objects of the charity) and fundraisers to enable them to carry out their duties effectively. The time incurred producing such information may therefore reasonably be included as a cost under support costs and cost of generating funds respectively. The remaining costs of the accounting function might then be included under management and administration but not – as is sometimes thought – *all* of the accounting costs.

Costs that SORP 2000 does recommend for inclusion in management and administration – i.e. costs not to be apportioned, but directly allocated – include:

- internal audit;
- external audit;
- legal advice for trustees; and
- costs associated with constitutional and statutory requirements.

There should also be an apportionment of indirect costs involved in managing and administering the charity as distinct from directly pursuing its charitable activities.

18.5 Summary

Whilst SORP 2000 does not state directly which costs should fall under which headings, it does stress that the methods used to classify costs should be reasonable, consistent and justifiable. Although there will inevitably be inconsistencies across charities with regards to the functional classification of certain costs, what is crucial in the first instance is that a charity follows a reasonable and consistent method of allocation and apportionment that is justifiable and shown to be so by means of adequate disclosure in the accounting policy note. This will allow the user to reasonably compare categories year on year.

Part IV
CC66 – SORP 2000:
Example accounts (extracts)

Extract from the Introduction to CC66 – SORP 2000

Purpose of this publication

This publication complements the Statement of Recommended Practice – Accounting and Reporting by Charities (SORP 2000). It contains seven examples of reports and financial statements demonstrating the practical application of the SORP 2000 issued by the Charity Commission in October 2000.

The Commission is also producing additional guidance for English and Welsh charities:

- Accounting and Reporting by Charities: Statement of Recommended Practice (Charities SORP 2000). Single copies available free on request; requests for multiple copies will attract a charge of £5 per extra copy.
- CC52 Charity Accounts: Charities Under the £10,000 Threshold
- CC61 Charity Accounts 2001: The framework
- CC62 Charities SORP 2000: What has changed
  (This is a summary of the differences between SORP 1995 and SORP 2000.)
- CC63 The Carrying Out of an Independent Examination: Directions and Guidance Notes. Revised.
- CC64 SORP 2000: Receipts and Payments Accounts Pack
  (This is a help-pack for charities with income of £100,000 or less which are eligible to prepare their accounts on a receipts and payments basis.)
- CC65 SORP 2000: Accruals Accounts Pack
  (This is a help-pack for charities with income of £250,000 or less which are preparing their accounts on an accruals basis.)

All the above are available on our internet site (www.charity-commission.gov.uk) or by phoning our publications order line on 01823 345427. All are free, but extra copies of SORP 2000 may be charged for.

Summary of the examples

These examples have been prepared as a general guide. They are not a substitute for professional advice, which would necessarily take account of particular circumstances, nor for reading the full text of SORP 2000 itself.

The examples are no more than illustrations of layouts and important principles. The charitable sector is very diverse and the examples do not attempt to deal with all types of charities, all issues that may arise or even all the matters in SORP 2000 itself. The examples do, however, provide a variety of presentations for trustees' reports, accounting policies, and particular types of transaction and balances for seven charities. These examples are also available on the Charity Commission's website. It is possible that additional examples may be added to the website over time.

Each example begins with a summary of the charity's:

- constitution and the law under which it reports;
- principal characteristics; and
- the significant SORP issues illustrated by that example.

To help readers of reports and financial statements understand their activities, many charities make voluntary disclosures in addition to those required by SORP 2000, accounting standards and applicable law. This is reflected in certain of the examples.

Statement of Financial Activities
The examples show the Statement of Financial Activities in the form required by SORP 2000. In accordance with paragraph 70 of SORP 2000, certain examples have been expanded to ensure they convey a proper understanding of the nature of all the charity's activities. In addition some examples use the subtotal "net incoming resources available for charitable application" and the subtotal "charitable expenditure" which are options described in paragraph 71 of SORP 2000.

Although it is possible for charities to show extra columns to highlight particular activities, none of the examples have taken advantage of this provision. Such columnar presentation could be useful in consolidated accounts to distinguish, for example, trading activities carried out by a trading subsidiary from the activities carried out by the charity itself.

Balance sheets
These show a variety of situations, including a columnar presentation by type of fund and consolidated balance sheets.

Cashflow statements
Cashflow statements are required by accounting standards for those entities above the thresholds specified in Financial Reporting Standard No 1. In the examples, a cashflow statement has not been prepared where it is not required.

One of the cashflow statements (example 5) shows the treatment of donations to a permanent endowment. It also shows the treatment of cash movements in investment assets which form part of an endowment fund (SORP 2000 – paragraph 275). Examples 6 and 7 demonstrate that sometimes the cashflow from investment income can be considered as arising from operating activities and sometimes as a return on investments.

Accounting policies
The accounting policies adopted by a charity "should be the most appropriate in the particular circumstances of each charity for the purpose of giving a true and fair view" (SORP 2000 – paragraph 277).

The accounting policies in the examples demonstrate a variety of different wording for similar policies. What the examples have in common is that they all show the accounting policies adopted and that the policies are appropriate to the particular circumstances of the individual charity.

Notes to the accounts
The notes to the accounts have been drafted to show various methods for presenting matters of a similar nature.

The detailed disclosures in the notes can vary according to whether the charity is:

- A smaller charity as defined by SORP 2000 and accounting regulations.
- A small company as defined for the purposes of the Companies Act 1985.
- Eligible to take advantage of certain exemptions, by virtue of size, in applying accounting standards.
- Required by the charity's own constitution to make certain disclosures.

The definition of a smaller charity as set out in SORP 2000 is given in the section on smaller charities below.

A small company for the purposes of the Companies Act 1985 is one which meets two of the following three conditions in any two of the current or two preceding financial years:

- Gross income not exceeding £2,800,000.
- Balance sheet total not exceeding £1,400,000.
- Average number of employees not exceeding 50.

The balance sheet total is the gross amount prior to deduction of liabilities or provisions.

Smaller charities

Smaller charities are defined for the purposes of SORP 2000 as those with gross income not exceeding £250,000 (England and Wales). A separate example has not been prepared on this basis. However, example 2 identifies the disclosures that would not be needed if that charity's gross income was £250,000 or less.

Unincorporated charities in England and Wales with gross income of £100,000 or less are eligible to prepare their accounts on a receipts and payments basis unless their constitution prevents them from doing so. Since the Charity Commission produces further guidance on the preparation of receipts and payments accounts in its publication CC64, this is not illustrated in these examples.

Consolidation of subsidiary undertakings

SORP 2000 recommends that the method of consolidation be on a line by line basis (paragraph 309).

The examples include consolidations of subsidiary undertakings which are trading entities to raise funds for the charity itself. They are not carrying out charitable activities. Therefore, all the costs of the subsidiary are included as "costs of generating funds". If, on the other hand, the subsidiary were carrying out some of the charity's activities on its behalf, a proportion of the expenditure of the subsidiary might be shown in the consolidated accounts as charitable expenditure within the classifications specified by paragraph 60(ii) of SORP 2000.

The examples have assumed that there are no intra-group charges which require elimination, for example rents charged to a trading subsidiary by a charity will be eliminated on consolidation.

A separate Statement of Financial Activities has not been **presented** for the charity itself in any of the examples of consolidated financial statements as reliance is being placed on exemptions available in the Companies Act 1985 and in paragraph 304 of SORP 2000. However, paragraph 304 of the SORP does not exempt the charity from **preparing** a SOFA for itself as an individual entity and the Charity Commission retains the power to require the production and filing of any individual charity Statement of Financial Activities and similarly members of the public have a legal right to request this Statement.

Example A

Arts Theatre Trust Limited
(A company limited by guarantee)

Report and Financial Statements (Extract)

Year ended: 31 March 2001

Charity no: 1234567
Company no: 89101112

Consolidated Statement of Financial Activities (including Income and Expenditure Account) for the year ended 31 March 2001

	Notes	Unrestricted Funds £'000	Restricted Funds £'000	Total Funds 2001 £'000	Total Funds 2000 £'000
Incoming resources					
Operation of theatre and arts centre	3	1,200	–	**1,200**	1,259
Activities for generating funds:					
Commercial trading operations	4	549	–	**549**	296
Donations		12	79	**91**	79
Interest receivable		18	1	**19**	16
Total incoming resources		1,779	80	**1,859**	1,650
Less cost of generating funds:					
Commercial trading operations	4	337	2	**339**	280
Net incoming resources available for charitable application		1,442	78	**1,520**	1,370
Charitable expenditure					
Cost of operation of theatre and arts centre	5	1,209	81	**1,290**	1,230
Managing and administering the charity	6	150	2	**152**	113
Total charitable expenditure		1,359	83	**1,442**	1,343
Total resources expended		1,696	85	**1,781**	1,623
Movement in total funds for the year – Net income/(expenditure) for the year		83	(5)	**78**	27
Total funds brought forward		1,294	17	**1,311**	1,284
Total funds carried forward	16, 17	1,377	12	**1,389**	1,311

The statement of financial activities includes all gains and losses recognised in the year.

All incoming resources and resources expended derive from continuing activities.

Consolidated and Charity Balance Sheets as at 31 March 2001

	Notes	Group 2001 £'000	Group 2000 £'000	Charity 2001 £'000	Charity 2000 £'000
Fixed assets					
Tangible assets	10	**830**	824	**830**	824
Investments	4	**–**	–	**1**	1
		830	824	**831**	825
Current assets					
Stock	11	**217**	213	**203**	212
Debtors	12	**207**	206	**272**	206
Cash at bank and in hand		**423**	319	**314**	319
		847	738	**789**	737
Creditors: amounts falling due within one year	13	**242**	195	**185**	195
Net current assets		**605**	543	**604**	542
Total assets less current liabilities		**1,435**	1,367	**1,435**	1,367
Creditors: amounts falling due after more than one year	15	**46**	56	**46**	56
		1,389	1,311	**1,389**	1,311
Unrestricted funds					
General	16	**1,210**	1,263	**1,210**	1,263
Designated	16	**167**	31	**167**	31
		1,377	1,294	**1,377**	1,294
Restricted funds	17	**12**	17	**12**	17
		1,389	1,311	**1,389**	1,311

Approved by the trustees on 16 June 2001 and signed on its behalf by

S A Bloggs, Chairman

Notes forming part of the financial statements for the year ended 31 March 2001

1. Accounting policies

The financial statements have been prepared under the historical cost convention and in accordance with the Statement of Recommended Practice, Accounting and Reporting by Charities (SORP 2000) issued in October 2000, applicable accounting standards and the Companies Act 1985. The principal accounting policies adopted in the preparation of the financial statements are as follows:

Group financial statements

These financial statements consolidate the results of the charity and its wholly-owned subsidiary HTC Limited on a line by line basis. A separate Statement of Financial Activities, or income and expenditure account, for the charity itself is not presented because the charity has taken advantage of the exemptions afforded by section 230 of the Companies Act 1985 and paragraph 304 of SORP 2000.

Incoming resources

Charitable trading activities

Income from theatre admission fees is included in incoming resources in the period in which the relevant show takes place.

Commercial trading activities

Income from commercial activities is included in the period in which the group is entitled to receipt.

Donations and grants

Income from donations and grants, including capital grants, is included in incoming resources when these are receivable, except as follows:

- When donors specify that donations and grants given to the charity must be used in future accounting periods, the income is deferred until those periods.
- When donors impose conditions which have to be fulfilled before the charity becomes entitled to use such income, the income is deferred and not included in incoming resources until the pre-conditions for use have been met.

When donors specify that donations and grants, including capital grants, are for particular restricted purposes, which do not amount to pre-conditions regarding entitlement, this income is included in incoming resources of restricted funds when receivable.

Intangible income

Intangible income, which comprises donated services, is included in income at a valuation which is an estimate of the financial cost borne by the donor where such a cost is quantifiable and measurable. No income is recognised when there is no financial cost borne by a third party.

Interest receivable

Interest is included when receivable by the charity.

Resources expended

Resources expended are included in the Statement of Financial Activities on an accruals basis, inclusive of any VAT which cannot be recovered.

Certain expenditure is directly attributable to specific activities and has been included in those cost categories. Certain other costs, which are attributable to more than one activity, are apportioned across cost categories on the basis of an estimate of the proportion of time spent by staff on those activities.

Pension costs

The charity participates in a defined benefit scheme. Pension costs are assessed in accordance with actuarial advice and based on the most recent actuarial valuation of the scheme. These costs are accounted for on the basis of charging the cost of providing pensions over the period during which the charity benefits from the employees' services.

Operating leases

Rentals payable under operating leases are charged to the Statement of Financial Activities as incurred over the term of the lease.

Tangible fixed assets

Individual fixed assets costing £1,000 or more are capitalised at cost.

Tangible fixed assets are depreciated on a straight-line basis over their estimated useful lives as follows:

	Annual rate
Long leasehold buildings	1%–2%
Plant, equipment and motor vehicles	10%–33%
Pianos	10%

Stock

Stock is included at the lower of cost or net realisable value.

Fund accounting

Funds held by the charity are either:

- *Unrestricted general funds* – these are funds which can be used in accordance with the charitable objects at the discretion of the trustees.
- *Designated funds* – these are funds set aside by the trustees out of unrestricted general funds for specific future purposes or projects.
- *Restricted funds* – these are funds that can only be used for particular restricted purposes within the objects of the charity. Restrictions arise when specified by the donor or when funds are raised for particular restricted purposes.

Further explanation of the nature and purpose of each fund is included in the notes to the financial statements.

Notes forming part of the financial statements for the year ended 31 March 2001

2. Legal status of the charity

The charity is a company limited by guarantee and has no share capital. The liability of each member in the event of winding-up is limited to £5.

3. Incoming resources from operation of theatre and arts centre

	2001 £'000	2000 £'000
Admission fees	**514**	489
Public authority service agreements for operation of theatre	**509**	601
Service agreements with other charities for workshops	**154**	150
Other income	**23**	19
	1,200	1,259

4. Commercial trading operations and investment in trading subsidiary

The wholly-owned trading subsidiary, HTC Limited, which is incorporated in the United Kingdom, pays all its profits to the charity by gift aid. HTC Limited operates the bars, restaurant, coffee lounge and all commercial trading operations carried on at the Arts Theatre Trust Limited. The charity owns the entire issued share capital of 1,000 ordinary shares of £1 each. A summary of the trading results is shown below.

Summary profit and loss account

	2001 £'000	2000 £'000
Turnover	**549**	296
Cost of sales and administrative expenses	**(337)**	(280)
Interest receivable	**4**	–
Net profit	**216**	16
Amount gifted to the charity	**(216)**	(16)
Retained in the subsidiary	**–**	–
The assets and liabilities of the subsidiary were:		
Current assets	**136**	1
Creditors: amounts falling due with one year	**(135)**	–
Total net assets	**1**	1
Aggregate share capital and reserves	**1**	1

Notes forming part of the financial statements for the year ended 31 March 2001

5. Cost of operation of theatre and arts centre

	2001 £'000	2000 £'000
Reception and housekeeping	**197**	215
Marketing	**204**	211
Courses	**63**	58
Activities	**54**	67
Promotions	**286**	272
ATC Park capital project – feasibility study	**73**	–
Depreciation	**66**	60
Piano fund expenditure	**4**	–
Administration of box office	**152**	176
Central premises costs	**191**	171
	1,290	1,230

6. Managing and administering the charity

	2001 £'000	2000 £'000
Salaries and wages	**86**	73
Meeting costs	**22**	6
Legal and professional expenses	**19**	12
Office costs	**25**	22
	152	113

7. Staff costs and trustees' remuneration

	2001 £'000	2000 £'000
Wages and salaries	**620**	603
Social security costs	**41**	39
Pension costs	**19**	11
Ex-gratia payments	**16**	–
	696	653

The ex-gratia payment was made to a former chief executive for whom no pension provision had been made. The Charity Commission approved payment on 15 December 2000.

No employee earned more than £50,000 per annum (2000 – nil).

The trustees were not paid or reimbursed for expenses during the year.

Notes forming part of the financial statements for the year ended 31 March 2001

8. Staff numbers

The average number of full-time equivalent employees (including casual and part-time staff) during the year was made up as follows:

	2001 No	2000 No
Arts department	**11**	11
Administration, marketing and commercial	**14**	13
Technical	**11**	10
Bars and coffee shop	**21**	17
Front of house, box office, cleaning	**20**	21
Course tutors, models	**31**	30
	108	102

9. Movement in total funds for the year

	2001 £'000	2000 £'000
This is stated after charging:		
Operating leases – equipment	**13**	13
Depreciation	**66**	60
Auditors' remuneration		
external audit	**8**	6
other services	**2**	6

10. Tangible fixed assets – group and charity

	Long Leasehold Property £'000	Equipment and Motor Vehicles £'000	Pianos £'000	Total £'000
Cost				
At 1 April 2000	1,597	869	32	**2,498**
Additions	–	72	–	**72**
At 31 March 2001	1,597	941	32	**2,570**
Depreciation				
At 1 April 2000	845	801	28	**1,674**
Provided for the year	23	42	1	**66**
At 31 March 2001	868	843	29	**1,740**
Net book value				
At 31 March 2001	**729**	**98**	**3**	**830**
At 31 March 2000	752	68	4	824

Notes forming part of the financial statements for the year ended 31 March 2001

11. Stock

	Group		Charity	
	2001	**2000**	**2001**	**2000**
	£'000	**£'000**	**£'000**	**£'000**
Finished goods for resale	**203**	212	**203**	212
Stationery	**14**	1	**–**	–
	217	213	**203**	212

12. Debtors

	Group		Charity	
	2001	**2000**	**2001**	**2000**
	£'000	**£'000**	**£'000**	**£'000**
Trade debtors	**33**	20	**14**	20
Other debtors	**119**	128	**119**	128
Prepayments and accrued income	**55**	58	**55**	58
Amount due from subsidiary undertaking	**–**	–	**84**	–
	207	206	**272**	206

13. Creditors: amounts falling due within one year

	Group		Charity	
	2001	**2000**	**2001**	**2000**
	£'000	**£'000**	**£'000**	**£'000**
Trade creditors	**117**	88	**80**	88
Other taxes and social security costs	**18**	19	**18**	19
Other creditors and accruals	**52**	42	**32**	42
Deferred income (Note 14)	**55**	46	**55**	46
	242	195	**185**	195

14. Deferred income

	Group	**Charity**
Balance at 1 April 2000	46	49
Amount released to incoming resources	(46)	(49)
Amount deferred in the year	55	46
Balance at 31 March 2001	**55**	**46**

Deferred income comprises admission fees received in advance and grants which the donor has specified must be used in future accounting periods.

Notes forming part of the financial statements for the year ended 31 March 2001

15. Creditors: amounts falling due after more than one year

	Group		Charity	
	2001 £'000	2000 £'000	2001 £'000	2000 £'000
Unsecured loan	**46**	56	**46**	56

The loan is provided by XYZ Limited, is interest free and is repayable in equal half yearly instalments between 2002 and 2007.

16. Unrestricted funds of the charity

	General Fund £'000	Designated Funds £'000	Total £'000
Balance at 1 April 2000	1,263	31	1,294
Movement in funds for the year	83	–	83
Transfer of amount designated for future repairs	(136)	136	–
Balance at 31 March 2001	**1,210**	**167**	**1,377**

The trustees have designated funds for repairs which may be required under the lease for property.

17. Restricted funds

	At 1 April 2000 £'000	Incoming Resources £'000	Outgoing Resources £'000	At 31 March 2001 £'000
Piano fund	10	3	5	8
Ceramics residency	3	–	3	–
Jazz course	–	1	1	–
Clay at the park	2	–	–	2
Kennel ride	2	–	–	2
The ugly show	–	1	1	–
ATC Park capital project	–	73	73	–
	17	78	83	12

The piano fund is for the purchase of a baby grand piano, which was acquired in June 2001.

The ceramics residency fund is to support the appointment of a resident ceramist. The appointment was made at the beginning of September 2000.

The jazz course fund is specifically to underwrite the costs of the jazz weekend held in March as an attempt to bring professional and amateur musicians together.

The clay at the park fund is to publish documents and create an archive relating to the development of clay craft in the Borough.

The kennel ride fund is to assist with the charity's project with the young people of Kennel Ride.

The ugly show fund was to underwrite the costs of an exhibition from five artists held in September and October 2000 which explored notions of beauty.

The ATC Park capital project was funded by the Arts Council of England, which gave the charity a grant of £73,000. This grant was towards the cost of a further feasibility study for alterations, refurbishment and a new extension to the Theatre, which is a Grade 2, listed building. It included the appointment of consultants and the payment of professional fees.

Notes forming part of the financial statements for the year ended 31 March 2001

18. Analysis of group net assets between funds

	General Fund £'000	Designated Fund £'000	Restricted Funds £'000	Total £'000
Tangible fixed assets	830	–	–	830
Cash at bank and in hand	244	167	12	423
Other net current assets	182	–	–	182
Long term liabilities	(46)	–	–	(46)
	1,210	167	12	1,389

19. Operating lease commitments

The amounts payable in the next year in respect of operating leases for equipment are shown below, analysed according to the expiry date of the leases.

	2001 £'000	2000 £'000
One year	1	8
Between two and five years	5	1
	6	9

20. Related parties

The charity has a very close relationship with N Arts, which is a charity, BF Borough Council and B Town Council, all of which nominate the majority of the trustees and provide funding to enable the charity to carry out its charitable objectives. The following is a summary of transactions with those entities:

	2001 £'000	2000 £'000
Revenue funding		
BF Borough Council	405	501
B Town Council	104	100
N Arts Trust	154	150
	663	751

All the above funding was received under contracts with the charity to provide services, eg training in drama production, and has been included in the financial statements under the heading *Incoming Resources: from Operation of theatre and arts centre*.

The charity also received a donation in kind, from BF Borough Council, for the rent of premises, the value of which could not be quantified and therefore has not been included in these financial statements.

There were no outstanding balances with related parties at 31 March 2001 (2000 – £NIL).

Notes forming part of the financial statements for the year ended 31 March 2001

21. Pensions

The charity operates a funded defined benefit scheme providing benefits based on final remuneration. The assets of the scheme are held separately from those of the charity. The staff are members of the County Pension Fund.

Contributions to the scheme are charged to SOFA so as to spread the cost of pensions over the employees' working lives with the charity. Contributions are determined by a qualified actuary on the basis of valuations using a market related method which derives the financial assumptions by considering various average yields in the twelve months leading up to the valuation date and values the assets of the fund at a value based on the average market value in the twelve months to the valuation date.

The pension charge for the year is £19,000. The assumptions used in the valuation were as follows:

Date of latest actuarial valuation	**31 March 2000**
Investment returns	6.7%–7.2%
Price inflation	3.4%
Earnings increases	5.4%
Market value of assets	£882m
Benefit cover	114%

Example B

Dorsetshire Drugs Advice Centre
(A company limited by guarantee)

Report and Financial Statements (Extract)

Year ended: 31 March 2002

Charity no: 1253687
Company no: 1032145

Statement of Financial Activities (including Income and Expenditure Account) for the year ended 31 March 2002

	Notes	Unrestricted Funds £	Restricted Funds £	Total Funds 2002 £	Total Funds 2001 £
Incoming resources					
Donations	2	–	5,000	**5,000**	6,796
Activities to further the charity's objects:					
Grants and contracts for advice and information, outreach work and training project	3	95,535	150,000	**245,535**	207,304
Activities to generate funds:					
Charity shop		19,465	–	**19,465**	17,242
Investment income and interest		900	765	**1,665**	1,324
Total incoming resources		115,900	155,765	**271,665**	232,666
Resources expended					
Costs of generating funds					
Charity shop		11,773	–	**11,773**	11,225
Fund-raising and publicity		5,798	–	**5,798**	1,893
Charitable expenditure					
Advice and information		–	67,008	**67,008**	59,876
Outreach work		–	68,391	**68,391**	53,316
Training project		80,836	–	**80,836**	63,606
Management and administration		10,108	1,250	**11,358**	7,372
Total resources expended	4	108,515	136,649	**245,164**	197,288
Net incoming resources – Net income for the year	5	7,385	19,116	**26,501**	35,378
Gain on revaluation of investments	9	762	–	**762**	202
Net movement in funds		8,147	19,116	**27,263**	35,580
Total funds at 1 April 2001		20,249	1,316	**21,565**	(14,015)
Total funds at 31 March 2002	13	28,396	20,432	**48,828**	21,565

Movements in funds are disclosed in Note 13 to the financial statements.

*(**Note:** If the gross income of the entity was less than £250,000, resources expended could be analysed by natural classification (ie salaries, wages etc) rather than by activity as shown above.)*

Balance Sheet as at 31 March 2002

	Notes	£	2002 £	2001 £
Fixed assets				
Tangible assets	8		**11,250**	10,000
Investments	9		**11,654**	10,892
			22,904	20,892
Current assets				
Debtors	10	**7,835**		5,628
Cash at bank and in hand		**26,473**		3,797
		34,308		9,425
Creditors: amounts falling due within one year	11	**8,384**		8,752
Net current assets			**25,924**	673
Net assets	12		**48,828**	21,565
Unrestricted funds				
Designated funds		**10,000**		–
Revaluation fund		**1,829**		1,067
General funds		**16,567**		19,182
			28,396	20,249
Restricted funds			**20,432**	1,316
Total funds	13		**48,828**	21,565

These accounts are prepared in accordance with the special provisions of Part VII of the Companies Act 1985 relating to small entities.

Approved by the management committee on 13 September 2002 and signed on its behalf by:

M Haliwell, Treasurer

Notes forming part of the financial statements for the year ended 31 March 2002

1. Accounting policies

(a) The financial statements have been prepared under the historical cost convention, as modified by the inclusion of fixed asset investments at market value, and in accordance with the Financial Reporting Standard for Smaller Entities (effective March 2000), the Companies Act 1985 and follow the recommendations in *Accounting and Reporting by Charities: Statement of Recommended Practice* issued in October 2000.

(b) Voluntary income is received by way of donations and gifts and is included in full in the Statement of Financial Activities when receivable. The value of services provided by volunteers has not been included.

(c) Grants, including grants for the purchase of fixed assets, are recognised in full in the Statement of Financial Activities in the year in which they are receivable.

(d) Incoming resources from the charity shop and from investments is included when receivable.

(e) Resources expended are recognised in the period in which they are incurred. Resources expended include attributable VAT which cannot be recovered.

(f) Resources expended are allocated to the particular activity where the cost relates directly to that activity. However, the cost of overall direction and administration on each activity, comprising the salary and overhead costs of the central function, is apportioned on the following basis which are an estimate, based on staff time, of the amount attributable to each activity:

Charity shop	0%
Fund-raising and publicity	15%
Advice and information	20%
Outreach work	20%
Training project	30%
Management and administration of the charity	15%

(g) Depreciation is provided at rates calculated to write off the cost of each asset over its expected useful life, which in all cases is estimated at 4 years. Items of equipment are capitalised where the purchase price exceed £500.

(h) Investments held as fixed assets are revalued at mid-market value at the balance sheet date and the gain or loss taken to the Statement of Financial Activities.

(i) Unrestricted funds are donations and other incoming resources receivable or generated for the objects of the charity without further specified purpose and are available as general funds.

(j) Designated funds are unrestricted funds earmarked by the management committee for particular purposes.

(k) Restricted funds are to be used for specific purposes as laid down by the donor. Expenditure which meets these criteria is charged to the fund, together with a fair allocation of management and support costs.

2. Donations

	Unrestricted £	Restricted £	2002 Total £	2001 Total £
Berrow Estate Charitable Trust	–	5,000	**5,000**	–
General donations	–	–	**–**	6,796
	–	5,000	**5,000**	6,796

3. Incoming resources from activities to further the charity's objects

	Unrestricted £	Restricted £	2002 Total £	2001 Total £
Dorsetshire County Council:				
Advice and information	–	70,000	**70,000**	60,000
Outreach work	–	80,000	**80,000**	66,132
Training project:				
Income from café	95,535	–	**95,535**	81,172
Total grants and contracts	95,535	150,000	**245,535**	207,304

Notes forming part of the financial statements for the year ended 31 March 2002

4. Total resources expended

	Charity Shop	Fund-raising & Publicity £	Advice & Information £	Outreach Work £	Training Project £	Management and Administration £	2002 Total £	2001 Total £
Staff costs (Note 6)	–	1,284	62,955	60,568	71,394	1,878	**198,079**	159,611
Recruitment	–	–	–	1,426	1,212	–	**2,638**	2,817
Travel	–	–	324	482	396	166	**1,368**	956
Premises	10,250	3,000	1,646	3,931	5,084	–	**23,911**	20,562
Communications	–	233	594	589	1,500	589	**3,505**	2,816
Legal and professional	–	–	–	–	–	1,250	**1,250**	1,429
Audit fees	–	–	–	–	–	2,000	**2,000**	1,800
Consultancy	–	–	–	770	–	2,336	**3,106**	–
Annual report	–	1,281	–	–	–	1,281	**2,562**	1,825
Volunteer expenses	1,523	–	864	–	–	–	**2,387**	2,520
Depreciation	–	–	625	625	1,250	1,250	**3,750**	2,500
Bank charges	–	–	–	–	–	608	**608**	452
Total resources expended	11,773	5,798	67,008	68,391	80,836	11,358	**245,164**	197,288

*(**Note:** If the gross income of the charity were less than £250,000, it would be sufficient to show the narrative on the left of this note and the totals for each year.)*

5. Net incoming resources for the year

This is stated after charging:

	2002 £	2001 £
Depreciation	**3,125**	2,500
Management committee's remuneration	**–**	–
Auditors' remuneration		
Audit services	**2,000**	1,800

Travel costs amounting to £166 (2001 – £184) were reimbursed to 4 (2001 – 5) members of the management committee.

Notes forming part of the financial statements for the year ended 31 March 2002

6. Staff costs and numbers

Staff costs were as follows:

	2002 £	2001 £
Salaries and wages	**180,072**	144,247
Social security costs	**18,007**	15,364
	198,079	159,611

No employee received emoluments of more than £50,000.

The average weekly number of employees during the year, calculated on the basis of full time equivalents, was as follows:

	2002 No	2001 No
Director	**1**	1
Advice and information	**3**	3
Outreach work	**3**	3
Training project	**5**	4
Administration and support	**1**	1
	13	12

7. Taxation

The charitable company is exempt from corporation tax on its charitable activities.

8. Tangible fixed assets

	Office Equipment £	Total £
Cost		
At 1 April 2001	15,000	**15,000**
Additions in year	5,000	**5,000**
At 31 March 2002	20,000	**20,000**
Depreciation		
At 1 April 2001	5,000	**5,000**
Charge for the year	3,750	**3,750**
At 31 March 2002	8,750	**8,750**
Net book value		
At 31 March 2002	11,250	**11,250**
At 31 March 2001	10,000	**10,000**

Notes forming part of the financial statements for the year ended 31 March 2001

9. Investments

	2002 £	2001 £
Charifund Unit Trust at mid-market value:		
At 31 March 2001	**10,892**	10,690
Gain on investments from change in value	**762**	202
At 31 March 2002	**11,654**	10,892
Historical cost of investments held at 31 March 2002	**9,825**	9,825

10. Debtors

	2002 £	2001 £
Contract income receivable	**6,709**	4,580
Other debtors and prepayments	**1,126**	1,048
	7,835	5,628

11. Creditors: amounts falling due within one year

	2002 £	2001 £
Taxation and social security	**4,458**	3,896
Other creditors and accruals	**3,926**	4,856
	8,384	8,752

12. Analysis of net assets between funds

	General Funds £	Designated Funds £	Restricted Funds £	Total Funds £
Tangible fixed assets	7,500	–	3,750	**11,250**
Investments	9,825	1,829	–	**11,654**
Current assets	5,170	10,000	19,138	**34,308**
Current liabilities	(5,928)	–	(2,456)	**(8,384)**
Net assets at 31 March 2002	**16,567**	**11,829**	**20,432**	**48,828**

Notes forming part of the financial statements for the year ended 31 March 2001

13. Movements in funds

	At 1 April 2001 £	Incoming Resources £	Outgoing Resources £	Transfers £	At 31 March 2002 £
Restricted funds:					
Computer equipment	–	5,000	(1,250)	–	**3,750**
Advice and information	1,316	70,000	(67,008)	–	**4,308**
Outreach	–	80,765	(68,391)	–	**12,374**
Total restricted funds	1,316	155,765	(136,649)	–	**20,432**
Unrestricted funds:					
Designated training project equipment fund	–	–	–	10,000	**10,000**
Designated revaluation fund	1,067	762	–	–	**1,829**
General funds	19,182	115,900	(108,515)	(10,000)	**16,567**
Total unrestricted funds	20,249	116,662	(108,515)	–	**28,396**
Total funds	**21,565**	**272,427**	**(245,164)**	**-**	**48,828**

Purposes of restricted funds

Computer equipment	The balance will fund future depreciation of computers which were originally purchased using restricted funds and which the donor specified must be retained.
Advice and information	The fund is for the advice and information activity as explained in the trustees' report.
Outreach	This is a fund for outreach work with young people who are vulnerable or falling into drug misuse. The balance arose from a delay in using grants which were given for the purpose of appointing new staff. Staff were appointed late in the year and all the fund will be utilised in forthcoming months.

Purposes of designated funds

Training project equipment	The management committee has designated funds for purchase of new equipment in the training project.
Revaluation fund	The revaluation fund is required by the Companies Act 1985 and represents the amount by which investments exceed their historical cost.

Example C

The Rosanna Grant Trust

Report and Financial Statements (Extract)

Year ended: 30 September 2001

Charity no: 98765432

Statement of Financial Activities for the year ended 30 September 2001

	Notes	Unrestricted Funds £'000	Restricted Funds £'000	Endowment Funds £'000	Total 2001 £'000	Total 2000 £'000
Incoming resources						
Investment income	2	634	103	–	**737**	680
Resources expended						
Costs of generating funds	3	14	20	90	**124**	112
Charitable expenditure:						
Grants payable	4	458	85	–	**543**	421
Support costs	5	105	5	–	**110**	81
Management and administration	6	48	3	15	**66**	63
Total resources expended		625	113	105	**843**	677
Net incoming resources/ (resources expended)		9	(10)	(105)	**(106)**	3
Other recognised gains and losses:						
Gain/(loss) on investments	10	8	12	447	**467**	(103)
Net movement in funds		17	2	342	**361**	(100)
Balance at 1 October 2000		378	5,982	20,223	**26,583**	26,683
Balance at 30 September 2001	14	395	5,984	20,565	**26,944**	26,583

Balance Sheet as at 30 September 2001

	Notes	Unrestricted Funds £'000	Restricted Funds £'000	Endowment Funds £'000	Total 2001 £'000	Total 2000 £'000
Fixed assets						
Tangible assets	8	14	1	–	**15**	17
Inalienable and historic assets	9	–	–	2	**2**	2
Investments	10	474	5,979	20,546	**26,999**	27,102
		488	5,980	20,548	**27,016**	27,121
Current assets						
Debtors	11	38	14	17	**69**	42
Cash at bank and in hand		15	8	–	**23**	11
		53	22	17	**92**	53
Creditors: amounts falling due within one year	12	(74)	(15)	–	**(89)**	(422)
Net current assets/(liabilities)		(21)	7	17	**3**	(369)
Total assets less current liabilities		467	5,987	20,565	**27,019**	26,752
Creditors: Amounts falling due after more than one year	13	(72)	(3)	–	**(75)**	(170)
Total net assets		395	5,984	20,565	**26,944**	26,582
Funds	14	395	5,984	20,565	**26,944**	26,583

Approved by the trustees on 12 January 2002 and signed on its behalf by:

M Hope (Chairman)

Notes forming part of the financial statements for the year ended 30 September 2001

1. Principal accounting policies

(a) **Accounting convention**
The financial statements are prepared under the historical cost convention as modified by the inclusion of investments at market value and in accordance with the Financial Reporting Standard for Smaller Entities (effective March 2000). In preparing the financial statements the charity follows best practice as laid down in the Statement of Recommended Practice "Accounting and Reporting by Charities" (SORP 2000) issued in October 2000.

(b) **Investment income**
Investment income is accounted for in the period in which the charity is entitled to receipt.

(c) **Resources expended**
Expenditure is included on an accruals basis.

Costs of generating funds comprise those costs directly attributable to managing the investment portfolio and raising investment income.

Grants payable are charged in the year when the offer is conveyed to the recipient except in those cases where the offer is conditional, such grants being recognised as expenditure when the conditions attaching are fulfilled. Grants offered subject to conditions which have not been met at the year end are noted as a commitment, but not accrued as expenditure.

Support costs comprise costs for processing grants and applications, including support to actual and potential applicants. Management and administration comprises costs for the running of the charity itself as an organisation. Where costs cannot be directly attributed to either of these two categories, it is estimated based on activity levels that 85% of staffing costs and 90% of the costs are attributable to support costs with the balance attributable to management and administration.

(d) **Tangible fixed assets and depreciation**
All assets costing more than £500 are capitalised.

Depreciation is not charged on historic artefacts as the residual value is considered to be higher than the carrying value. Furniture and equipment is written off on a straight-line basis over their estimated useful life of four years.

(e) **Fixed asset investments**
Investments are included at closing mid-market value at the balance sheet date. Any gain or loss on revaluation is taken to the Statement of Financial Activities.

(f) **Fund accounting**
Details of the nature and purpose of each fund is set out in note 14.

2. Investment income

	2001 £'000	2000 £'000
Dividends – UK equities	**430**	385
Interest – UK fixed interest securities	**287**	278
Interest on cash deposits	**20**	17
	737	680

Transitional tax relief amounting to £125,000 (2000 – £67,000) is included above.

3. Costs of generating funds

	2001 £'000	2000 £'000
Legal fees	**6**	5
Investment management fees	**118**	107
	124	112

Notes forming part of the financial statements for the year ended 30 September 2001

4. Grants payable

	2001		2000	
	£'000	**£'000**	**£'000**	**£'000**
The amount payable in the year comprises:				
Education and research				
Manchester Institute of Technology				
4 grants (2000 – 4) as follows:				
to fund educational post	**51**		36	
genetic research	**31**		31	
research into awareness of symptoms of Alzheimer's in general practitioners	**20**		20	
the impact of Alzheimer's on family and carers	**21**		21	
		123		108
University of Slough				
2 grants to fund educational posts (2000 – 1 grant)		**91**		57
University of Taunton				
2 grants (2000 – 3) as follows:				
research into drug therapies	**51**		49	
research on nursing homes caring for patients with Alzheimer's	**34**		30	
compilation of registry of practitioners and hospitals specialising in Alzheimer's	**–**		24	
		85		103
Total institutional grants		**299**		268
PhD scholarships – grants to 79 individuals (2000 – 52 individuals)		**244**		153
		543		421
Reconciliation of grants payable:				
Commitments at 1 October 2000		**545**		281
Commitments made in the year	**561**		431	
Grants cancelled or recovered	**(18)**		(10)	
Grants payable for the year		**543**		421
Grants paid during the year		**(929)**		(157)
Commitments at 30 September 2001		**159**		545
Commitments at 30 September are payable as follows:				
Within one year (note 12)		**84**		375
After more than one year (note 13)		**75**		170
		159		545

Commitments

In addition to the amounts committed and accrued noted above, the trustees have also authorised certain grants which are subject to the recipient fulfilling certain conditions. The total amount authorised but not accrued as expenditure at 30 September 2001 was £184,000 (2000: £191,000).

Notes forming part of the financial statements for the year ended 30 September 2001

5. Support costs

	2001 £'000	2000 £'000
Staff costs	**63**	54
Office rental and costs	**25**	19
Computer costs	**17**	4
Depreciation	**5**	4
	110	81

6. Management and administration

	2001 £'000	2000 £'000
Staff costs	**11**	10
Office rental and costs	**25**	19
Auditor's fees for audit services	**5**	4
Auditor's fees for other services	**1**	–
Legal fees	**10**	12
Computer costs	**6**	6
Costs of meetings	**6**	10
Depreciation	**2**	2
	66	63

7. Staff costs and trustees' remuneration

	2001 £'000	2000 £'000
Salaries	**67**	59
Social security costs	**7**	5
	74	64
The average weekly number of employees during the year, calculated on a full time equivalent basis, was:	**2**	2

No employee received remuneration amounting to more than £50,000 in either year.

Trustees received no remuneration (2000 – £Nil) and were not reimbursed for any of their expenses in the year (2000 – £Nil).

Notes forming part of the financial statements for the year ended 30 September 2001

8. Tangible fixed assets

	Furniture and equipment £'000
Cost	
At 1 October 2000	**26**
Additions	**5**
Disposals	**(2)**
At 30 September 2001	**29**
Depreciation	
At 1 October 2000	**9**
Charge for the year	**7**
On disposals	**(2)**
At 30 September 2001	**14**
Net book value	
At 30 September 2001	**15**
At 30 September 2000	**17**

9. Inalienable and historic assets

The trustees estimated the value of the historic artefacts, comprising paintings and busts, depicting Mrs Grant, as at 30 September 1999 at £2,000. All other assets are held at cost.

10. Investments

	2001 £'000	2000 £'000
Market value at 1 October 2000	**27,102**	27,501
Acquisitions at cost	**5,150**	4,013
Sales proceeds from disposals	**(5,720)**	(4,309)
Gain/(loss) in the year	**467**	(103)
Market value at 30 September 2001	**26,999**	27,102
Investments at market value comprised:		
UK equities	**18,897**	18,168
UK fixed interest securities	**8,102**	8,934
	26,999	27,102
Historical cost as at 30 September 2001	**14,303**	14,121

All investments are listed UK securities.

Notes forming part of the financial statements for the year ended 30 September 2001

11. Debtors

	2001 £'000	2000 £'000
Other debtors	**17**	8
Prepayments and accrued income	**52**	34
	69	42

12. Creditors: Amounts falling due within one year

	2001 £'000	2000 £'000
Grants payable (note 4)	**84**	375
Other creditors	**–**	40
Accruals	**5**	7
	89	422

13. Creditors: Amounts falling due after more than one year

	2001 £'000	2000 £'000
Grants payable (note 4)	**75**	170

14. Funds

Unrestricted funds comprise those funds which the trustees are free to use in accordance with the charitable objects.

Restricted funds are funds which have been given for particular purposes and projects. The restricted fund must be used wholly to provide grants to PhD students carrying out research into Alzheimer's Disease.

The **endowment fund** represents those assets which must be held permanently by the charity, principally investments. Income arising on the endowment fund can be used in accordance with the objects of the charity and is included as unrestricted income. Any capital gains or losses arising on the investments form part of the fund. Investment management charges and legal advice relating to the fund are charged against the fund.

Example D

Aid Overseas

Report and Financial Statements (Extract)

Year ended: 30 September 2001

Charity no: 98765432

Consolidated Statement of Financial Activities for the year ended 30 September 2001

	Notes	Unrestricted Funds £'000	Restricted Funds £'000	2001 Total £'000	2000 Total £'000
Incoming resources					
Donations, legacies and similar incoming resources	2	**6,897**	3,797	**10,694**	10,991
Activities in furtherance of the charity's objects:					
Contracts for operational programmes	3	–	4,746	**4,746**	4,567
Activities for generating funds:					
Shop income	4	**8,573**	–	**8,573**	6,596
Investment income and interest	5	**190**	39	**229**	202
Total incoming resources		**15,660**	**8,582**	**24,242**	**22,356**
Less: Cost of generating funds					
Shop expenditure	4	**6,494**	–	**6,494**	6,029
Fund-raising costs	6	**1,646**	113	**1,759**	1,584
		8,140	**113**	**8,253**	**7,613**
Net incoming resources available for charitable application		**7,520**	**8,469**	**15,989**	**14,743**
Charitable expenditure					
Costs of activities in furtherance of the objects of the charity:	7				
Grants payable to partner organisations	7, 8	**1,286**	2,239	**3,525**	3,829
Operational programmes	7	**1,032**	4,578	**5,610**	5,892
Gifts in kind	7	**239**	1,092	**1,331**	1,296
Information, campaigning & education	7	**984**	9	**993**	917
Support costs	9	**1,502**	404	**1,906**	1,845
Managing and administering the charity	10	**470**	2	**472**	466
Total charitable expenditure		**5,513**	**8,324**	**13,837**	**14,245**
Total resources expended		**13,653**	**8,437**	**22,090**	**21,858**
Net incoming resources	11	**2,007**	**145**	**2,152**	**498**
Total funds brought forward		**4,006**	2,695	**6,701**	6,203
Total funds carried forward	21, 22	**6,013**	**2,840**	**8,853**	**6,701**

The statement of financial activities includes all gains and losses recognised in the year.

All incoming resources and resources expended derive from continuing activities.

Consolidated and Charity Balance Sheets as at 30 September 2001

	Notes	2001 Group £'000	2000 Group £'000	2001 Charity £'000	2000 Charity £'000
Fixed assets					
Tangible assets	14	**2,403**	2,258	**2,356**	2,224
Investments	15	**35**	43	**37**	45
		2,438	**2,301**	**2,393**	**2,269**
Current assets					
Stocks	16	**784**	969	**260**	245
Debtors	17	**3,150**	2,281	**3,554**	2,941
Cash at bank and in hand	18	**5,094**	3,248	**5,081**	3,218
		9,028	6,498	**8,895**	6,404
Creditors: amounts falling within one year	19	**(2,276)**	(1,315)	**(2,098)**	(1,189)
Net current assets		**6,752**	**5,183**	**6,797**	**5,215**
Total assets less current liabilities		**9,190**	**7,484**	**9,190**	**7,484**
Creditors: amounts falling due after more than one year	20	**(337)**	(783)	**(337)**	(783)
Net assets	23	**8,853**	**6,701**	**8,853**	**6,701**
Funds					
Unrestricted funds: General reserves	21	**2,708**	**1,293**	**2,755**	**1,327**
Designated funds					
fixed assets	21	**2,403**	2,258	**2,356**	2,224
other	21	**902**	455	**902**	455
		3,305	**2,713**	**3,258**	**2,679**
Restricted funds	22	**2,840**	**2,695**	**2,840**	**2,695**
		8,853	**6,701**	**8,853**	**6,701**

Approved by the Board of Trustees:

S C Bourne

Date: 12 December 2001

Consolidated Statement of Cash Flow for the year ended 30 September 2001

	Notes	2001 £'000	2001 £'000	2000 £'000	2000 £'000
Net cash inflow from operating activities	26(a)		**1,659**		**827**
Returns on investments and servicing of finance					
Deposit interest received		221		195	
Investment income		8		7	
			229		**202**
Capital expenditure and financial investment					
Payments to acquire tangible fixed assets		(488)		(266)	
Receipts from sales of tangible fixed assets		46		–	
Disposal of fixed asset investments		8		–	
			(434)		**(266)**
Net cash inflow before management of liquid resources and financing			**1,454**		**763**
Management of liquid resources					
Cash added to short term deposits			(1,391)		(1,170)
Increase /(decrease) in cash in the year			**63**		**(407)**
Net cash resources at 1 October 2000			1,394		1,801
Net cash resources at 30 September 2001	26(b)		**1,457**		**1,394**

Notes forming part of the financial statements for the year ended 30 September 2001

1. Principal accounting policies

(a) **Accounting convention**
The financial statements are prepared under the historical cost convention as modified by the inclusion of investments at market value and in accordance with applicable accounting standards. In preparing the financial statements the charity follows best practice as set out in the Statement of Recommended Practice "Accounting and Reporting by Charities" (SORP) issued in October 2000.

(b) **Group financial statements**
These financial statements consolidate the results of the charity and its wholly-owned trading subsidiary, Aid Overseas Trading Limited, on a line by line basis. It also includes the results of all the charity's branches, including those overseas. A separate statement of financial activities (SOFA) is not presented because the charity has taken advantage of the provisions of paragraph 304 of the SORP.

(c) **Incoming resources**
Income is recognised in the period in which the charitable group is entitled to receipt and the amount can be measured with reasonable certainty. Income is deferred only when the charity has to fulfil conditions before becoming entitled to it or where the donor has specified that the income is to be expended in a future period.

Grants from the government and other agencies have been included as income from activities in furtherance of the charity's objects where these amount to a contract for services, but as donations where the money is given in response to an appeal or with greater freedom of use, for example government block grants.

In accordance with this policy, legacies are included when the charity is advised by the personal representative of an estate that payment will be made or property transferred and the amount involved can be quantified.

(d) **Resources expended and basis of allocation of costs**
Expenditure is included when incurred.

Grants payable to partner organisations for relief and development projects are included in the SOFA when approved by the trustees and agreed with the other organisation. The value of such grants unpaid at the year end is accrued. Grants where the beneficiary has not been informed or has to meet certain conditions before the grant is released are not accrued but are noted as financial commitments.

Expenditure on operational programmes is recognised in the period in which it is incurred. A designated fund is established for expenditure which has been committed to projects, but remains unspent at the year end.

The majority of costs are directly attributable to specific activities. Certain shared costs are apportioned to activities in furtherance of the objects of the charity. Office costs and property related costs are apportioned on the proportion of floor area occupied by the activity. Staff costs and office costs are allocated in the same proportion as directly attributed staff costs.

(e) **Fund-raising costs**
These include the salaries, direct expenditure and overhead costs of the staff in offices in the UK who promote fund-raising, including events.

(f) **Support costs**
Support costs represent the cost of core field offices and the costs incurred by UK based staff, directly providing support for the international programme, including management, policy and advocacy work and supervision and technical support for emergency programmes.

(g) **Costs of managing and administering the charity**
These represent costs incurred by finance, human resources, internal audit and directorate departments, attributable to the management of the charity's assets, organisational administration and compliance with constitutional and statutory requirements.

(h) **Gifts in kind**
Blankets and clothing etc received and given to overseas projects are included in the financial statements at market value at the time of export. Food aid from the World Food Programme, for which the charity accepts full responsibility for distribution, is included in income at its market value and as resources expended at the same value when distributed. Properties, investments, and other fixed assets donated to the charity are included as donation income at market value at the time of receipt. Items donated for resale are included in shop income when sold and no value is placed on stock at the year end.

(i) **Capitalisation and depreciation of tangible fixed assets**
All assets costing more than £1,000 are capitalised.

Freehold land is not depreciated. The cost of other tangible fixed assets is written-off by equal annual instalments over their expected useful lives as follows:

Notes forming part of the financial statements for the year ended 30 September 2001

Freehold buildings	50 years
Leasehold property	5–10 years
Furniture, fixtures, and equipment	3–10 years
Motor vehicles	4 years

Vehicles and equipment for use in overseas operational programmes are not capitalised but charged in full to 'Resources expended' when purchased. This is because the expected useful life is significantly reduced in such programmes and is generally less than one year for the majority of these assets.

(j) **Fixed asset investments**
Fixed asset investments, including investment property, are included at market value at the balance sheet date. Any gain or loss on revaluation is taken to the SOFA.

(k) **Stocks**
Purchased stocks are valued at the lower of cost or net realisable value after making due allowance for any obsolete or slow-moving items.

(l) **Funds accounting**
Funds held by the charity are:

Unrestricted general funds – these are funds which can be used in accordance with the charitable objects at the discretion of the trustees.

Designated funds – these are funds set aside by the trustees out of unrestricted general funds for specific future purposes or projects.

Restricted funds – these are funds that can only be used for particular restricted purposes within the objects of the charity. Restrictions arise when specified by the donor or when funds are raised for particular restricted purposes.

Further explanation of the nature and purpose of each fund is included in the notes to the accounts.

(m) **Foreign currencies**
Transactions in foreign currencies are translated at rates prevailing at the date of the transaction. Balances denominated in foreign currencies are translated at the rate of exchange prevailing at the year end.

(n) **Pension scheme**
The charity operates a pension scheme providing benefits based on final pensionable pay. The assets of the scheme are held and managed separately from those of the charity. The expected cost of providing pensions, as calculated periodically by professionally qualified actuaries, is charged to the SOFA, so as to spread the cost of pensions over employees' working lives with the charity, in such a way that the pension cost is a substantially level percentage of current and expected future pensionable payroll.

(o) **Operating leases**
Rentals applicable to operating leases where substantially all the benefits and risks of ownership remain with the lessor are charged to the SOFA as charged.

Notes forming part of the financial statements for the year ended 30 September 2001

2. Donations, legacies and similar incoming resources

	Unrestricted £'000	Restricted £'000	2001 Total £'000	2000 Total £'000
Donations				
Committed giving	4,147	–	**4,147**	4,032
Legacies	1,043	–	**1,043**	1,928
Donations, appeals and fund-raising events	1,468	854	**2,322**	1,136
	6,658	**854**	**7,512**	**8,096**
Grants from UK Government				
Department for International Development	–	**500**	**500**	**500**
Grants from other agencies				
Disaster Emergencies Committee	–	1,341	**1,341**	1,091
Other UK agencies		10	**10**	10
	–	**1,351**	**1,351**	**1,101**
Gifts in kind				
Blankets and clothing	239	–	**239**	240
Food Aid received from World Food Programme	–	582	**582**	556
Food Aid received from European Union	–	510	**510**	498
	239	**1,092**	**1,331**	**1,294**
Total	**6,897**	**3,797**	**10,694**	**8,991**

3. Activities in furtherance of the charity's objectives

	2001 £'000	2000 £'000
Contracts for operational programmes		
UK Government – Department for International Development	**1,415**	1,296
Other UK agencies – National Lottery Charities' Board	**25**	25
European Union	**1,933**	1,901
United Nations agencies	**269**	276
Non-UK governments	**1,020**	991
Other international agencies	**132**	128
Less deferred income	**(48)**	(50)
	4,746	**4,567**

All the income arising under the above contracts is considered to be restricted to particular projects, an outline of which are given in note 7.

Notes forming part of the financial statements for the year ended 30 September 2001

4. Shop income and expenditure

	Aid Overseas Trading Ltd £'000	Charitable Trading £'000	2001 Total Shop Activities £'000	2000 Total Shop Activities £'000
Turnover from donated goods	–	6,985	**6,985**	5,366
Turnover from purchased goods	1,588	–	**1,588**	1,230
Total shop income	**1,588**	**6,985**	**8,573**	**6,596**
Operating expenses	(1,012)	(4,626)	**(5,638)**	(5,187)
Management expenses	(452)	(404)	**(856)**	(842)
Shop expenditure	**(1,464)**	**(5,030)**	**(6,494)**	**(6,029)**
Net income from trading	**124**	**1,955**	**2,079**	**567**

This represents income from the sale of donated and bought-in goods through the charity's shops.

The profit of Aid Overseas Trading Limited is gifted to the charity so that there is no liability to Corporation Tax for that entity. Further details are set out in note 15 to the accounts.

5. Investment income and interest

	Unrestricted £'000	Restricted £'000	2001 Total £'000	2000 Total £'000
Deposit interest	182	39	**221**	196
Investment income from quoted investments	8	–	**8**	6
	190	**39**	**229**	**202**

6. Fund-raising costs

	Unrestricted £'000	Restricted £'000	2001 Total £'000	2000 Total £'000
Staff costs	640	100	**740**	721
Consultancy costs	501	6	**507**	427
Brochures and material	264	2	**266**	249
Office costs and other overheads	241	5	**246**	187
	1,646	**113**	**1,759**	**1,584**

Notes forming part of the financial statements for the year ended 30 September 2001

7. Cost of activities in furtherance of the objects of the charity

	Grants Payable to Partner Organisations £'000	Operational Programmes £'000	Gifts in Kind £'000	Information Campaigning and Education £'000	2001 Total £'000	2000 Total £'000
Health and nutrition	1,013	637	1,092	–	**2,742**	2,882
Water supply and sanitation	1,015	1,264	–	–	**2,279**	2,576
Agriculture	641	814	–	–	**1,455**	1,498
Institutional development and social organisation	556	546	–	–	**1,102**	1,076
Shelter	176	416	239	–	**831**	880
Information/lobbying	–	–	–	520	**520**	529
Income generation/ production	–	680	–	–	**680**	702
Education and legal aid	124	322	–	202	**648**	639
Logistics support	–	601	–	–	**601**	576
Other	–	330	–	271	**601**	576
	3,525	**5,610**	**1,331**	**993**	**11,459**	**11,934**

Grants payable to partner organisations are considered to be part of the costs of activities in furtherance of the objects of the charity because much of the charity's development programme is carried out through grants to local organisations which support long-term, sustainable benefits for a community, which are monitored by the charity. Grants are also made to fund immediate emergency relief provision in times of crisis, catastrophe or natural disaster. Further details are given in Note 8.

The operational programme is work undertaken overseas by the charity and includes the provision of specialist services (eg to address the water and sanitation needs of refugees) and training and networking for local organisations.

The charity's information, campaigning and education programme has several key objectives. One is to contribute the experience which comes from the international programme to the curricula and methods of school teaching and youth work in the UK. Another is to inform our supporters and the wider UK public about our international experience of work with poor people. We also carry out research and analysis of the issues raised by our work, as a contribution to public debate and policy-making in the UK and the European Union, in the interests of alleviating poverty and suffering world-wide. The trustees see the programme as an important ancillary activity which furthers the charitable purposes.

Resources expended on operational programmes comprised:	2001 £'000	2000 £'000
Staff costs	**2,327**	2,228
Travel and subsistence	**981**	993
Projects	**2,302**	2,671
	5,610	**5,892**

Notes forming part of the financial statements for the year ended 30 September 2001

8. Grants payable to partner organisations

Location and name of institution	2001 £'000	2000 £'000
Africa:		
Horn of Africa: World Food Programme	**1,309**	1,570
Sudan: Operation Lifeline/UNICEF	**130**	140
Angola: Asociacion de Organizaciones No Gubernamentales	**155**	160
West Africa: Association Nationale des Maisons Familiales Rurales	70	60
Asia:		
District Education Department, Vietnam	**255**	238
Tamil Women's Association	**72**	0
The Americas:		
Brazil: Conselho Indigena De Roraima	**90**	95
Central America: Fundacion para la Cooperacion con Desplazados y Repoblados Salvadorenos	**78**	–
Caribbean: Service Formation Action pour le Developpement Economique et Social	**75**	85
Eastern Europe:		75
Balkan Rehabilitation Association	**1,260**	1,350
Other grants	**31**	56
	3,525	3,829

A full list of the individual grants and the projects that are funded is available from our principal office and on our website at: www.aidoverseas.org.uk.

9. Support Costs

	2001 £'000	2000 £'000
Staff costs	**1,167**	1,124
Office costs	**401**	376
Communications	**338**	345
	1,906	**1,845**

10. Costs of managing and administering the charity

	2001 £'000	2000 £'000
Staff costs	**166**	180
Office costs	**106**	97
Communications	**102**	105
Legal and professional fees	**98**	84
	472	**466**

Notes forming part of the financial statements for the year ended 30 September 2001

11. Net incoming resources

	£'000	£'000
This is stated after charging:		
Hire of vehicles and equipment	**71**	68
Property rental	**1,804**	1,775
Auditors' remuneration – statutory audit	**25**	23
– audit (overseas)	**2**	2
– other	**2**	4

12. Employees and staff costs

	2001 No	2000 No
The average number of UK contracted employees throughout the year, calculated on a full time equivalent basis, was:		
Trading operation	**98**	96
Marketing operation	**47**	45
Corporate functions	**18**	17
Programmes in the UK	**38**	38
Programmes overseas	**11**	13
	212	209
Staff based overseas on local contracts	**192**	194
	404	403

	2001 £'000	2000 £'000
The costs of employing those staff was:		
Salaries and wages	**3,395**	3,286
National insurance	**325**	315
Pension scheme	**160**	154
	3,880	**3,755**

In addition, a great amount of time, the value of which it is impossible to reflect in these financial statements, is donated by thousands of volunteers throughout the UK.

The emoluments of one member of staff, including benefits in kind, are within the range of £50,000 to £59,999 (2000 - one in range £60,000 to £69,999), not including retirement benefits which are accruing under a defined benefit scheme.

Notes forming part of the financial statements for the year ended 30 September 2001

13. Trustees' remuneration

Trustees are not remunerated. £2,142 was reimbursed for directly incurred travel expenses to 8 trustees (2000 – £1,896 to 7 trustees).

14. Tangible fixed assets

Group	Freehold Property £'000	Leasehold Property £'000	Furniture, Fixtures and Equipment £'000	Motor Vehicles £'000	Total £'000
Cost					
At 1 October 2000	1,585	3,382	2,431	379	**7,777**
Additions	52	205	218	13	**488**
Disposals	–	(18)	(32)	(88)	**(138)**
At 30 September 2001	**1,637**	**3,569**	**2,617**	**304**	**8,127**
Depreciation					
At 1 October 2000	303	2,963	1,962	291	**5,519**
Charge for the year	19	112	155	11	**297**
Disposals	6	(5)	(27)	(66)	**(92)**
At 30 September 2001	**328**	**3,070**	**2,090**	**236**	**5,724**
Net book value					
At 30 September 2001	**1,309**	**499**	**527**	**68**	**2,403**
At 30 September 2000	1,282	418	469	88	**2,258**

Charity:	Freehold Property £'000	Leasehold Property £'000	Furniture, Fixtures and Equipment £'000	Motor Vehicles £'000	Total £'000
Cost					
At 1 October 2000	1,585	3,317	2,279	351	**7,532**
Additions	52	199	211	–	**462**
Disposals	–	(18)	(32)	(81)	**(131)**
At 30 September 2001	**1,637**	**3,498**	**2,458**	**270**	**7,863**
Depreciation					
At 1 October 2000	303	2,915	1,823	267	**5,308**
Charge for the year	19	109	149	7	**284**
Disposals	6	(5)	(27)	(59)	**(85)**
At 30 September 2001	**328**	**3,019**	**1,945**	**215**	**5,507**
Net book value					
At 30 September 2001	**1,309**	**479**	**513**	**55**	**2,356**
At 30 September 2000	1,282	402	456	84	**2,224**

Notes forming part of the financial statements for the year ended 30 September 2001

15. Fixed asset investments

Group	Freehold Investment Property £'000	Quoted £'000	Unquoted £'000	Total £'000
Market value:				
At 1 October 2000	42	1	–	**43**
Disposals	(8)	–	–	**(8)**
At 30 September 2001	**34**	**1**	**-**	**35**
Charity				
Market value:				
At 1 October 2000	42	1	2	**45**
Disposals	(8)	–	–	**(8)**
At 30 September 2001	**34**	**1**	**2**	**37**

All the fixed asset investments are held in the UK. Quoted investments comprise Treasury stock. The investment property was professionally revalued by Surveyor & Co, Quantity Surveyors, on 30 September 2001.

At 30 September 2001, the charity owned all of the ordinary share capital, consisting of 2,000 ordinary shares, of Aid Overseas Trading Limited, a company registered in the UK, which promotes fair trade and raises funds through trading activities. The trading results are set out in note 4. At 30 September 2001 the aggregate amount of this company's assets, liabilities, share capital and reserves was:

	2001 £'000	2000 £'000
Current assets	**768**	662
Creditors: amounts falling due within one year	**766**	660
	2	2
Represented by:		
Share capital and reserves	**2**	2

16. Stocks

	2001 Group £'000	2000 Group £'000	2001 Charity £'000	2000 Charity £'000
Finished goods:				
Trading stocks for resale	**524**	724	–	–
Emergency stocks	**174**	166	**174**	166
Other stocks	**86**	79	**86**	79
	784	**969**	**260**	**245**

Notes forming part of the financial statements for the year ended 30 September 2001

17. Debtors

	2001 Group £'000	2000 Group £'000	2001 Charity £'000	2000 Charity £'000
Other debtors	**2,385**	1,583	**2,232**	1,583
Prepayments	**765**	698	**734**	698
Amounts due from subsidiary	**–**	–	**588**	660
	3,150	**2,281**	**3,554**	**2,941**

Other debtors include £1.6 million of amounts due from institutional donors for approved project expenditure.

Amounts due from subsidiary includes a loan of £0.2 million to Aid Overseas Trading Limited. The loan is secured by a fixed and floating charge. Interest was charged on the outstanding balance of the loan at 6% during the year. The loan is all repayable after more than one year.

18. Cash at bank and in hand

	2001 Group £'000	2000 Group £'000	2001 Charity £'000	2000 Charity £'000
Short term deposits	**3,953**	2,319	**3,953**	2,319
Cash and bank balances	**1,141**	929	**1,128**	899
	5,094	**3,248**	**5,081**	**3,218**

19. Creditors: amounts falling due within one year

	2001 Group £'000	2000 Group £'000	2001 Charity £'000	2000 Charity £'000
Bank overdraft	**494**	102	**466**	70
Grants payable	**257**	198	**257**	198
Trade creditors	**674**	344	**625**	297
Deferred income	**48**	68	**48**	68
Accruals	**682**	496	**581**	449
Other tax and social security	**96**	107	**96**	107
Interest-free loans to partner organisations	**25**	–	**25**	–
	2,276	**1,315**	**2,098**	**1,189**

20. Creditors: amounts falling due after more than one year

	2001 Group £'000	2000 Group £'000	2001 Charity £'000	2000 Charity £'000
Grants payable within two years	**337**	**783**	**337**	**783**

Notes forming part of the financial statements for the year ended 30 September 2001

21. Unrestricted funds

	General Reserves £'000	Designated Funds Fixed Assets Funds £'000	Designated Funds Projects Fund £'000	Total £'000
Balance at 1 October 2000	1,293	2,258	455	**4,006**
Surplus for the year	2,007	–	–	**2,007**
Transfers between funds	(592)	145	447	**-**
Balance at 30 September 2001	**2,708**	**2,403**	**902**	**6,013**

The designated fixed assets fund represents the net book value of tangible fixed assets. Each year an amount is transferred to or from the fund representing the movement in the net book value of tangible fixed assets in the year.

The designated projects fund represents the amount committed by the trustees to specific charitable projects at the year end, the principal of which are the water and sanitation projects in Africa.

22. Restricted funds

	Balance at 1 Oct 2000 £'000	Incoming Resources £'000	Programme Expenditure £'000	Fund-raising Costs £'000	Balance at 30 Sept 2001 £'000
Central Africa	310	960	(705)	(12)	**553**
South Sudan and Horn of Africa	561	941	(904)	(13)	**585**
Southern Africa	186	201	(110)	(5)	**272**
Central America Hurricane	–	567	(472)	(7)	**88**
Latin America and Caribbean	61	587	(569)	(8)	**71**
Bangladesh	–	205	(177)	(5)	**23**
East Asia	–	129	(127)	(6)	**(4)**
South Asia	298	655	(677)	(10)	**266**
Middle East	683	19	(313)	–	**389**
Kosovo	–	534	(145)	(16)	**373**
Eastern Europe	265	1,204	(1,402)	(20)	**47**
Humanitarian emergencies	331	1,488	(1,631)	(11)	**177**
Food aid	–	1,092	(1,092)	–	**-**
	2,695	**8,582**	**(8,324)**	**(113)**	**2,840**

All restricted funds are for specific humanitarian or education projects in particular areas of the world. These projects include development programmes to provide long-term sustainable benefits for a community, including health and nutrition, water supply and sanitation projects, agricultural projects and educational projects. The charity also holds certain restricted funds raised through appeal for emergency relief provision in times of crisis.

Notes forming part of the financial statements for the year ended 30 September 2001

23. Analysis of group net assets between funds

	Unrestricted Funds £'000	Designated Funds £'000	Restricted Funds £'000	Total Funds £'000
Fund balances at 30 September 2001 are represented by:				
Tangible fixed assets	–	2,403	–	**2,403**
Investment assets	35	–	–	**35**
Current assets	5,238	902	2,888	**9,028**
Current liabilities	(2,276)	–	–	**(2,276)**
Long-term liabilities	(289)	–	(48)	**(337)**
Total net assets at 30 September 2001	**2,708**	**3,305**	**2,840**	**8,853**

24. Commitments

	2001 Group £'000	2000 Group £'000	2001 Charity £'000	2000 Charity £'000
At 30 September 2001, the charity had commitments as follows:				
Capital expenditure authorised but not contracted for:	**79**	**200**	**79**	**200**
Commitments in respect of grants approved for projects which have not been accrued in the financial statements but will form part of grants:				
Within one year	472	319	472	319
Between one and two years	180	165	180	165
Between two and three years	42	38	42	38
	694	**522**	**694**	**522**
Annual commitments under non-cancellable operating leases for land and buildings which expire:				
Within 1 year	185	138	137	101
In two to five years	416	281	416	281
Over five years	393	574	372	553
	994	**993**	**925**	**935**
Annual commitments under non-cancellable operating leases for motor vehicles which expire:				
Within one year	1	–	–	–
In two to five years	45	46	28	28
	46	**46**	**28**	**28**

Notes forming part of the financial statements for the year ended 30 September 2001

25. Pension scheme

The charity operates a final salary (ie defined benefit) pension scheme for its employees. The assets of the scheme are held separately from those of the charity.

The pension cost is determined on the advice of independent qualified actuaries, XYZ. The pension cost for 2000/01 is based on the results of the actuarial valuation of the scheme as at 31 March 2001 using the projected unit method. The previous valuation took place on 31 March 1998.

The valuation of the scheme was based on the following assumptions:

Rate of return on investments	8.0% pa
Rate of earnings increases	5.5% pa
Rate of pension increases	4.0% pa
Rate of inflation	3.5% pa

The market value of the scheme's assets at 31 March 2001 was £3.8 million. On the assumptions used to calculate the pension cost, the actuarial value of the assets at that date represented 107% of the value of the members' accrued benefits. These accrued benefits include all benefits for pensioners and other former members as well as benefits based on service completed to date for active members allowing for future pay rises.

Employer contributions during the year were 8% of earnings and employees contribution were 5% of earnings.

Debtors include a pension prepayment account resulting from excess employer's contributions in previous years of £121,000 (previously £159,000). The actuary has taken account of the prepayment in the setting employer's contributions and this prepayment will be released against employer's contributions over the period to the next valuation.

26. Notes to consolidated cash flow statement

(a) **Reconciliation of surplus of income to net cash inflow from operating activities**

	2001 £'000	**2000 £'000**
Net movement in funds for the year	**2,152**	498
Investment income	**(229)**	(202)
Depreciation charges	**297**	291
Decrease in stocks	**185**	56
Increase in debtors	**(869)**	(21)
Increase in creditors	**569**	102
(Decrease)/increase in grants payable	**(446)**	103
Net cash inflow from operating activities	**1,659**	827

(b) **Analysis of net cash resources**

	2000 £'000	**Cashflow £'000**	**2001 £'000**
Cash in hand (note 18)	929	**212**	1,141
Deposits on one day notice (note 18)	567	**243**	810
Overdrafts	(102)	**(392)**	(494)
	1,394	**63**	1,457

Short term deposits on more than one days notice are considered to be liquid resources.

Example E

The Edinburgh Educational Trust

Report and Financial Statements (Extract)

Year ended: 31 March 2001

Charity no: SC012345

Statement of Financial Activities for the year ended 31 March 2001

	Notes	Unrestricted Funds £'000	Restricted Funds £'000	Endowment Funds £'000	2001 Total £'000	2000 Total £'000
Incoming resources						
Donations and legacies	2	123,328	–	–	**123,328**	28,565
Millennium appeal income	2	–	1,490,367	–	**1,490,367**	372,525
Activities in furtherance of the charity's objects:						
Grants and fees for care and education of children	3	1,381,047	–	–	**1,381,047**	1,491,997
Activities for generating funds – rental income		11,761	–	–	**11,761**	15,576
Investment income	4	258,266	–	–	**258,266**	205,181
Total incoming resources		1,774,402	1,490,367	–	**3,264,769**	2,113,844
Cost of generating funds	5	–	(82,975)	–	**(82,975)**	(242,282)
Net incoming resources available for charitable application		1,774,402	1,407,392	–	**3,181,794**	1,871,562
Charitable expenditure						
Costs of activities in furtherance of charitable objectives:						
Teaching and care of children	6(a)	794,227	–	–	**794,227**	733,870
Running costs and maintenance of school	6(b)	793,340	–	149,621	**942,961**	706,524
Management and administration	7	69,950	14,321	–	**84,271**	62,242
Total charitable expenditure		1,657,517	14,321	149,621	**1,821,459**	1,502,636
Total resources expended		1,657,517	97,296	149,621	**1,904,434**	1,502,636
Net incoming/(outgoing) resources before transfers		116,885	1,393,071	(149,621)	**1,360,335**	368,926
Transfers in respect of fixed assets additions	14		(1,401,229)	1,401,229	**–**	–
Gains on investments		–	–	209,329	**209,329**	2,550,912
Net movement in funds for the year		116,885	(8,158)	1,460,937	**1,569,664**	2,919,838
Total funds at 1 April 2000	14	194,224	(135,085)	8,185,985	**8,245,124**	5,325,286
Total funds at 31 March 2001	14	311,109	(143,243)	9,646,922	**9,814,788**	8,245,124

Income and expenditure account for the year ended 31 March 2001

	Notes	2001 £'000	2000 £'000
Income			
Donations, legacies and Millennium Appeal income	2	**1,613,695**	401,090
Grant from Scottish Executive	3	**902,978**	923,854
Local authority fees	3	**478,069**	568,143
Investment income	4	**258,266**	205,181
Rental income		**11,761**	15,576
		3,264,769	2,113,844
Charitable expenditure			
Costs of generating funds	5	**82,975**	242,282
Teaching and care of children	6	**794,227**	733,870
Running costs and maintenance of school	6	**942,961**	706,524
Management and administration expenses	7	**84,271**	62,242
		1,904,434	1,744,918
Operating surplus for the year		**1,360,335**	368,926
Realised (loss)/gain on sale of investments		**(29,843)**	109,434
Surplus for the year		**1,330,492**	478,360

Statement of Total Recognised Gains and Losses

		2001 £'000	2000 £'000
Surplus for the year		**1,330,492**	478,360
Unrealised gain on investment	10	**239,172**	2,441,478
Total gains and losses recognised since 31 March 2000		**1,569,664**	2,919,838

All activities relate to continuing operations.

There is no difference between the surplus on ordinary activities for the year stated above and its historical cost equivalent.

Balance Sheet as at 31 March 2001

	Notes	2001 £'000	2001 £'000	2000 £'000	2000 £'000
Fixed assets					
Tangible assets	9		**2,588,412**		1,336,804
Investments	10		**7,058,510**		6,849,181
			9,646,922		8,185,985
Current assets					
Debtors	11	**125,346**		160,326	
Cash at bank and in hand		**1,131,923**		601,454	
		1,257,269		761,780	
Creditors: Amounts falling due within one year	12	**(1,089,403)**		(702,641)	
Net current assets			**167,866**		59,139
Total assets less current liabilities			**9,814,788**		8,245,124
Funds					
Unrestricted funds – Reserve fund	14		**311,109**		194,224
Restricted funds					
Millennium Appeal fund	14		**(143,243)**		(135,085)
Permanent Endowment funds	14		**9,646,922**		8,185,985
			9,814,788		8,245,124

These accounts were approved by the board of trustees on 31 July 2001 and signed on their behalf by:

R Bruce

Cashflow Statement for the year ended 31 March 2001

	Notes	2001 £'000	2001 £'000	2000 £'000	2000 £'000
Net cash inflow from operating activities	**16(a)**		**280,361**		164,270
Returns on investments and servicing of finance					
Investment income received		**258,266**		205,181	
			258,266		205,181
Capital expenditure and financial investment					
Payments to acquire investments		**(909,534)**		(442,837)	
Payments to acquire tangible fixed assets		**(1,401,229)**		(265,328)	
Receipts from sale of investments		**919,045**		480,185	
Net movement in cashflows attributable to endowment fund investments		**(9,511)**		(37,348)	
			(1,401,229)		(265,328)
Net cash flow before financing			**(862,602)**		(104,123)
Financing					
Donations received and utilised for additions to endowment assets		**1,393,071**		130,344	
Net movement in cashflows attributable to endowment fund investments		**9,511**		37,348	
			1,402,582		167,692
Increase in cash in the year	**16(b)**		**539,980**		271,815

Notes forming part of the financial statements for the year ended 30 September 2001

1. Accounting policies

(a) **Basis of accounting**
The accounts have been prepared under the historical cost convention as modified by the revaluation of investment assets and are in accordance with applicable accounting standards, the Charities Accounts (Scotland) Regulations 1992 and Accounting and Reporting by Charities: Statement of Recommended Practice (SORP) issued in October 2000.

(b) **Donations, legacies and similar incoming resources**
Donations, legacies and similar incoming resources are included in the year in which they are receivable, which is when the charity becomes entitled to the resource.

(c) **Grants receivable and local authority fees**
Grants receivable and local authority fees are credited to the Statement of Financial Activities (SOFA) in the year for which they are received. Deferred income represents amounts received for future periods and is released to incoming resources in the period for which it has been received.

(d) **Investment income and rental income**
Income from investments and from rental income is included in the SOFA in the year in which it is receivable.

(e) **Expenditure**
All expenditure is included on an accruals basis and is recognised when there is a legal or constructive obligation to pay for expenditure. All costs have been directly attributed to one of the functional categories of resources expended in the SOFA. The Trust is not registered for VAT and accordingly expenditure is shown gross of irrecoverable VAT.

(f) **Tangible fixed assets**
Until 31 December 1991 neither the original cost nor improvements to freehold land and buildings were capitalised because the buildings are historic, inalienable and form part of a permanent endowment which means that these cannot be sold but must be held in perpetuity.

The original cost of the assets and improvements thereto is not available. The users of the accounts are principally the trustees, parents of children attending the school and various donors. The trustees consider the cost of carrying out a professional valuation to include these assets at a value in the accounts to be considerable compared to the limited additional benefit derived by the users of the accounts.

Since 1 January 1992, all improvements to land and buildings costing more than £1,000 are capitalised and depreciated. Other tangible fixed assets costing more than £1,500 are capitalised and depreciated over 4 years. At 31 March 2001, all such assets have been fully depreciated and eliminated from these accounts.

(g) **Depreciation**
Depreciation is charged to write off the cost less estimated residual value of property improvements over 20 years.

(h) **Investments**
Investments are included at market value at the year end.

Gains and losses on disposal and revaluation of investments are charged or credited to the SOFA.

(i) **Pensions**
Teaching staff employed by the charity are eligible for membership of the Teachers Pension Scheme, which is a national, statutory contributory, unfunded defined benefit scheme administered by the Teachers Pension Agency, an executive agency of the Department for Education and Employment. Pension costs are assessed in accordance with the advice of the Government Actuary.

The charity has arranged a defined contribution pension scheme for those members of staff who are not eligible to join the Teachers Pension Scheme. The assets of this scheme are held separately from those of the charity, being invested with insurance companies. Pension costs charged in the Statement of Financial Activities represent the contributions payable by the charity in the year.

(j) **Fund Accounting**
The nature and purpose of each fund are explained in note 14.

Notes forming part of the financial statements for the year ended 30 September 2001

2. Donations, legacies and Millennium Appeal income

	2001 £'000	2000 £'000
Legacies	**96,000**	–
Donations	**27,328**	28,565
	123,328	28,565
Millennium appeal income:		
Individuals	**596,781**	156,329
Trusts	**679,000**	167,000
Corporate	**214,586**	49,196
	1,490,367	372,525
Total	**1,613,695**	401,090

3. Activities in furtherance of the charity's objects

	2001 £'000	2000 £'000
Grant from Scottish Executive	**902,978**	923,854
Local authority fees	**478,069**	568,143
	1,381,047	1,491,997

4. Investment income

	2001 £'000	2000 £'000
Dividends and interest on listed investments	**258,119**	205,022
Interest on cash deposits	**147**	159
	258,266	205,181

5. Cost of generating funds

	2001 £'000	2000 £'000
Legal fees	**–**	14,360
Fund-raising consultancy	**36,000**	109,576
Staff	**24,361**	18,617
Literature	**12,367**	88,362
Investment management charges	**10,247**	11,367
	82,975	242,282

Notes forming part of the financial statements for the year ended 30 September 2001

6. Costs of activities in furtherance of charitable objectives

	2001 £'000	2000 £'000
(a) Teaching and care of children		
Teaching and care staff	**691,303**	670,590
Books, apparatus, stationery	**29,108**	22,703
Educational consultancy	**26,909**	–
Food and board	**33,791**	34,991
Clothing and laundry	**2,218**	3,594
Medical expenses	**3,010**	1,746
Sport and recreation	**331**	246
Training	**7,557**	–
	794,227	733,870
(b) Running costs and maintenance of school		
Premises maintenance staff	**471,135**	416,838
Temporary accommodation	**116,309**	–
Insurance	**28,510**	18,861
Fuel and light	**115,430**	88,789
Cleaning	**9,144**	10,096
Maintenance, repairs etc	**38,491**	71,351
Furniture	**10,467**	5,086
Garden	**1,579**	13,015
Transport	**2,275**	2,928
	793,340	626,964
Depreciation (charged to Endowment Fund)	**149,621**	79,560
	942,961	706,524

7. Management and administration

	2001 £'000	2000 £'000
Salaries – Bursar's office	**38,391**	35,456
Bursars department expenses	**16,998**	12,167
Audit fee	**4,200**	4,000
Legal expenses	**10,361**	10,619
	69,950	62,242
Project management expenses for Millennium Appeal Fund	**14,321**	–
	84,271	62,242

Notes forming part of the financial statements for the year ended 30 September 2001

8. Staff numbers and costs

	2001 £'000	2000 £'000
Wages and salaries	**1,074,886**	1,006,108
Social security costs	**87,486**	76,365
Pension costs	**38,457**	40,411
	1,200,829	1,122,884

The average weekly number of employees, calculated as full time equivalents, during the period was:	Number	Number
Teachers	**29**	29
Domestic	**27**	24
Maintenance	**7**	8
Cleaners	**10**	11
	73	**72**

No employee received remuneration of more than £50,000.

Trustees are not remunerated. Four trustees received reimbursement of expenses for attending meetings amounting to £1,500 (2000: £1,400).

9. Tangible fixed assets

	Furniture and equipment £'000	Improvements to property £'000	Total £'000
At cost			
Balance at 1 April 2000	341,206	1,591,208	1,932,414
Additions in year	–	1,401,229	1,401,229
Balance at 31 March 2001	**341,206**	**2,992,437**	**3,333,643**
Depreciation			
Balance at 1 April 2000	341,206	254,404	595,610
Charged in the year	–	149,621	149,621
Balance at 31 March 2001	**341,206**	**404,025**	**745,231**
Net book value			
At 31 March 2001	–	**2,588,412**	**2,588,412**
At 31 March 2000	–	1,336,804	1,336,804

The Trust owns the original Georgian Mansion House built in 1757 and the Victorian Hospital designed by Hippolyte Whyte and built in 1874, both of which are "A" listed. These properties were originally gifted to the Trust to be held in perpetuity in accordance with the Trust Deed and they form part of the permanent endowment funds. The original value of the assets and the cost of improvements to them until 1991 has not been included in the balance sheet because, in the opinion of the trustees, the cost of professionally valuing these assets to include a value in the accounts outweighs the benefits to the users of the accounts. They are insured for £20,000,000 which is an estimate of their replacement cost.

Notes forming part of the financial statements for the year ended 30 September 2001

10. Investments

	2001 £'000	2000 £'000
Market value at 1 April 2000	**6,811,833**	4,355,998
Add: Acquisitions at cost	**909,534**	442,837
Less: Disposals at opening book value	**(948,888)**	(428,480)
Net gains on revaluation at 31 March 2001	**239,172**	2,441,478
	7,011,651	6,811,833
Cash at bank awaiting investment	**46,859**	37,348
Market value at 31 March 2001	**7,058,510**	6,849,181
Cost as at 31 March 2001	**3,287,089**	2,610,427

Investments in individual entities held at 31 March 2001 which are over 5% of portfolio by value are:

BP Amoco – Market value £400,000

All investments held are listed UK Securities.

11. Debtors

	2001 £'000	2000 £'000
Revenue Grants – Scottish Executive	**87,400**	89,162
Local authority fees	**5,200**	46,598
Other debtors	**12,264**	15,781
Prepayments and accrued income	**20,482**	8,785
	125,346	160,326

12. Creditors: Amounts falling due within one year

	2001 £'000	2000 £'000
Trade creditors	**239,933**	263,534
Other creditors	**233,813**	–
Deferred income (note 13)	**353,564**	389,179
Accruals	**262,093**	49,928
	1,089,403	702,641

13. Deferred income

	2001 £'000	2000 £'000
Balance at 1 April 2000	**389,179**	352,244
Local authority fees received	**442,454**	605,078
Released to statement of financial activities	**(478,069)**	(568,143)
Balance at 31 March 2001	**353,564**	389,179

Notes forming part of the financial statements for the year ended 30 September 2001

14. Funds

	Reserve Fund £'000	Appeal Fund £'000	Endowment Funds £'000	Total £'000
Opening balance at 1 April 2000	194,224	(135,085)	8,185,985	**8,245,124**
Net (outgoing)/incoming resources before transfers and investment gains	(141,381)	1,393,071	108,645	**1,360,335**
Transfers:				
Investment income arising on endowment funds for unrestricted purposes	258,266	–	(258,266)	–
Fixed assets additions	–	(1,401,229)	1,401,229	–
Investment gains	–	–	209,329	**209,329**
Balance at 31 March 2001	**311,109**	**(143,243)**	**9,646,922**	**9,814,788**
Represented by:				
Tangible fixed assets	–	–	2,588,412	**2,588,412**
Investments	–	–	7,058,510	**7,058,510**
Inter-fund loans	143,243	(143,243)	–	–
Net current assets	521,430	–	–	**521,430**
Deferred income	(353,564)	–	–	**(353,564)**
	311,109	**(143,243)**	**9,646,922**	**9,814,788**

The Reserve fund represents the unrestricted funds which the Trustees are free to use in accordance with the charitable objects.

The Millennium Appeal Fund was launched to raise £5,000,000 for the purpose of providing modern sports facilities and a swimming pool for the children and must be used for these purposes. Capital expenditure relating to inalienable and historic assets, which form part of the permanent endowment funds, is transferred from the appeal fund to the endowment fund when it is spent. At 31 March 2001 £1,862,892 has been raised out of £3,750,000 which has been promised to that date. The fund has returned to a surplus since the year end, as a further £600,000 has been raised which has not yet been spent.

The Endowment funds represent those assets which must be held permanently by the charity, in this case additions to inalienable and historic assets and investments both of which must be held permanently. Additions to inalienable and historic assets are added to the fund and depreciation on those assets is charged against the fund. In accordance with the Trust deed, £3,600,000 of the amount invested is expendable, that is the capital can be converted into income, when a specific set of circumstances arise, the principal of which is that Grants from the Scottish Executive or its successor organisations fall below £700,000.

15. Capital commitments

	2001 £'000	2000 £'000
Amount contracted for but not provided in the accounts	**3,309,000**	980,000
Funding committed by third parties under contracts with the Trust	**(3,206,000)**	–
Net capital commitment	**103,000**	**980,000**

Notes forming part of the financial statements for the year ended 30 September 2001

16. Note to the cashflow statement

(a) Reconciliation of net incoming resources to net cashflow from operating activities

	2001 £'000	2000 £'000
Net incoming resources	**1,360,335**	368,926
Decrease in debtors	**34,980**	19,770
Increase/(decrease) in creditors	**422,377**	(5,396)
(Decrease)/increase in deferred income	**(35,615)**	36,935
Depreciation	**149,621**	79,560
Investment income	**(258,266)**	(205,181)
Donations received and utilised for additions to endowment fund assets	**(1,393,071)**	(130,344)
Net cash inflow from operating activities	**280,361**	164,270

(b) Analysis of changes in net cash resources

	2000 £'000	Cashflow £'000	2001 £'000
Cash at bank and in hand	601,454	**530,469**	1,131,923
Cash at bank awaiting investment	37,348	**9,511**	46,859
	638,802	**539,980**	1,178,782

17. Pension costs

Under the Teacher's Pension Scheme, teachers' contributions, on a pay-as-you go basis, and employer's contributions are credited to the Exchequer. An annual account, the Teachers Pension Account, is kept of receipts and expenditure. Any excess of income over expenditure is deemed to be invested in Government securities. Notional interest on the deemed investment is added to the Account, and the resultant balance is known as the Notional Fund. Expenditure debited to the Account excludes the cost of pension increases paid under the Pension (Increases) Act.

Every 5 years the Government actuary conducts an actuarial review of the Scheme, using normal actuarial principles. The cost of pension increases is excluded from the valuation and consequently neither teachers nor employers contribute to this added value, which is met directly by the Exchequer. The most recent review of the Scheme, covering the 5 years ended 31 March 1991, was published in 1997 and showed liabilities of £49,444 million compared with assets of £48,192 million. The Government Actuary concluded that the deficiency of £1,252 million would require supplementary contributions from employers of 0.5% per annum from 1 April 1997. The charity contributed 8.05% of pensionable salaries to the scheme until 30 June 1997, when the rate was reduced to 7.2%.

Non-teaching staff are eligible for participation in a defined contribution scheme managed by Agreeable Life Assurance Society. The charity contributes 7.2% of pensionable salary.

Example F

The Higher College Charity

Report and Financial Statements (Extract)

Year ended: 31 August 2001

Charity no: 279654

Consolidated Statement of Financial Activities for the year ended 31 August 2001

	Notes	Unrestricted Funds £'000	Restricted Funds £'000	Endowed Funds £'000	2001 Total Funds £'000	2000 Total Funds £'000
INCOMING RESOURCES						
Charitable activities						
School fees	2(a)	8,439	–	–	**8,439**	*8,236*
Other income	4	140	–	–	**140**	*121*
Other activities to generate funds						
Commission and lettings income	4	99	–	–	**99**	*46*
Trading income	3	1,583	–	–	**1,583**	*1,192*
Investment income	5	362	292	–	**654**	*547*
Donations		21	320	8	**349**	*36*
Other incoming resources	4	34	–	–	**34**	–
Total Incoming resources		**10,678**	**612**	**8**	**11,298**	*10,178*
RESOURCES EXPENDED						
Costs of generating funds						
Trading expenses	3	1,466	–	–	**1,466**	*1,093*
Financing costs		217	–	–	**217**	*232*
Investment management		6	4	–	**10**	*10*
Fund-raising costs		–	90	–	**90**	–
		1,689	**94**	**–**	**1,783**	*1,335*
Net incoming resources available for charitable application		**8,989**	**518**	**8**	**9,515**	8,843
Charitable expenditure						
Teaching		3,380	–	–	**3,380**	*3,181*
Welfare		1,797	–	–	**1,797**	*1,686*
Premises		2,502	–	–	**2,502**	*2,133*
Support costs		729	–	–	**729**	*584*
Grants, awards and prizes	2(b)	–	251	–	**251**	*239*
Management and administration		45	–	–	**45**	*41*
Total charitable expenditure		**8,453**	**251**	**–**	**8,704**	*7,864*
Total resources expended	6, 7	**10,142**	**345**	**–**	**10,487**	*9,199*
NET INCOMING RESOURCES		**536**	**267**	**8**	**811**	*979*
Investment gains/losses		(13)	15	62	**64**	*206*
NET MOVEMENT IN FUNDS		**523**	**282**	**70**	**875**	*1,185*
Fund balances at 1 September 2000		8,738	804	3,963	**13,505**	*12,320*
FUND BALANCES at 31 August 2001	14	**9,261**	**1,086**	**4,033**	**14,380**	*13,505*

All amounts derive from continuing activities.

All gains and losses recognised in the year are included in the Statement of Financial Activities.

Consolidated and Charity Balance Sheets as at 31 August 2001

	Notes	Group 2001 £'000	Group 2000 £'000	Charity 2001 £'000	Charity 2000 £'000
FIXED ASSETS					
Tangible assets	9	**9,570**	*9,386*	**9,562**	*9,374*
Investments	10	**7,033**	*6,937*	**7,040**	*6,944*
		16,603	*16,323*	**16,602**	*16,318*
CURRENT ASSETS					
Stocks		**169**	*178*	**74**	*86*
Debtors	11	**661**	*619*	**595**	*497*
Cash		**597**	*566*	**596**	*565*
		1,427	*1,363*	**1,265**	*1,148*
CREDITORS: due within one year	12	**(1,775)**	*(2,238)*	**(1,620)**	*(2,023)*
NET CURRENT LIABILITIES		**(348)**	*(875)*	**(355)**	*(875)*
TOTAL ASSETS LESS CURRENT LIABILITIES		**16,255**	*15,448*	**16,247**	*15,443*
CREDITORS: due after more than one year					
Advance fees	13	**(1,831)**	*(1,858)*	**(1,831)**	*(1,858)*
Final term deposits		**(44)**	*(85)*	**(44)**	*(85)*
TOTAL NET ASSETS		**14,380**	*13,505*	**14,372**	13,500
ENDOWED FUNDS	14a	**4,033**	*3,963*	**4,033**	*3,963*
RESTRICTED FUNDS	14b	**1,086**	*804*	**1,086**	*804*
UNRESTRICTED FUNDS					
Designated & general funds	14c	**9,253**	*8,733*	**9,253**	*8,733*
Non-charitable trading funds		**8**	*5*	**–**	–
TOTAL FUNDS	14	**14,380**	*13,505*	**14,372**	*13,500*

Approved by the Board of Governors of Higher College on 7th November 2001 and signed on its behalf by:

Sir A H Critchton-Hall (Chairman)

Date: 12 December 2001

Notes forming part of the financial statements for the year ended 31 August 2001

5. Investment income

	2001 £'000	2000 £'000
Interest on cash deposits held for investment	**10**	*8*
On listed investments	**644**	*539*
	654	*547*

Transitional tax relief included above amounted to £106,000 (2000 – £31,000)

6. Expenditure

	2001 £'000	2000 £'000
Charitable expenditure includes:		
Refurbishment of pupil accommodation	**335**	*555*
Loss on disposal of tangible fixed assets	**–**	*3*
Depreciation	**392**	*375*
Auditors' remuneration:		
for audit services	**15**	*14*
for other services	**1**	*7*
Governors' liability insurance	**1**	*–*

	2001 £'000	2000 £'000
Total staff costs comprised:		
Wages and salaries	**4,572**	*4,488*
Social security costs	**379**	*372*
Pension contributions	**280**	*270*
	5,231	*5,130*

The average number of employees in the year, calculated on a full time equivalent basis, was 276 (2000 – 287) of which 100 (102) were teaching staff. Neither the governors nor persons connected with them received any remuneration, other benefits or reimbursement of expenses from the School or any connected organisation.

The number of higher paid employees was:	2001 No	2000 No
£50,000 – £60,000	**2**	*2*
£60,000 – £70,000	**1**	*1*

Contributions were made to the Teachers' Superannuation Scheme, which is a defined benefits scheme, for two higher paid employees and contributions amounting to £3,750 (2000 – £3,650) were made to a defined contribution scheme for one employee.

Notes forming part of the financial statements for the year ended 31 August 2001

7. Analysis of total resources expended

	Staff costs £'000	Other costs £'000	Depreciation £'000	Total £'000
Charitable activities				
Teaching	3,068	250	62	**3,380**
Welfare	997	746	54	**1,797**
Premises	567	1,671	264	**2,502**
Support costs	310	408	11	**729**
Grants, awards and prizes	–	251	–	**251**
Management and administration	–	45	–	**45**
	4,942	3,371	391	**8,704**
Costs of generating funds:				
Financing costs	–	217	–	**217**
Investment management	–	10	–	**10**
Fund-raising	49	41	–	**90**
Total for charity	**4,991**	**3,639**	**391**	**9,021**
Trading costs of the subsidiary	240	1,225	1	**1,466**
Total for group	**5,231**	**4,864**	**392**	**10,487**

8. Management and administration

	2001 £'000	2000 £'000
Auditors' remuneration (see note 6)	**16**	*21*
Governors' liability insurance	**1**	–
Staff costs	**20**	*18*
Office costs	**8**	*2*
	45	*41*

Notes forming part of the financial statements for the year ended 31 August 2001

9. Tangible fixed assets

	Freehold land £'000	Freehold buildings £'000	Motor vehicles £'000	Furniture & equipment £'000	Charity total £'000	Subsidiary: furniture & equipment £'000	Group total £'000
Cost							
1 September 2000	6,000	4,403	40	1,500	**11,943**	58	**12,001**
Additions	–	490	14	142	**646**	–	**646**
Disposals	–	(69)	(9)	(21)	**(99)**	(6)	**(105)**
31 August 2001	6,000	4,824	45	1,621	**12,490**	52	**12,542**
Depreciation							
1 September 2000	–	1,331	35	1,203	**2,569**	46	**2,615**
Charge for year	–	232	5	154	**391**	1	**392**
Disposals	–	(10)	(9)	(13)	**(32)**	(3)	**(35)**
31 August 2001	–	1,553	31	1,344	**2,928**	44	2,972
Net book values							
31 August 2001	6,000	3,271	14	277	**9,562**	8	**9,570**
31 August 2000	*6,000*	*3,072*	*5*	*297*	***9,374***	*12*	***9,386***

Inalienable and historic assets (College Treasures)

In addition to the capitalised fixed assets held for the Charity's own use, Higher College also has a substantial endowment of assets bequeathed on trust for retention in perpetuity as a permanent record of the College's history. These comprise a unique collection of busts, paintings and cartoons depicting the College's 15 Heads since its founding in 1903, together with many other artefacts whose intrinsic value is also bound up with the College's history. These are irreplaceable originals to which no reliable cost or value can be attributed and accordingly these assets have not been capitalised in the financial statements.

Notes forming part of the financial statements for the year ended 31 August 2001

10. Investments

Group:	**Unrestricted £'000**	**Restricted £'000**	**Endowment £'000**	**Advance fees £'000**	**Total £'000**
Balance at 1 September 2000	203	744	3,963	2,027	**6,937**
Additions	20	73	1,402	–	**1,495**
Disposals at book value	–	(33)	(1,605)	(41)	**(1,679)**
Revaluations	27	27	273	(47)	**280**
Balance at 31 August 2001	**250**	**811**	**4,033**	**1,939**	**7,033**
Listed on UK Stock Exchange (Historical cost: £6,150,000)	250	711	3,783	1,939	**6,683**
Cash deposits	–	100	250	–	**350**
Charity: as above					**7,033**
Investment in Subsidiary Company (see Note 3 and below)					**7**
					7,040

The assets and liabilities of the subsidiary were:	**2001 £'000**	**2000 £'000**
Tangible fixed assets	**8**	12
Current assets	**162**	215
	170	227
Creditors: amounts falling due within one year	**(155)**	(215)
	15	12
Representing:		
Share capital	**7**	7
Profit and loss account	**8**	5
	15	12

Details of the subsidiary's profit and loss account are given in note 3.

11. Debtors

	Group		**College**	
	2001 £'000	**2000 £'000**	**2001 £'000**	**2000 £'000**
School fees	**166**	175	**166**	175
Trade debtors	**53**	74	–	–
Sundry debtors	**384**	322	**378**	279
Prepayments	**58**	48	**51**	42
	661	619	**595**	496

Notes forming part of the financial statements for the year ended 31 August 2001

12. Creditors: amounts falling due within one year

	Group		College	
	2001	**2000**	**2001**	**2000**
	£'000	**£'000**	**£'000**	**£'000**
Bank overdraft	**235**	375	**221**	284
Amounts due from subsidiary company	–	–	**23**	88
Fees received in advance	**420**	353	**420**	353
Trade creditors	**25**	38	–	–
Taxation and social security	**61**	62	**43**	–
Refurbishment costs	**10**	290	**11**	290
Other creditors and accruals	**519**	490	**397**	378
	1,270	1,608	**1,115**	1,393
Advance fees scheme (see note 13 below)	**505**	630	**505**	630
	1,775	2,238	**1,620**	2,023

The bank overdraft is the amount currently drawn down on a standing facility of £2,000,000 secured on the freehold property to provide additional working capital as the need arises.

13. Advance fees scheme

Parents may enter into a contract to pay to the school up to the equivalent of seven years' tuition fees in advance. The money may be returned subject to specific conditions on the receipt of one year's notice. Assuming pupils will remain in the school, advance fees will be applied as follows:

	2001	**2000**
	£'000	**£'000**
After 5 years	**108**	*129*
Within 2 to 5 years	**1,316**	*1,291*
Within 1 to 2 years	**407**	*438*
	1,831	*1,858*
Within 1 year	**505**	*630*
	2,336	*2,488*

The balance represents the accrued liability under the contracts. The movements during the year were:

	£'000	**£'000**
Balance at 1 September 2000		2,488
New contracts		423
Amounts accrued to contracts		165
		3,076
Amounts utilised in payment of fees:		
To the school	(646)	
To other schools	(52)	
		(698)
Capital repaid		(42)
Balance at 31 August 2001		**2,336**

Notes forming part of the financial statements for the year ended 31 August 2001

14. Net assets of the group's funds

The group's net assets belong to the various funds (including Advance Fees) as follows:

	Fixed assets £'000	Investments £'000	Net current assets £'000	Long-term liabilities £'000	Fund balances £'000
Endowment funds	–	4,033	–	–	**4,033**
Restricted funds	–	811	275	–	**1,086**
Unrestricted funds:					
Designated funds					
Advance fees	–	1,939	185	(1,831)	**293**
Tangible fixed assets fund	9,562	–	(2,000)	–	**7,562**
Heritage fund	–	250	2	–	**252**
Non-charitable trading funds	8	–	–	–	**8**
General Reserve	–	–	1,190	(44)	**1,146**
	9,570	7,033	(348)	(1,875)	14,380

Net current assets for Advance Fees comprised:	
Cash	**397**
Advance fees due within one year	**(505)**
	(108)

14A. Endowed funds: movements in the year

	Balance at 1 September 2000 £'000	Incoming endowments £'000	Amounts expended £'000	Transfers and investment gains/(losses) £'000	Balance at 31 August 2001 £'000
Permanent endowments:					
Foundation capital	563	–	–	15	**578**
Other Special Trusts:					
Grants and allowances	1,772	8	–	66	**1,846**
Scholarships, bursaries	1,460	–	–	(17)	**1,443**
Prize and other funds	168	–	–	(2)	**166**
	3,963	**8**	**–**	**62**	**4,033**

The Foundation Capital represents the original endowment to provide free education. The income of this fund contributes to the free education of pupils whose parents live in Newshire.

The other Special Trusts consist of a number of individual trusts and prize funds set up by individual donors.

Each fund is allocated its proportion of investment income and gains and losses and bears its own expenses.

Notes forming part of the financial statements for the year ended 31 August 2001

14B. Restricted funds: movements in the year

	Balance at 1 September 2000 £'000	Income £'000	Expended £'000	Transfers and investment gains/(losses) £'000	Balance at 31 August 2001 £'000
New building fund	–	320	(90)	–	**230**
Grants and allowances	157	112	(112)	(8)	**149**
Scholarships and bursaries	504	113	(86)	20	**551**
Prize and other funds	99	28	(21)	4	**110**
Foundation	44	39	(36)	(1)	**46**
	804	**612**	**(345)**	**15**	**1,086**

Included above is a transfer of £3,700 from a bursary fund to the grants and allowances fund.

14C. Unrestricted funds: movements in the year

	Balance at 1 September 2000 £'000	Income £'000	Expended £'000	Transfers and investment gains/(losses) £'000	Balance at 31 August 2001 £'000
Designated funds:					
Advance fee income	250	248	(165)	(40)	**293**
Tangible fixed assets fund	7,374	–	–	188	**7,562**
Heritage fund	219	20	–	13	**252**
General reserve	890	8,716	(8,511)	51	**1,146**
Charity	**8,733**	**8,984**	**(8,676)**	**212**	**9,253**
Non-charitable trading funds	5	1,694	(1,466)	(225)	**8**
Group	**8,738**	**10,678**	**(10,142)**	**(13)**	**9,261**

Advance fee income represents the amount set aside to cover any future shortfall on the accrued liability for advance fees.

The tangible fixed assets fund represents the net book value of tangible fixed assets less the bank facilities secured on those assets.

The Governors are setting aside, in the Heritage Fund, monies towards the costs of extensions and refurbishment of the school buildings in preparation for the school's centenary celebrations in 2006.

The general reserve fund represents those funds which are unrestricted and not designated for other purposes.

15. Contracts

No capital expenditure has been contracted for at 31 August 2001.

Notes forming part of the financial statements for the year ended 31 August 2001

16. Reconciliation of group net incoming resources to net cash inflow from group operations

	2001		2000	
	£'000	**£'000**	**£'000**	**£'000**
Net Incoming resources		**811**		*979*
Non-operating cashflows eliminated:				
Investment income		**(654)**		*(547)*
Endowment donations		**(8)**		–
Gain on disposal of tangible fixed assets		**(27)**		*3*
Financing costs		**217**		*232*
Depreciation charges added back		**392**		*375*
Decrease in stocks		**9**		*10*
Increase in debtors		**(42)**		*(20)*
(Decrease)/increase in creditors	**(323)**		*158*	
Movement in advance fees due within 1 year	**125**		*(25)*	
		(198)		*133*
(Increase)/decrease in Final Term Deposits		**(41)**		*20*
Net cash inflow from group operations		**459**		*1,185*

17. Analysis of changes in net cash resources of the group

	Cash £'000	Bank overdraft £'000	Total £'000
Balance 1 September 1999	441	(400)	41
Net cash inflow for 1999/00	*125*	*25*	*150*
Balance 31 August 2000	566	(375)	191
Net cash inflow for the year	**31**	**140**	**171**
Balance 31 August 2001	597	(235)	362

18. Pension costs

Teachers are required to join the Teachers' Pension Scheme. Under the Teachers' Pension Scheme, teachers' contributions, on a pay-as-you go basis, and employer's contributions are credited to the Exchequer. An annual account, the Teachers' Pension Account, is kept of receipts and expenditure. Any excess of income over expenditure is deemed to be invested in Government securities. Notional interest on the deemed investment is added to the Account, and the resultant balance is known as the Notional Fund. Expenditure debited to the Account excludes the cost of pension increases paid under the Pension (Increases) Act.

Every 5 years the Government actuary conducts an actuarial review of the Scheme, using normal actuarial principles. The cost of pension increases is excluded from the valuation and consequently neither teachers nor employers contribute to this added value, which is met directly by the Exchequer. The most recent review of the Scheme, covering the 5 years ended 31 March 1991, was published in 1997 and showed liabilities of £49,444 million compared with assets of £48,192 million. The Government Actuary concluded that the deficiency of £1,252 million would require supplementary contributions from employers of 0.5% per annum from 1 April 1997. During the year, the College contributed 7.2% of pensionable salaries to the scheme.

Non-teaching staff are eligible to participate in a defined contribution scheme managed by Scottish Friendly Society. The assets of the scheme are held separately from the College. With effect from 1 April 1997 this scheme ceased to be contracted out of the State Earnings Related Pension Scheme and the employers' contribution was reduced to 5.75%.

There were no amounts unpaid or prepaid to either scheme at the year end.

Example G

The ABC Charity

(A company limited by guarantee)

Report and Financial Statements (Extract)

Year ended: 31 March 2001

Charity no: 87654321
Company no: 12345678

Consolidated Statement of Financial Activities (incorporating an Income and Expenditure Account) for the year ended 31 March 2001

	Notes	Unrestricted Funds £'000	Restricted Funds £'000	Totals 2001 £'000	Totals 2000 £'000
Incoming resources					
Donations and gifts	2	4,130	3,200	**7,330**	6,000
Legacies	3	2,150	–	**2,150**	1,330
Building appeal	17	–	400	**400**	900
Activities in furtherance of the charity's objects:					
Government grants for residential care	17	–	700	**700**	400
Fees for residential care		1,200	–	**1,200**	1,000
Activities for generating funds:					
Merchandising income	4	1,140	–	**1,140**	900
Investment income	5	350	50	**400**	475
Net gain on disposal of fixed assets		20	–	**20**	30
Total incoming resources		8,990	4,350	**13,340**	11,035
Resources expended					
Cost of generating funds:					
Fund-raising costs		480	210	**690**	550
Building appeal costs	17	–	45	**45**	110
Merchandising costs	4	870	–	**870**	710
Investment management fees		80	10	**90**	110
		1,430	265	**1,695**	1,480
Charitable expenditure:					
Costs of activities in furtherance of the charity's objects:					
Residential care costs		1,400	1,030	**2,430**	2,545
Childcare		1,000	2,400	**3,400**	3,150
Emergency services		1,800	1,300	**3,100**	2,800
Information and Education		90	10	**100**	300
Support costs		110	80	**190**	180
Management and administration		210	60	**270**	230
		4,610	4,880	**9,490**	9,405
Total resources expended	6	6,040	5,145	**11,185**	10,885
Net incoming resources/(resources expended) before transfers		2,950	(795)	**2,155**	150
Transfers between funds	17	15	(15)	–	–
Net incoming resources/(resources expended)		2,965	(810)	**2,155**	150
Net gains on investment assets	11	100	–	**100**	250
Net movement in funds		3,065	(810)	**2,255**	400
Fund balances brought forward at 1 April	17	6,300	3,900	**10,200**	9,800
Fund balances carried forward at 31 March	17	9,365	3,090	**12,455**	10,200

All of the above results are derived from continuing activities. All gains and losses recognised in the year are included above. The surplus for the year for Companies Act purposes comprises the net incoming resources for the year plus realised gains on investments and was £2,225,000 (2000: £230,000). Page 10 gives details of changes in resources applied for fixed assets for charity use.

Consolidated and Charity Balance Sheets as at 31 March 2001

	Notes	Group 2001 £'000	Group 2000 £'000	Charity 2001 £'000	Charity 2000 £'000
Fixed assets					
Tangible assets	10	**5,500**	4,000	**5,500**	4,000
Investments	11	**2,000**	3,000	**2,001**	3,001
		7,500	7,000	**7,501**	7,001
Current assets					
Stocks		**300**	400	**100**	150
Debtors	12	**1,765**	1,000	**1,465**	800
Short term deposits		**3,400**	3,000	**3,400**	3,000
Cash at bank and in hand		**1,090**	200	**1,000**	180
		6,555	4,600	**5,965**	4,130
Creditors: amounts falling due within one year	13	**(1,500)**	(1,260)	**(911)**	(791)
Net current assets		**5,055**	3,340	**5,054**	3,339
Total assets less current liabilities		**12,555**	10,340	**12,555**	10,340
Creditors: amounts falling due after more than one year	14	**(100)**	(140)	**(100)**	(140)
Net assets		**12,455**	10,200	**12,455**	10,200
Funds:					
Unrestricted funds					
General funds – includes revaluation reserve of £140,000 (2000: £110,000)	17	**4,785**	2,900	**4,785**	2,900
Designated funds	17	**4,580**	3,400	**4,580**	3,400
		9,365	6,300	**9,365**	6,300
Restricted funds	17	**3,090**	3,900	**3,090**	3,900
Total funds	17	**12,455**	10,200	**12,455**	10,200

The financial statements on pages 9 to 20 were approved by the trustees on 16 June 2001 and signed on their behalf by:

H Singh (Chairman)

Consolidated Cashflow Statement for the year ended 31 March 2001

	Notes	2001 £'000	2000 £'000
Net cash inflow from operating activities	20	**2,090**	595
Capital expenditure and financial investment			
Payments to acquire tangible fixed assets		**(1,990)**	(1,000)
Proceeds from sale of tangible fixed assets		**130**	170
Purchase of investments		**(1,200)**	(865)
Proceeds from sales of investments		**2,300**	915
		(760)	(780)
Cash inflow/(outflow) before increase in liquid resources and financing	20	**1,330**	(185)
Financing			
Finance lease payments		**(40)**	(40)
Management of liquid resources			
Increase in short term deposits		**(400)**	(200)
Increase/(decrease) in cash in the year	20	**890**	(425)

Statement of changes in resources applied for fixed assets for charity use for the year ended 31 March 2000

	Unrestricted Funds £'000	Restricted Funds £'000	Totals 2001 £'000	Totals 2000 £'000
Net movement in funds for the year	3,065	(810)	**2,255**	400
Resources used for net acquisitions of tangible fixed assets	(1,100)	(400)	**(1,500)**	(590)
Net movement in funds available for future activities	1,965	(1,210)	**755**	(190)

Notes forming part of the financial statements for the year ended 31 March 2001

1. Accounting policies

(a) **Basis of preparation**
The financial statements have been prepared under the historical cost convention, with the exception of investments which are included at market value. The financial statements have been prepared in accordance with the Statement of Recommended Practice (SORP), "Accounting and Reporting by Charities" published in October 2000 and applicable accounting standards.

The statement of financial activities (SOFA) and balance sheet consolidate the financial statements of the charity and its subsidiary undertaking. The results of the subsidiary are consolidated on a line by line basis.

The charity has availed itself of Paragraph 3 (3) of Schedule 4 of the Companies Act and adapted the Companies Act formats to reflect the special nature of the charity's activities. No separate SOFA has been presented for the charity alone as permitted by Section 230 of the Companies Act 1985 and paragraph 304 of the SORP.

(b) **Company status**
The charity is a company limited by guarantee. The members of the company are the trustees named on page 1. In the event of the charity being wound up, the liability in respect of the guarantee is limited to £1 per member of the charity.

(c) **Fund accounting**
General funds are unrestricted funds which are available for use at the discretion of the trustees in furtherance of the general objectives of the charity and which have not been designated for other purposes.

Designated funds comprise unrestricted funds that have been set aside by the trustees for particular purposes. The aim and use of each designated fund is set out in the notes to the financial statements. Restricted funds are funds which are to be used in accordance with specific restrictions imposed by donors or which have been raised by the charity for particular purposes. The cost of raising and administering such funds are charged against the specific fund. The aim and use of each restricted fund is set out in the notes to the financial statements.

Investment income and gains are allocated to the appropriate fund.

(d) **Incoming resources**
All incoming resources are included in the SOFA when the charity is legally entitled to the income and the amount can be quantified with reasonable accuracy. For legacies, entitlement is the earlier of the charity being notified of an impending distribution or the legacy being received.

Gifts in kind donated for distribution are included at valuation and recognised as income when they are distributed to the projects. Gifts donated for resale are included as income when they are sold. Donated facilities are included at the value to the charity where this can be quantified and a third party is bearing the cost. No amounts are included in the financial statements for services donated by volunteers.

(e) **Resources expended**
All expenditure is accounted for on an accruals basis and has been classified under headings that aggregate all costs related to the category. Where costs cannot be directly attributed to particular headings they have been allocated to activities on a basis consistent with use of the resources. Premises overheads have been allocated on a floor area basis and other overheads have been allocated on the basis of the head count.

Fund-raising costs are those incurred in seeking voluntary contributions and do not include the costs of disseminating information in support of the charitable activities. Support costs are those costs incurred directly in support of expenditure on the objects of the charity and include project management carried out at Headquarters. Management and administration costs are those incurred in connection with administration of the charity and compliance with constitutional and statutory requirements.

(f) **Tangible fixed assets and depreciation**
Tangible fixed assets costing more than £1,000 are capitalised and included at cost including any incidental expenses of acquisition.

Depreciation is provided on all tangible fixed assets at rates calculated to write off the cost on a straight line basis over their expected useful economic lives as follows:

Freehold land	nil
Freehold buildings	over 50 years
Project and office equipment	over 5 years
Computer equipment	over 3 years
Motor vehicles	over 4 years
Equipment held under finance leases	over the life of the lease

(g) **Investments**
Investments are stated at market value at the balance sheet date. The SOFA includes the net gains and losses arising on revaluations and disposals throughout the year.

Notes forming part of the financial statements for the year ended 31 March 2001

(h) **Stock**
Stock consists of purchased goods for resale. Stocks are valued at the lower of cost and net realisable value. Items donated for resale or distribution are not included in the financial statements until they are sold or distributed.

(i) **Pension costs**
The cost of providing pension and related benefits is charged to the SOFA over the employees' service lives on the basis of a constant percentage of earnings which is an estimate of the regular cost. Variations from regular cost, arising from periodic actuarial valuations are allocated over the expected remaining service lives of current employees on the basis of a constant percentage of current and estimated future earnings. Any difference between the charge to the statement of financial activities and the contributions payable to the scheme is shown as an asset or a liability in the balance sheet.

(j) **Finance and operating leases**
Rentals applicable to operating leases are charged to the SOFA over the period in which the cost is incurred. Assets purchased under finance lease are capitalised as fixed assets. Obligations under such agreements are included in creditors. The difference between the capitalised cost and the total obligation under the lease represents the finance charges. Finance charges are written-off to the SOFA over the period of the lease so as to produce a constant periodic rate of charge.

(k) **Foreign currencies**
Transactions in foreign currencies are recorded at the rate ruling at the date of the transaction. Monetary assets and liabilities are retranslated at the rate of exchange ruling at the balance sheet date. All differences are taken to the SOFA.

2. Donations and gifts

	2001 £'000	**2000 £'000**
Individuals	**2,106**	1,678
Charitable foundations	**4,100**	3,500
Corporate donors	**1,100**	800
Gifts in kind	**24**	22
	7,330	6,000

Gifts in kind comprise free accommodation for the charity's Childcare team in Wimbledon kindly provided by the Packwood Foundation. A corresponding amount is included within Childcare expenditure.

3. Legacies

The charity is the residuary beneficiary of a farm in Kent. This is occupied by a life tenant and has not been included in the financial statements. The existing unencumbered value of the farm is estimated at £400,000.

In addition, legacies with a probate value of £1,600,000 have not been included in the financial statements as no notification of impending distribution has been received.

Notes forming part of the financial statements for the year ended 31 March 2001

4. Merchandising income and costs

	Donated goods £'000	Sale of puchased goods through ABC Enterprises Limited (see note 19) £'000	Total 2001 £'000	Total 2000 £'000
Merchandising income	280	860	**1,140**	900
Cost of sales	–	700	**700**	620
Administrative expenses	100	70	**170**	90
Merchandising expenses	100	770	**870**	710
Surplus	180	90	**270**	190

5. Investment income

	2001 £'000	2000 £'000
Interest receivable	**260**	300
Dividends receivable from equity shares	**90**	105
Dividends receivable from investments and unit trusts	**50**	70
	400	475

The transitional tax credit included above was £14,000 (2000 – £5,000).

Notes forming part of the financial statements for the year ended 31 March 2001

6. Total resources expended

	Staff Costs £'000	Other Direct Costs £'000	Other Allocated Costs £'000	Total 2001 £'000	Total 2000 £'000
Fund-raising costs	210	360	120	**690**	550
Building appeal costs	25	5	15	**45**	110
Merchandising costs	80	560	230	**870**	1,040
Investment management fees	–	90	–	**90**	110
Residential care costs	2,000	330	100	**2,430**	2,545
Childcare	2,800	345	255	**3,400**	3,150
Emergency services	1,980	870	250	**3,100**	2,800
Information and education	25	65	10	**100**	300
Support costs	45	110	35	**190**	50
Management and administration	85	145	40	**270**	230
Total resources expended	7,250	2,880	1,055	**11,185**	10,885

Other direct costs include:	2001 £'000	2000 £'000
Auditors' remuneration:		
Audit fee	**14**	13
Accountancy, taxation and other services	**6**	9
Operating lease rentals – Land and buildings	**110**	110
– Plant and equipment	**70**	70
Depreciation	**380**	270
Finance lease interest	**12**	14

7. Trustees' remuneration

The trustees neither received nor waived any emoluments during the year (2000: £Nil). Out of pocket expenses were reimbursed to trustees as follows.

	2001 Number	2000 Number	2001 £'000	2000 £'000
Travel	2	3	**640**	530
Visit to Sudan Project	1	–	**1,200**	–
Other	1	1	**40**	65
	4	4	**1,880**	595

During the year payments of £2,500 were made to the Harvey Print Company for the printing of the Annual Report. Mrs W. Williams, a trustee of this charity, is a director of that company. Mr H. Singh a trustee is also a trustee of the Packwood Foundation that provided free accommodation to the charity during the year valued at £24,000.

Notes forming part of the financial statements for the year ended 31 March 2001

8. Staff costs

	2001 £'000	2000 £'000
Wages and salaries	**6,050**	5,820
Social security costs	**700**	650
Pension costs	**500**	480
	7,250	6,950

The number of employees whose emoluments as defined for taxation purposes amounted to over £50,000 in the year was as follows:

	2001 Number	2000 Number
£50,001 – £60,000	1	1
£60,001 – £70,000	1	2

All employees earning more than £50,000 participated in the pension scheme.

The average number of employees, calculated on a full-time equivalent basis, analysed by function was:

	2001 Number	2000 Number
Charitable activities	**264**	260
Cost of generating funds	**12**	10
Management and administration of the charity	**3**	3

9. Pension costs

The charity operates a defined benefit pension scheme for the benefit of the employees. The assets of the Scheme are administered by Pension Scheme Trustees in a fund independent from that of the charity.

Pension costs are assessed in accordance with the advice of a qualified actuary using the Projected Unit Method. The assumptions which have the most significant effect on the results of the valuation are:

Rate of investment	–	10% per annum compound
Rate of pensionable salary increases including promotions	–	8.5% per annum compound
Rate of increase to pensions in payment	–	5.5% per annum compound
Rate of increase in dividends	–	5.0% per annum compound

The most recent actuarial valuation of the Scheme was at 1 October 1999 and showed the market value of the Scheme's assets was £9,100,000 and that the actuarial value of the assets was 110% of the liabilities accrued to 1 October 1999 allowing for future increases to salaries.

The pension cost for the year was £500,000 (2000: £480,000). The surplus is being recognised over 12 years being the average remaining service life of employees. The balance sheet includes £40,000 (2000: £37,000) in respect of accrued pension costs.

Notes forming part of the financial statements for the year ended 31 March 2001

10. Tangible fixed assets

	Freehold land and buildings £'000	Project and office equipment £'000	Computer equipment £'000	Motor vehicles £'000	Total £'000
Cost					
At 1 April 2000	4,350	400	250	200	**5,200**
Additions	1,700	180	100	10	**1,990**
Disposals	(300)	–	–	–	**(300)**
At 31 March 2001	5,750	580	350	210	**6,890**
Depreciation					
At 1 April 2000	800	200	150	50	**1,200**
Charge for year	90	150	88	52	**380**
Disposals	(190)	–	–	–	**(190)**
At 31 March 2001	700	350	238	102	**1,390**
Net book value					
At 31 March 2001	5,050	230	112	108	**5,500**
At 31 March 2000	3,550	200	100	150	**4,000**

Project and office equipment includes assets with a net book value of £140,000 (2000: £180,000) held under finance leases. Freehold land and buildings includes freehold land of £1.2 million that is not depreciated.

Capital expenditure contracted for, but not provided in the financial statements, was £250,000 (2000: £190,000).

11. Fixed asset investments

	2001 £'000	2000 £'000
Group:		
Market value as at 1 April 2000	**3,000**	2,800
Additions	**1,200**	865
Disposal proceeds	**(2,300)**	(915)
Net investment gains	**100**	250
Market value at 31 March 2001	**2,000**	3,000
Historical cost at 31 March 2001	**1,860**	2,890
UK listed investments are represented by:		
Fixed interest securities	**900**	1,600
Equity shares	**620**	580
Investment trusts and unit trusts	**480**	820
Total	**2,000**	3,000

Investments held by the charity also include an additional £1,000 (2000: £1,000) investment in the subsidiary company at cost (see note 19).

Notes forming part of the financial statements for the year ended 31 March 2001

12. Debtors

	Group 2001 £'000	Group 2000 £'000	Charity 2001 £'000	Charity 2000 £'000
Trade debtors	**560**	505	**290**	325
Legacies	**755**	170	**755**	170
Other debtors	**225**	205	**125**	125
Amount owed by subsidiary undertaking	–	–	**100**	80
Prepayments and other accrued income	**225**	120	**195**	100
	1,765	1,000	**1,465**	800

The amount owed by the subsidiary undertaking is secured by a charge over the assets of the subsidiary.

13. Creditors: amounts falling due within one year

	Group 2001 £'000	Group 2000 £'000	Charity 2001 £'000	Charity 2000 £'000
Trade creditors	**525**	580	**325**	400
Taxation and social security costs	**355**	315	**46**	66
Other creditors	**190**	125	**160**	105
Obligations under finance leases	**40**	40	**40**	40
Accruals and deferred income	**390**	200	**340**	180
	1,500	1,260	**911**	791

14. Creditors: amounts falling due after more than one year

Group and charity	2001 £'000	2000 £'000
Obligations under finance leases	**100**	140

15. Obligations under finance leases

Group and charity	2001 £'000	2000 £'000
The amounts fall due as follows:		
Within one year	**40**	40
In the second to fifth year inclusive	**100**	140
	140	180

Notes forming part of the financial statements for the year ended 31 March 2001

16. Financial commitments

At 31 March 2001 the group has annual commitments under non-cancellable leases as follows:

	2001		2000	
Expiry date:	**Land and buildings £'000**	**Other £'000**	**Land and buildings £'000**	**Other £'000**
Two to five years	**40**	**70**	–	70
Over five years	**70**	–	110	–
	110	**70**	110	70

17. Statement of funds

	At 1 April 2000 £'000	Income £'000	Expenditure £'000	Investment gains £'000	Transfers £'000	At 31 March 2001 £'000
General reserve	2,900	8,990	5,995	100	(1,210)	**4,785**
Designated funds						
Cyclical repair fund	300	–	45	–	95	**350**
Fixed asset fund	3,100	–	–	–	1,130	**4,230**
Total unrestricted funds	6,300	8,990	6,040	100	15	**9,365**
Restricted funds:						
Building appeal	900	400	30	–	–	**1,270**
Anita House	100	75	125	–	–	**50**
Other residential care	375	700	1,010	–	–	**65**
Childcare	2,400	1,775	2,535	–	(15)	**1,625**
Emergency services	105	1,100	1,350	–	–	**(145)**
Information and education	20	100	95	–	–	**25**
The E J Marf fund	–	200	–	–	–	**200**
Total restricted funds	3,900	4,350	5,145	–	(15)	**3,090**
Total funds	10,200	13,340	11,185	100	–	**12,455**

The General reserve represents the free funds of the charity which are not designated for particular purposes.

The Cyclical repair fund has been designated by the trustees for the major refurbishment and repairs to Bailey House. It is expected that the repairs will be carried out in 2002.

The Fixed asset fund has been set up to assist in identifying those funds that are not free funds and it represents the net book value of tangible fixed assets except for the residential care facility in Wimbledon, which has been funded from the capital appeal.

The Building appeal fund represents the net book value of the new residential care facility in Wimbledon. The fund balances are reduced by the depreciation charged on the facility.

The Anita House fund represents funds raised by the Friends of Anita House for use at Anita House.

The Childcare fund was established in 1994 by a gift from the Darlaston Foundation to be used solely for the Childcare projects. Since then sundry restricted gifts for child care have been added to the Fund. During the year an unexpended balance of £15,000 has been transferred to the general fund with the permission of the donor.

The negative balance on the Emergency services fund represents the excess amount that has been spent on emergency services in anticipation of an appeal that was launched after the year end. By June 2001 the appeal raised £180,000.

The E J Marf fund was received during the year to support a sustainable development programme around the Jim Corbett National Park in India. The fund is represented by short-term deposits and is expected to be applied during 2001.

Notes forming part of the financial statements for the year ended 31 March 2001

18. Analysis of group net assets between funds

	Restricted funds £'000	Designated funds £'000	General funds £'000	Total £'000
Fund balances at 31 March 2001 are represented by:				
Tangible fixed assets	1,270	4,230	–	**5,500**
Investments	–	–	2,000	**2,000**
Current assets	1,820	350	4,385	**6,555**
Current liabilities	–	–	(1,500)	**(1,500)**
Long term liabilities	–	–	(100)	**(100)**
Total net assets	3,090	4,580	4,785	**12,455**

19. Subsidiary company

The charity owns the whole of the issued ordinary share capital of ABC Enterprises Ltd, a company registered in England. The subsidiary is used for non-primary purpose trading activities, namely the mail order retail operation and the sale of bought in goods through the charity's shops. In addition corporate sponsorships and non-tax exempt events are also carried out by the subsidiary. All activities have been consolidated on a line by line basis in the SOFA. The total net profit is gifted to the charity. Corporate income is treated as donations. A summary of the results of the subsidiary is shown below:

ABC Enterprises Ltd	Mail Order 2001 £'000	Shops 2001 £'000	Corporate 2001 £'000	Total 2001 £'000	Total 2000 £'000
Turnover	400	460	350	**1,210**	1,300
Cost of sales	390	310	150	**850**	900
Gross profit	10	150	200	**360**	400
Administrative expenses	30	40	40	**110**	130
Net profit/ (loss)	(20)	110	160	**250**	270

The aggregate of the assets, liabilities and funds was:

	2001	2000
Assets	**590**	470
Liabilities	**(589)**	(469)
Funds (representing 1000 ordinary shares of £1 each)	**1**	1

Notes forming part of the financial statements for the year ended 31 March 2001

20. Cash flow information for the group

(a) Reconciliation of changes in resources to net inflow from operating activities

	2001 £'000	2000 £'000
Net incoming resources before revaluations	**2,155**	150
Gain on sale of tangible fixed assets	**(20)**	(30)
Depreciation	**380**	270
Decrease in stocks	**100**	450
Increase in debtors	**(765)**	(225)
Increase/(decrease) in creditors	**240**	(20)
Net cash inflow from operating activities	**2,090**	595

(b) Reconciliation of net cash flow to movement in net funds/debt

	2001 £'000	2000 £'000
Increase/(decrease) in cash in the period	**890**	(425)
Cash outflow from decrease in lease financing	**40**	40
Cash outflow from increase in liquid resources	**400**	200
Movement in net funds and debt in the year	**1,330**	(185)
Net funds and debt at 1 April 2000	**3,020**	3,205
Net funds and debt at 31 March 2001	**4,350**	3,020

(c) Analysis of net funds/debt

	1 April 2000 £'000	Cashflow £'000	31 March 2001 £'000
Cash at bank and in hand	200	**890**	1,090
Liquid resources	3,000	**400**	3,400
Finance leases	(180)	**40**	(140)
	3,020	**1,330**	4,350

Index

All references are to chapter and paragraph, Example or Table number, e.g. 9.1.2 refers to Chapter 9, section 1.2; Example 3.1 refers to Chapter 3, Example 1; Table 4.1 refers to Chapter 4, Table 1. Examples A–G are located at the end of the book after the main text.